Rural Transformation in Tropical Africa

Edited by

Douglas Rimmer

Belhaven Press
(a division of Pinter Publishers)
London

© Douglas Rimmer, 1988

First published in Great Britain in 1988 by
Belhaven Press (an imprint of Pinter Publishers Limited)
25 Floral Street, London WC2E 9DS

British Library Cataloguing in Publication Data

A CIP catalogue record for this book is available from the British Library.

ISBN 082140895X ✓

Typeset by Wordbook Ltd London
Printed by Biddles of Guildford Ltd

Contents

List of Tables

List of Figures

Acknowledgements

Earlier versions of the papers, other than the Introduction, that are published in this volume, were presented at a Conference on Rural Transformation in Tropical Africa held at the University of Birmingham on 23–24 September 1986. That Conference was an initiative of the International Activities Committee, chaired by Professor Robert Steel, of the Economic and Social Research Council, London. I am grateful to Professor Steel and to his colleagues on the Committee, Professor Meghnad Desai and Dr Ralph Grillo, for their encouragement. My thanks are also due to Kim Davies and Mrs Joy Dike for the assistance they gave me in convening the Conference. In addition, Kim Davies willingly helped in preparation of the papers for publication.

The support of the Economic and Social Research Council is acknowledged, but responsibility for the contents of and opinions expressed and conclusions reached in the papers in this volume rests with the individual authors and should not be attributed to the Council.

Douglas Rimmer

Contributors to this volume

John Borton is Research Associate, Relief and Development Institute, London

Sandy Cairncross is Senior Lecturer in Tropical Public Health Engineering, Department of Tropical Hygiene, London School of Hygiene and Tropical Medicine

Edward Clay is Director of the Relief and Development Institute, London, and Fellow of the Institute of Development Studies at the University of Sussex

Richard Crook is Lecturer in Politics, University of Glasgow

Walter Elkan is Professor of Economics at Brunel, the University of West London

W.T.S. Gould is Senior Lecturer in Geography and a member of the Centre of African Studies, University of Liverpool

Allan G. Hill is Senior Lecturer in the Department of Medical Demography, London School of Hygiene and Tropical Medicine

Carol P. MacCormack is Senior Lecturer in Social Anthropology, Evaluation and Planning Centre for Health Care, London School of Hygiene and Tropical Medicine

Douglas Rimmer is an Honorary Senior Research Fellow of the Centre of West African Studies, University of Birmingham

Ken Swindell is Senior Lecturer in Geography and an Associate of the Centre of West African Studies, University of Birmingham

List of copyright permissions

Table 2.1 is reproduced with permission from *Population Growth and Policies in Sub-Saharan Africa*, Washington D.C., The World Bank, 1986; material in **Table 2.2** and **Table 2.3** from J. Casteline *et al*, 'The proximate determinants of fertility', *Comparative Studies no. 39*, World Fertility Survey, Voorburg, ISI, 1984; **Table 2.4** from S. Singh and B. Ferry, 'Biological and traditional factors that influence fertility: results from WFS Surveys', *Comparative Studies no. 40*, World Fertility Survey, Voorburg, ISI, 1984; **Table 2.5** from A.A. Way, A.R. Cross and S. Kumar, 'Family planning in Botswana, Kenya and Zimbabwe', *International Family Planning Perspectives*, vol. 13, no. 1, March 1987; **Table 2.6** from *Mortality of Children under Age 5: World Estimates and Projections 1950–2025*, New York, United Nations, Department of International Economic and Social Affairs, 1987; **Figure 2.1** from S.C. Randall, *A Comparative Study of Three Sahelian Populations*, unpublished Ph.D. thesis, University of London, 1984; **Figure 2.2** from B. van Norren and H.A.W. van Vianen, 'The malnutrition and infections syndrome and its demographic outcome in developing countries', Publication No. 4, PCDR, Department of Demography, State University, Groningen; **Tables 4.3** and **4.5** from S. Cairncross and J.L. Cliff, 'Water use and health in Mueda, Mozambique', *Transactions of the Royal Society of Tropical Medicine and Hygiene*, vol. 81, 1987; and **Table 4.4** and **Figure 4.2** from R. Feachem *et al*, *Water, Health and Development: an Inter-Disciplinary Evaluation*, London, Tri-Med Books, 1978.

1 Introduction

Douglas Rimmer

Of all the principal populated regions of the world, tropical Africa is the least urbanized. Nearly four-fifths of the total of some 375 million people in this region are believed to live outside towns, even though African towns are usually defined modestly in population size. From the 1940s until at least the 1970s, the urban populations were growing much faster than territorial or national totals — around two to three times as fast — as a result, chiefly, of migration. Even so, the weight of tropical African population lies in the countryside, and will remain there for many years to come. To address the subject of rural transformation is therefore to study change in the ways of life of most people in tropical Africa.

As W.T.S. Gould and Ken Swindell point out in their contributions to this volume, these rural livelihoods and life styles cannot be neatly distinguished and separated from their urban counterparts. The division of town and country illustrates a commonplace analytical fondness for dichotomy. Other examples are agriculture and industry, traditional and modern, formal and informal, indigenous and alien. Such conceptual oppositions simplify reality, but can obstruct the understanding of it, if much individual behaviour obstinately straddles the dividing line. People make their livings and live their lives regardless of the boundaries postulated by theorists of social change or adopted for statistical estimation. Life in a big African city may be a world away from life in the bush, but individuals circulate between these worlds, and many households and families have interests in both. So rural transformation is not a process limited to the countryside, any more than the effects of urbanization are felt only in the towns. And, so far as the movement of people between places in Africa is free, or at least not effectively controlled, we had best think of the distribution of the gains and losses from these processes of change occuring among people rather than among places or economic sectors.

Rural transformation was not defined when papers were commissioned for the Conference of which this volume is an outcome, and none of the authors found it necessary to give an exact meaning to the term. It was not used as a synonym for rural development, in the sense of change consciously planned and engineered through investments or by policy inducements. Such policy interventions might rather be regarded as changes in data to which people react as they would also react to chance happenings or to opportunities arising more spontaneously. Rural transformation might then be construed as adaptations to changes

in circumstances arising from a variety of causes. These changes may
be gradual and continuous, like the growth of population, or large and
abrupt, as with the building of a big dam, an influx of refugees, or an
important advance in productive techniques; and the adaptations made
to them may be more or less radical and more or less constructive. Passive
adaptation implies an economic life that merely expands or contracts in
well-worn grooves. More active adjustments to changing circumstances,
provided they are large enough and sustained long enough, produce
the qualitative changes in economy and society for which the term
transformation appears more appropriate.

Commercialization as a transforming force

Historically, rural societies in Africa have been transformed by
commercialization of their economic life, or by what the Marxists
call commodity production. Labour and land have been switched
from production of goods for the direct consumption of their users
to production for markets, whether local or distant, urban or rural.
Migrations and tendencies towards economic specialization have been
among the consequences, and considerations of cost and returns, profit
or loss, have assumed increasing importance relatively to other
criteria of resource use.

Commercialization is a matter of degree. Rarely is it altogether absent,
and nowhere is it complete. But in Africa the pace of commercialization
is generally believed to have been greatly accelerated from the later years
of the nineteenth century by European colonialism. There was always
disagreement among observers of this process, though not necessarily
among the participants, about how far it was desirable, and the debate
continues today. Production for the market, or the sale of labour for hire,
exposes the supplier to risks of a kind he or she would not otherwise face
and to the possibility of exploitation by buyers. Commercialization is also
a disequalizing force in society.

On the other hand, subsistence production is not without risks of its
own, exploitation through selling or buying depends on the presence of
monopoly power rather than being intrinsic to exchange, and societies
in which disequalizing forces are repressed are unlikely to experience
much economic progress.

Recent events have shown commercialization not to be an irreversible
process in Africa. If the real earnings obtained from selling products or
factors of production fall persistently in relation to supply costs, a point
may be reached where incentives to sell disappear for some sellers,
and resources are switched from exchange to subsistence. Warfare in
countries including Mozambique, Angola and Uganda has had this result
through increasing the costs, reducing the returns and raising the risks of
production for markets; but experience elsewhere, perhaps most notably

in Ghana during the decade following 1974, has shown that maladroit economic policies can decommercialize economic life in tropical Africa even in the absence of war.

Economically reactionary politics

Decommercialization is the starkest evidence of the negative economic consequences, especially for agriculture, characteristic of African politics for many years. The more prevalent illustrations show the diversion of farming resources from their socially most profitable uses in export-cropping. Richard Crook's chapter in this volume examines two explanations of these perversions. One is that governments have pursued political rather than economic objectives in their agricultural measures: political dividends are won from actions that appear economically irrational. The second explanation is that public functionaries have diverted state power from collective ends into networks of private patronage, in which case political interventions become politically as well as economically destructive. These explanations are rivals in the literature but they are not mutually exclusive. Actual results can be the outcome of both sets of causes.

The currently most influential critics of African policy-making urge that market forces should be substituted for public administration. Other critics distrust the market as well as the state and express populist ideals. But the need to diminish the economic power of the state is generally agreed — even now, and under pressure from their foreign creditors, by African governments themselves. Dr Crook observes that this prescription evades the puzzle that agricultural performance is not uniformly unsatisfactory in all tropical African countries. Some states — he instances the Ivory Coast — appear capable of sustaining both public policies and markets while sharing, or at least not notably diverging from, the political culture of states where agricultural performance has been dismal. The presence of large farmers, and therefore of a politically organized and influential agricultural interest, is one possible explanation of the difference (Bates, 1981, p. 95). Another is the inhibitions on policy-making, especially in the monetary sphere, which some governments have accepted through their international connections; it is significant that African countries using the CFA franc maintained monetary sobriety and realistic exchange rates in the 1960s and 1970s while others did not. Perhaps it should be conceded that there are really differences in political culture, if some governments are more inhibited in their behaviour than others, but we are still left asking why.

Population growth as a transforming force

Commercialization, checked and trammelled by politics as it has been, is one transforming force in rural Africa. Potentially at least, population growth is another. It is believed to have been accelerating in tropical Africa since the 1930s, as a result of death-rates falling, especially in early childhood, without a compensating decline in birth-rates. The current annual rate of growth for the region as a whole is estimated to be around 3 per cent; for Kenya, the estimate is 4 per cent. Allan Hill observes in his chapter in this volume that such rates of growth over so wide an area are unique in demographic history. Probably in no other way have outside forces so deeply affected the conditions of life in Africa. Not only have numbers risen but also the age composition of populations has altered as infant and child mortality rates have fallen and life expectancy has lengthened. Currently 40 to 50 per cent of the national totals are people aged less than 15 years. African societies have had to adapt to rising survival rates among children, as later they may have to adapt to rising survival rates among elderly people. These changes in composition attract less notice than the change in numbers, but their effects on human behaviour and values are profound.

Attention is mostly concentrated on the question of when population growth will decelerate as a result of falling fertility. Dr Hill notes that, while the proximate determinants of fertility — marriage patterns, breastfeeding practice, contraception and abortions — are fairly well established, these findings provide no basis for understanding when the behavioural changes that reduce fertility occur. Among more fundamental causes of fertility reduction, schooling is the leading candidate, especially schooling that assumes and inculcates belief in equality between the sexes. Schooling converts children from assets to liabilities in the economies of their parents. Continued long enough, it reverses the inter-generational flow of income and other benefits (Caldwell, 1982).

The macro-economic effects of African population growth are less evident than postulated. The World Bank expresses (most categorically in McNamara, 1985) a neo-Malthusian view that the ability of African peoples to obtain food cannot possibly increase as fast as their numbers will increase if fertility is not brought down. There is little empirical evidence to support this view, and reliance is placed instead on projections. The study by Edward Clay and John Borton in this volume gives no special prominence to population pressure as a cause of the African food crisis of 1982–86, and none of the countries in which that crisis was manifest most (Ethiopia, Sudan, Mozambique, Chad and Mali) could be called thickly populated, even by African standards. Migration to towns, or between rural areas, seems to be more generally impelled by rising aspirations and a perception of differences in economic opportunities than by the pressure of people on available land. The sign of the relationship between population growth in Africa and food supply per head, or between population growth and economic growth in general, is much less certain than the

World Bank suggests; hence the general importance of this relationship may also be questioned.

The effects of population growth on resources previously free

But this is not to say that population growth in tropical Africa has been, or will be, economically insignificant. Combined with the trend towards commercialization of economic activity, it has conferred scarcity value upon agricultural land that was formerly free or nominally priced. Dr Swindell's chapter shows the development of this process on the principal urban peripheries and the creation there of a land-poor class having to supplement the output of inadequate plots by day-labour. Traffic in land has evolved elsewhere despite customary proscriptions as the growth of an effective demand for its use has ended its abundance. Rapid population growth is certain to continue, and land scarcity and individualization of tenure can be expected to occur over widening areas, with attendant social differentiation and political tension, however uncertain the timing of these changes in particular places in our present state of knowledge. In Kenya, land tenure has already been explicitly individualized, and one result has been the creation of landless people; that consequence may be deplored, but economic progress does not occur in countries where everyone remains an agriculturalist. The alternative to putting land into the market in places where it has become scarce is to tolerate its individual appropriation through political power or influence. That too is occurring as many African governments shrink from the legal implications and political consequences of recognizing closure of the frontier of settlement and land utilization in parts of their territories.

Population growth may also strongly affect human ecology. It is well to remember that on balance these effects have been highly beneficial in the past, so far as the human populations themselves are concerned. But, here again, current expectations are at variance with history. In Africa, attention is drawn particularly to deforestation and its direct and possible indirect consequences for soil fertility. Trees are lost partly because of their economic exploitation as fuel or industrial material. Writing on rural energy in this volume, Walter Elkan considers particularly the depletion of woodlands through the use of trees for fuel.

Like land, timber in the form of fuelwood commands prices in some places, particularly in cities and in districts from which urban markets are accessible, but is free elsewhere. Where fuelwood is free to its users or cheap relatively to its substitutes, it tends to be used wastefully. The same is true of any other good so characterized. Assuming rising demand and a constrained, and possibly diminishing, supply, fuelwood will cease to be free, or even relatively cheap, over widening areas. The fuelwood problem as we know it now will thus progressively disappear, becoming subsumed in the wider economic problem of scarcity. The current problem is that profligate use of a resource presently abundant will bring nearer, and is likely to aggravate, the future scarcity.

Yet, as Professor Elkan observes, the principal reason why defor-estation is occurring appears to be not the consumption of fuelwood but the enlargement and intesification of agriculture. To some extent, and in some areas. the abundance of wood as fuel is an incidental consequence of the advancing frontier of cultivation; indeed, trees in areas newly cleared may even be burned for want of uses for the timber. In this light, the current fuelwood problem appears as an aspect of the wider questions of whether agriculture is expanding with sufficient safeguarding of its future.

This agricultural expansion is probably much less the result of cash-cropping for export, a favourite target for denigration in some of the literature on Africa, than of food production to supply the increasing population. We should be readier than we are to acknowledge that tropical Africa could not have sustained the estimated doubling of its population in the last thirty years without remarkable growth in its output of food.

In all places and at all times, a balance needs to be kept between the immediate returns from cultivation and the guarding of future returns through maintaining the fertility of the soil. The pressure against this safeguard of a growing need or incentive to produce food and other crops is one source of rising productivity in agriculture. The private interest in keeping this balance diverges from the social interest only through ignorance or through a difference in the period of time over which the maintenance of returns is desired. As to the latter point, local communities and individual proprietors might be expected usually to take longer views than governments do. As to the former, officials have long been disposed to assume African farmers ignorant of the need for conservation (see, e.g., Anderson, 1984), but it is not clear why the accumulated wisdom of generations of practitioners should be any more deficient in this respect than in others.

There may nevertheless occur involuntary depletion of timber resources and tree cover because of inadequate definition and policing of rights over land, whether these rights are public or private. Communities, individual proprietors or authorities may have correct appreciations of the importance of conservation, but suffer frustration of their intentions through inadequate laws or silvan piracy. Bill Gould refers to the 'robber economy' of urban fuelwood suppliers in eastern Africa. The problem is not ignorance or lack of care for the future, but rather the long-standing inability of governments in Africa to legislate for changing economic conditions and effectively to maintain the law. The burden of law enforcement can hardly have been eased by the growing number of people seeking access to land, and the changes in values inevitably arising from alteration in the age-composition of populations and in their geographical distributions.

The real costs of free labour

Even 'free' fuelwood involves real costs, consisting largely in the time women and children spend collecting it; as Professor Elkan suggests, reduction in these costs is unlikely to be a priority when decisions on fuelwood use are taken. Other important real costs, to which Sandy Cairncross draws attention in this book, are incurred in fetching water and in food preparation, especially the grinding or pounding of starchy staples. Again, these costs lie outside commercial exchanges and are borne mostly by women and children.

As with land and fuelwood, so with people's time, the process of commercialization may confer money-value on what was previously gratuitous, and lead to economy in its use. But the labour available for household chores is increasing as African populations grow and their average age falls. It follows almost certainly that more than commercialization is needed, if the vast expenditure of the time and energy of women and children on water and fuelwood collection and food preparation is to be reduced. The extension of schooling — socially, geographically and in age — is one such additional requirement; and it is worth remarking that in recent times schooling, at least at primary level, does seem to have been extended in individual countries regardless of their rates of economic growth (Reynolds, 1985, p. 394). But schooling alone may merely shift some part of the burden from children to women, and probably from boys to girls. If resources are to be deployed so as to curtail the time that needs to be spent in rural Africa on household chores, the social, economic and political inequalities between the sexes will have to be reduced.

Until recently, these inequalities were little explored in rural Africa or, indeed, anywhere else. The great contribution of feminist scholars has been to persuade us that socio-economic analysis ought not to stop at the boundaries of households or families. It is an error to suppose the relationships among members of these entities (such as the division of labour, income distribution and property rights) to be irrelevant to an understanding of the functioning of society or of social change. Relationships within households, in particular, should rank high on the list of priorities of economic and social research in tropical Africa. The reasons are practical as well as scientific. For example, provision of social overheads causes reallocation in the time of women and children; income distribution within households affects migration; and the sexual division of labour conditions choice of crops and constrains total agricultural supply. (A paper by Dr Ann Whitehead on the sexual division of labour in rural production was presented at the Conference from which this volume is derived, but regretably could not be revised in time for inclusion here.)

The findings reported by Dr Cairncross suggest that not much of the women's time that could be saved by improvements in water supply would be used in agricultural production. The reasons might include limitations on women's access to land and agricultural inputs. But also there are other claims on women's time saved from fetching water. The time that mothers (and other family members) are able to give to the nurture of children is an important contribution to what it was fashionable, in the 1960s, to describe as human capital formation; it is not by chance that persons of superior capacities come disproportionately from leisured households. Dr Cairncross mentions the improvements in domestic hygiene, and therefore in health, that may follow from better access to water, because of savings in women's time as well as of the greater use of water, and the possibility that gains in the nutritional status of children may be sometimes attributed to these savings. He adds that the time-savings should be reckoned as benefits, however they are used; they improve the quality of women's lives, and are a step towards women's emancipation.

Increases in leisure are one of the three principal ways in which societies have advanced; the others are increases in population and in economic production. Gains are often recognized in only the last of these directions. In the first, they tend to be disregarded; reduction in drudgery, or more particularly domestic drudgery, has never been a great political cause. In the second, they tend to be misrepresented — regarded as an offset to production averaged per head. It is true that social and economic problems are associated with rapid population increase (though it seems that every other kind of population change has also caused concern at some time). But population increase attributable chiefly to falling mortality in early childhood, and associated with lengthening life expectancy, must be reckoned a gain whatever it does to GNP per head or to the burdens of public administration.

Influences on morbidity and mortality

In spite of the downward trend in child mortality rates, they remain relatively very high in rural tropical Africa. One child in every five still dies before its fifth birthday. Influences on mortality and morbidity include sanitation, health care, nutrition, customs, education and living standards in general. Dr Hill shows the difficulty of arriving at any general ordering of the relative importance of these influences in Africa, when experience is seemingly so various. Also, the influences are not always separable in practice. Outside Africa, there is a popular belief that nutrition, or the lack of it, is of decisive importance, but water may in fact be of more general significance than food. Many fewer African children die or are sick from under-nourshiment *per se* than suffer from deficient hygiene owing to shortage of water. Improving the quality of domestic water is desirable, since many diseases are water-borne or water-based, but greater gains are currently to be won, Dr Cairncross suggests, by increasing the quantities of water used, thus checking the principal transmission routes of faeco-oral diseases. Use of water can be increased only by making it more accessible, and in particular, empirical studies have shown, by making it more nearly accessible to people who presently live more than about one kilometre (or a thirty-minute journey) away from a source of water. Thus the same implication for practice seems to follow whether better health or the saving of time is taken to be the objective of improving water supply; priority should be given to people who live farthest from their present source of water. For those within the 1-km radius, use of water would be expected to increase only if piped connections were made with dwellings.

There have been broadly two approaches to primary health care in rural Africa: a selective one, imparting a quick 'technical fix' through programmes of, for example, immunization or oral rehydration therapy, and an approach integrating control of the variables generally affecting health, emphasizing prevention rather than cure, requiring community participation, and using techniques appropriate to local circumstances. Carol MacCormack's chapter in this book argues the merits of the second approach and explains the contribution that social anthropologists can make to it in assessing the social feasibility of measures of health care in particular cultures and localities. In her view, rural health is best promoted by teamwork among epidemiologists, social scientists and village health workers, including traditional practitioners. Since the causes of morbidity are inter-connected, they cannot with success be dealt with severally. And, so far as those causes are specific to places or communities, they resist general remedy.

One is reminded of the insistence on complementarities in the analyses of industrialization that were made in the 1950s (Nurkse, 1953, Chap. 1; Scitovsky, 1954), and the uncomfortable conclusion that everything needed to be done at once. Complementarities in health care are at least as marked as they are in industry, and from the standpoint of policy they are more important since their satisfaction usually cannot be left to market inducements. There is a strong case in principle for integrated programmes to secure simultaneous and mutually reinforcing improvements in public hygiene, water use, nutrition, housing, the education of women, and preventive and curative medicine; and no doubt these programmes would be even more effective if they were finely adjusted to localized cultures. In practice, it has not been in this way that disease has been diminished and lives lengthened, but in more singular or general ways, albeit more imperfect ones, such as sanitary engineering, easy access to water and rising living standards.

If the sway of central governments in Africa is to be diminished, either from ideological conviction or, perhaps more probably, from financial stringency, local institutions assume correspondingly more importance. Dr MacCormack considers the responsibility for primary health care best discharged locally anyway, and Dr Cairncross points out that water supply and other infrastructural provision have generally been the foundation of local government. But the experience of local government in the modern states of tropical Africa has not been a happy one. Newly elected or appointed bodies have taken rights away from the older communal institutions but frequently failed to acquire their authority. In Nigeria the attempt of 1976 to make local units an effective third tier of government led instead to enhancement of the power of the States and further proliferations of patronage. Another attempt is to be made in the late 1980s. Possibly local authorities that were both empowered and obliged to be financially self-sufficient would be more durable and effective. Anthropological research into the functioning of localized communities has been unfashionable since African countries became independent states. Perhaps the time has come to revive this work, in order to assess how communal institutions could be effectively integrated with structures of local administration, and their potential in raising revenues, maintaining or improving rural standards, and managing rural change.

African disasters

Nobody will be surprised to learn that calamity was what drew world-wide attention to Africa in recent years. Sensitivity to disaster in far-off places has been heightened by technical advances in the transmission of news. Thus the effects of (in particular) drought and famine in Ethiopia and the Sahel in the early 1970s, and over wider areas of tropical Africa a decade later, excited intense popular concern where previously there would have been ignorance or indifference (see Harrison & Palmer, 1986).

Edward Clay and John Borton discuss the second of these calamities in this volume. They use the adoption by governments and international agencies of extraordinary, or emergency, measures to distinguish the food crisis perceived in Africa in the early 1980s from any deeper-lying or more persistent agrarian or economic malaise.

The relevant statistics are very weak, but, if they are to be believed, there was a dramatic fall in African food production in 1980–82 and a dramatic rise in 1985–86. That the food problem in many African countries should have become one of surplus disposal by 1986 suggests that, even in Africa, agriculture is volatile rather than in decay. The severity of the earlier food deficiencies is virtually impossible to judge objectively. Statistics may have been politicized in the bad years since they were used to trigger international relief; emergency food aid was wanted to supplement government resources as well as to feed people. Of the five countries generally agreed to have been worst affected, all but Mali were experiencing warfare or insurgency. There appears nevertheless to have been no single cause of the crisis but rather several partial explanations and possible precipitants. As previously mentioned, the worst-affected countries were not densely populated. Nor were they strongly commercialized.

Weathering the crisis (for those who weathered it) was not just a matter of outside relief. John Borton's case studies of Kenya and Botswana, both of which countries were badly affected by drought, bring out the effectiveness of domestic policies and institutions in those places — in contrast to, for example, Ethiopia. The success stories are not less instructive than the failure, though the latter tend to engross attention. Kenya was able to purchase large imports of food during the drought years because it produced then the largest coffee crops in its history.

People with money in their pockets do not go hungry. It has been argued (e.g. in East Africa Royal Commission, 1955, pp. 46, 65–6) that the acquisition of purchasing power, or commercialization, is the surest insurance against famine. In this way, according to one view, famine in Africa had been brought under control by the end of the colonial period, but since then there has been a breakdown in some areas. A contrary view (see, e.g., Watts, 1983) is that the commercialization of Africa, far from removing food insecurity, actually created this hazard: that African communities were able regularly to secure their food, droughts notwithstanding, until they became caught in the web of international commerce. Ethiopian experience provides singularly bad support for this second view, as Edward Clay and John Borton point out. Credence is nevertheless given to it in official circles, and to the corollary that self-sufficiency in food is desirable, as was often so in the colonial period (Rimmer, 1983, pp. 151–2). Historical research could make an important contribution to intelligent policy-making by investigating just how secure in their food relatively uncommercialized African societies were.

Some reflections on research into African rural transformation

Consideration of the food crisis exposes the shortcomings of highly aggregated statistics in tropical Africa. For example, there was doubt about the severity of the impending Ethiopian famine because of a 20 per cent disagreement in the estimates of population used. Figures of African agricultural output are regularly produced by governments, the FAO and the US Department of Agriculture, but it has been said of the estimates for some of the larger countries (Zaire, Nigeria, Ethiopia, Sudan) that they are little better than random numbers (Fieldhouse, 1986, p. 98, quoting Michael Lipton). Statistics of food consumption per head are an even worse case, if that is conceivable, since population totals are uncertain, population growth rates may be substantially in error, calorie conversion factors are inexact, and losses in storage and in processing have to guessed (Farnsworth, 1961). Estimates are scarcely more robust in other areas. It is often said that one person out of every four in tropical Africa is a Nigerian, but there has been no genuine census of population in Nigeria since 1952–53, and the results of that census were regarded as nowhere near accurate. It has been suggested that the margin of error averages 20 per cent in African GDP estimates, and that some of the sectoral components of these estimates (including agricultural output) could be out by up to 50 per cent (Blades, 1980). Ironically, some production data are inferred from population estimates. Others are inferred from balance-of-payments figures, but it has been remarked that in some countries they too are necessarily part fantasy (Berg, 1975, p. 4). To say that many macro-economic estimates in Africa are very weak may be to exaggerate their value. There appears no ground for expecting any trend of improvement in the quality of such estimates. Their inadequacy is itself a datum of economic and social research in tropical Africa.

Our ideas about aggregative change in rural Africa are therefore quantitatively very rough. Much meaning has been read into recorded export volumes. This reliance may not be misleading in most cases, provided that domestic produce is not extensively smuggled, since economic growth appears historically to be more closely and positively correlated with exports than with anything else (Reynolds, 1985, pp. 409–13) and the exports of most African countries are mainly of rural origin. It is export performance that has chiefly divided the relatively successful from other African economies. Often the high performers have been mineral exporters (Nigeria, Gabon, Congo, Botswana) but arguably the more general case is of agricultural exports: thus the Ivory Coast has been contrasted with Ghana, Kenya with Tanzania, Malawi with Zambia. Policies are commonly regarded as central to explanations of these differences, but, as Dr Crook reminds us, we still understand too little why the politics of some countries and some regimes have facilitated commercial agriculture and the politics of others have not.

Contemporary Africa has the misfortune to provide several kinds of experimental conditions for investigating the effects of political upheaval on agriculture and rural society. First, there are countries (Uganda, Mozambique, Angola, the Central African Republic, Equatorial Guinea) that have experienced, or continue to experience, economic and administrative collapse. What conditions would have to be satisfied, and how long would it take, to restore in these countries such levels of performance as were attained in the late colonial period? Economic life in some parts of the world has shown amazing resilience in recovering from catastrophe. But might it be that in tropical Africa, where levels of economic and administrative performance were low even when were good, a ratchet effect will be present? Second, other countries (Ethiopia, Sudan, Somalia, Mali, Chad) have come to depend heavily on external aid in money and kind to alleviate hunger and supplement public resources during the occurrence (and recurrence) of famine. What will be the long-run effects on society and its economic and political functioning of these repeated interventions? Third, in the last few years a large number of African countries (including Nigeria, Ghana, Zaire, Tanzania, Zambia) have been obliged by pressure from their external creditors to undertake seemingly fundamental reforms by devaluing their currencies, removing or reducing producer and consumer subsidies, liberalizing their import regimes, holding down budget deficits and dismantling parastatal enterprises. So far as these reforms are sustained, African economic policies in the later 1980s will be quite different in character from those commonly followed in the first quarter-century of independence. Another rich field awaits investigation in exploring the effects of these new measures and of the political strains imposed by adhering to them.

Economic and social research in tropical Africa started late in the day and still provides a relatively shallow base of knowledge. In its early stages, which are still within living memory, it was mostly anthropological and linguistic work related to the needs of colonial administration. Research in economics, economic history, politics and urban sociology did not begin until the 1940s or even later. Research peaked in the 1960s. For financial, logistic and political reasons, it has become more difficult to conduct, and less extensive, as the years have passed since then.

A consequence of this limited and faltering research effort is that our portfolio of findings relevant to rural transformation resembles an album of snapshots. Mostly, they are not even snapshots of the same people at different points in time, for it is exceptional for data to be available in detail to allow inter-temporal comparisons of the same community or locality (see Lawson, 1972, for one of the exceptions). The longitudinal studies which are the necessary record of change are few and far between. We try to understand processes of change in the rural areas when we have only fragmentary knowledge of what changes have occured.

Although there can be little doubt that economic and social research in tropical Africa has been diminishing in recent years, the decline is not as steep as it appears to be (Eicher, 1985, p. 2). The reason is that much of the research that is currently undertaken is done under the auspices of aid agencies — bodies that have the resources to overcome the obstacles faced by independent researchers. African researchers in particular have often done their work under the shelter of these umbrellas. There are several weaknesses in this sector of current research. First, it is tied to aims that are both directly practical and short-term in their understanding of useful findings. Second, the findings are not always — perhaps not usually — widely disseminated. Often they appear in the so-called grey literature that international and other aid agencies print but do not publish. Third, because these findings are not subjected to the normal process of scholarly publication, they tend to escape serious critical scrutiny. In short, while we should be even more ignorant in the absence of this aid-related research, it is far from being an ideal way of enlarging our knowledge.

In many African countries, universities and research institutions are in disarray — starved of funds, increasingly detached from current developments in science and scholarship, rocked by political commotions. There is a danger that two classes of African specialists will evolve: those who are in Africa but out of touch with their subjects, and those outside Africa who can keep up with the development of their disciplines but possess diminishing first-hand experience of the places they are studying (Crowder, 1987).

One purpose of this book is to show something of the richness of African material for social and economic enquiry and the practical value of such research — not only for the peoples of Africa themselves but for the rest of us whose lives cannot be unaffected by what happens in Africa — and thus to assist in a reawakening of interest in these studies and the allocation of funds to support them. The chapters that follow are addressed to selected nodes of research: population growth, primary health care, domestic water supply, energy, rural–urban interaction, agrarian change on peri-urban fringes, the relations between farmers and government agencies, the food crisis of the early 1980s. This list is not, of course, exhaustive. Other topics (such as education, transport and communications, market-places and storage, rural industrialization) might have been chosen as aspects of rural transformation. For those topics that were selected, each contributor reports and comments on the current state of our knowledge and shows its importance, both scientific and practical. The contributors write dispassionately, but do not forget that their concern is with the welfare and aspirations of people whose fortitude in contending with an environment often hostile and institutions often defective demand our understanding and deserve our respect.

References

Anderson, David (1984), 'Depression, dust bowl, demography and drought: the colonial state and soil conservation in East Africa during the 1930s', *African Affairs*, **83**: 321–43.

Bates, Robert H. (1981), *Markets and States in Tropical Africa: the political basis of agricultural policies*, Berkeley, University of California Press.

Berg, Elliot (1975), *The Recent Economic Evolution of the Sahel*, Ann Arbor, Center for Research on Economic Development, University of Michigan.

Blades, D.W. (1980), 'What do we know about levels and growth of output in developing countries? A critical analysis with special reference to Africa' in *Economic Growth and Resources*, Vol. 2, London, Macmillan for the International Economic Association, R.C.O. Matthews, (ed.).

Caldwell, John C. (1982), *Theory of Fertility Decline*, London, Academic Press.

Crowder, Michael (1987), "Us" and "them": the International African Institute and the current crisis of identity in African Studies', *Africa*, **57**: 109-22.

East Africa Royal Commission 1953–1955 (1955), *Report*, London, HMSO, Cmd. 9475.

Eicher, Carl K. (1985), *Agricultural Research for African Development: problems and priorities for 1985–2000*, Paper prepared for a World Bank conference on Research Priorities for Sub-Saharan Africa, Bellagio, 25 February–1 March 1985.

Farnsworth, Helen C. (1961), 'Defects, uses and abuses of national food supply and consumption data', *Food Research Institute Studies*, **2**: 179–201.

Fieldhouse, D.K. (1986), *Black Africa 1945–80: Economic Decolonization and Arrested Development*, London, Allen & Unwin.

Harrison, Paul & Palmer, Robin (1986), *News out of Africa*, London, Hilary Shipman.

Lawson, Rowena (1972), *The Changing Economy of the Lower Volta 1954–67*, London, Oxford University Press for the International African Institute.

McNamara, Robert S. (1985), *The Challenges for Sub-Saharan Africa*, Sir John Crawford Memorial Lecture, Washington DC, 1 November 1985.

Nurkse, Ragnar (1953), *Problems of Capital Formation in Underdeveloped Countries*, Oxford, Basil Blackwell.

Reynolds, Lloyd G. (1985), *Economic Growth in the Third World, 1850–1980*, New Haven and London, Yale University Press.

Rimmer, Douglas (1983), 'The economic imprint of colonialism and domestic food supplies in British tropical Africa' in *Imperialism, Colonialism and Hunger: East and Central Africa*, Lexington, D.C. Heath, Robert I. Rotberg (ed.).

Scitovsky, Tibor (1954), 'Two concepts of external economies', *Journal of Political Economy*, 72: 143–51.

Watts, Michael (1983), *Silent Violence: Food, Famine and Peasantry in Northern Nigeria*, Berkeley, University of California Press.

2 Population Growth and Rural Transformation in Tropical Africa

Allan G. Hill

The statistical data on population growth in sub-Saharan Africa indicate rates unique in demographic history. Moreover, mortality levels in Africa are still relatively high, indicating a considerable potential for future continuation of these high rates of natural increase unless fertility rates decline very rapidly. The bare facts of this demographic explosion are widely reported, producing much shaking of heads in the international development agencies (e.g. World Bank, 1981 and 1986a).

A collation of demographic data for sub-Saharan Africa has been produced by the World Bank, together with estimates of the future population of African countries using some quite general assumptions about future trends in fertility and mortality. The annual growth rates and the projected populations in millions are shown in the first six columns of Table 2.1. The size of the stationary populations, for which birth- and death-rates have been equal and constant for some time, appears in column 7. The estimated dates when there is no change in the size of the generations are shown in column 8. Finally, in column 9, we see by how much each of the populations will continue to grow even when the net reproduction rate has reached unity. The overall impression given by this table is that sub-Saharan Africa is only at the beginning of a fairly long period of substantial population growth. Moreover, the growth in number is by no means restricted to the poorer countries; even in the middle-income countries, annual rates of population growth may continue to be around 3 per cent per year because modest fertility declines can be offset by improvements in mortality.

There is a gap in our understanding of the causes and consequences of rapid population growth in anything other than very gross terms. In part, our ignorance is explained by the nature of population growth itself which is simultaneously an exogenous and an endogamous variable in most models of economic development and social change. Further confusion arises from the conflicting findings obtained from macro- and micro-level research. How much mortality improvement or fertility change can be anticipated when interventions are directed at individuals rather than aimed at altering the social, economic and cultural context of decision-making?

Most of these larger issues are unlikely to be resolved by empirical research in the field. Decisions about interventionist policies, whether about family planning and induced abortion service, for example, or about universal access to primary education, are likely to be taken with ideological considerations paramount. Also important, however, are the mundane considerations of cost and feasibility. Whilst, for example, wholesale revolutionary change may be necessary to eradicate sex, caste and class differentials in child mortality, in practice the only politically acceptable intervention may involve a more conservative approach — say an enlarged programme of immunization. Thus, on the one hand, the role of social science research on population growth in sub-Saharan Africa is to exploit the many 'natural experiments' undertaken by African governments of various hues in an attempt to discern the demographic consequences of different ideologies. A subsidiary question is of course whether demographic circumstances have affected public policy in any important way. On the other hand, there is a need to consider the consequences for natural increase and population movement of a selection of policies that African governments regard as practical and worthwhile. Here, there is a broad range of choice available to the socially-minded state, some, like decisions regarding health care provision and family planning, bearing directly on the demographic indicators; others, such as labour laws and taxation systems, with an indirect effect.

To date, we have relatively few definitive answers to the key questions referred to above. In this stocktaking, therefore, it seems more sensible to begin with the results of the more mechanical research on sub-Saharan African demography, in which fertility and mortality are treated simply as outcome, or dependent variables, rather than attempting to speculate on larger issues such as the interactions between public policy and demographic factors about which we know comparatively little.

Fertility

Fertility is in many ways the key variable in the study of the social and economic transformation of traditional societies. Although the classic theoretical work on 'natural' (i.e. not deliberately controlled) fertility was completed many years ago (Henry, 1953), it has taken longer to develop a manageable set of indicators to describe the factors directly affecting both natural and controlled fertility that can be derived from the results of questionnaire surveys.

This work on the 'proximate' or intermediate determinants of fertility (Bongaarts & Potter, 1983) has helped our understanding of African fertility patterns in two important ways. It has taught us, first, what proximate factors in a mechanical sense can be left out of

Table 2.1   Population growth and projections for sub-Saharan Africa

Country	Average annual growth of population (percent)			Population (millions)			Hypothetical size of stationary population (millions)	Assumed year of reaching net reproduction rate of 1	Population momentum 1985
	1965–73	1973–83	1980–2000	1983	1990	2000			
Low-income economies	2.6w	2.8w	3.1w	248t	305t	411t			
Low-income semi-arid	2.5w	2.5w	2.7w	30t	36t	48t			
1 Mali	2.6	2.5	2.5	7	9	11	37	2035	1.9
2 Burkina	2.0	1.9	2.0	6	7	9	32	2040	1.8
3 Niger	2.6	3.0	3.2	6	8	11	40	2040	2.0
4 Somalia	3.5	2.8	3.0	5	6	8	31	2040	1.9
5 Gambia, The	3.0	3.6	2.7	1	1	1	3	—	1.9
6 Chad	1.8	2.1	2.4	5	6	7	22	2040	1.8
Other low-income	2.6w	2.9w	3.1w	218t	269t	363t			
7 Ethiopia	2.6	2.7	2.6	41	48	64	181	2035	1.9
8 Zaire	2.1	2.5	3.1	30	37	50	145	2030	1.9
9 Guinea-Bissau	1.2	4.3	2.1	1	1	1	4		1.8
10 Malawi	2.8	3.0	3.1	7	8	11	38	2040	2.0
11 Uganda	3.4	2.8	3.3	14	18	25	83	2035	2.0
12 Burundi	1.4	2.2	2.9	4	5	7	24	2035	1.9
13 Tanzania	3.1	3.3	3.4	21	27	37	125	2035	2.0
14 Rwanda	3.1	3.4	3.4	5	7	10	40	2040	2.0
15 Central African Rep.	1.6	2.3	2.7	2	3	4	12	2035	1.9
16 Togo	2.8	2.6	3.2	3	4	5	16	2035	2.0
17 Benin	2.6	2.8	3.1	4	5	6	21	2035	2.0
18 Guinea	1.8	2.0	2.1	6	7	8	25	2045	1.8
19 Ghana	2.2	3.1	3.5	13	17	23	64	2025	2.0
20 Madagascar	2.4	2.6	3.1	9	12	16	55	2035	1.9
21 Sierra Leone	1.7	2.1	2.3	4	4	5	17	2045	1.8
22 Kenya	3.7	4.0	3.9	19	25	36	120	2030	2.1
23 Sudan	2.6	3.2	2.8	21	25	33	102	2035	1.9
24 Mozambique	2.3	2.6	2.9	13	16	22	70	2035	2.0

	3.1w	3.3w	3.4w	39t	49t	67t			
Middle-income oil importers	3.1w	3.3w	3.4w	39t	49t	67t			
25 Senegal	2.4	2.8	2.9	6	8	10	30	2035	1.9
26 Lesotho	2.1	2.5	2.6	1	2	2	6	2030	1.8
27 Liberia	2.8	3.3	3.1	2	3	3	11	2035	1.9
28 Mauritania	2.3	2.2	2.6	2	2	3	8	2035	1.8
29 Zambia	3.0	3.2	3.3	6	8	11	33	2030	2.0
30 Ivory Coast	4.6	4.6	3.6	9	13	17	47	2030	2.0
31 Zimbabwe	3.4	3.2	3.6	8	10	14	39	2025	2.1
32 Swaziland	3.1	3.4	3.3	1	1	1	5	—	2.0
33 Botswana	3.0	4.5	3.5	1	1	2	6	—	1.9
34 Mauritius	2.0	1.4	1.6	1	1	1	2	—	1.8
35 Namibia	2.5	2.8	3.3	1	1	2	6	—	1.9
Middle-income oil exporters	2.5w	2.7w	3.3w	114t	144t	197t			
36 Nigeria	2.5	2.7	3.3	94	118	163	532	2035	2.0
37 Cameroon	2.4	3.1	3.2	10	12	17	52	2030	1.9
38 Congo, People's Rep.	2.6	3.1	3.7	2	2	3	9	2020	1.9
39 Gabon	0.2	1.4	2.6	1	1	1	3	—	1.7
40 Angola	2.2	2.6	2.8	8	10	13	44	2040	1.9
Upper-middle-income	2.6w	2.4w	2.7w	32t	39t	49t			
41 South Africa	2.6	2.4	2.7	32	39	49	104	2020	1.8
Countries with poulations less than 500,000	2.3w	2.5w	2.7w	3t	3t	5t			
42 Sao Tomé and Principe	2.1	2.1	3.1	0.1	0.1	0.2	—	—	—
43 Cape Verde	2.1	1.5	2.4	0.3	0.4	0.5	—	—	1.9
44 Seychelles	3.3	1.3	1.6	0.1	0.1	0.1	—	—	—
45 Comoros	2.3	2.5	3.5	0.4	0.5	0.7	—	—	1.9
46 Djibouti	3.6	7.1	3.1	0.4	0.4	0.6	—	—	—
47 Equatorial Guinea	1.7	1.7	2.3	0.4	0.4	0.5	2	—	1.8
48 Réunion	2.2	1.1	1.6	0.5	0.6	0.7	1	—	1.8
Sub-Saharan Africa	2.6w	2.9w	3.1w	436t	539t	729t			

Note: In this table, totals weighted by population size are followed by 'w'; simple summations are followed by 't'.
Source: World Bank (1986b), Table 19.

our calculations. The following few variables appear to explain most of the population-level variations in human fertility over time and space: patterns of co-habitation and marriage; breastfeeding practice; and use of contraception or induced abortion. Sterility and coital frequency only assume importance at the aggregate level when their average levels are highly exceptional. Secondly, in an African context, we have begun to appreciate how fertility can vary widely even in societies in which fertility is not deliberately controlled (Page & Lesthaeghe, 1981; Bongaarts, Frank & Lesthaeghe, 1984). The peculiarly African dimension of these proximate variables is being examined in several centres; some recent results are available on African marriage systems (Lesthaeghe, Kaufmann & Meekers, 1986) which form part of a much larger project on African fertility undertaken by the Vrije Universiteit Brussel.

Table 2.2 Fertility and its proximate determinants in selected African rural populations

Population	Total Fertility Rate	C_m	C_i	C_c	C_s	'Potential Fertility'
Ghana (1980)	6.5	0.84	0.64	0.94	—	12.9
Kenya (1978)	7.7	0.81	0.64	0.94	—	15.8
Senegal (1978)	7.3	0.92	0.65	0.98	—	12.5
N. Sudan (1978)	6.4	0.79	0.69	0.98	—	12.0
Mali (1981–3):						
Bambara	8.1	0.92	0.63	1.0	0.90	15.5
Delta Tamasheq	6.6	0.67	0.65	1.0	0.92	16.5
Gourma Tamasheq	5.2	0.68	0.61	1.0	0.86	14.6
Seno-Fulbe	6.0	0.89	0.61	1.0	0.88	12.6
Rimaibe	6.3	0.89	0.65	1.0	0.85	12.8
Masina-Fulbe	7.5	0.88	0.68	1.0	0.83	15.1
Rimaibe	6.6	0.86	0.69	1.0	0.89	12.5

Notes: C_m is the index of non-marriage; $1-C_m$ is the proportional reduction in potential fertility attributable to this variable alone. The other indices – C_i (post-partum amenorrhoea), C_c (contraception) and C_s (spousal separation) are interpreted in the same way.

'potential fertility' (a theoretical concept) = the total fertility rate/$(c_m \times C_i \times C_c \times C_s)$

Sources: Casterline *et al.* (1984), Appendix C; Hill (1985) Table 2 and survey data.

Since the focus here is on rural transformation, we turn to consider the recent direction of change in fertility and in the indices of the proximate fertility determinants in sub-Saharan Africa, particularly the rural areas. A few measures of the total fertility rate and the main

proximate determinants are shown for selected rural African populations in Table 2.2. The striking feature of this table is the similarity in
the values of two of the variables affecting the level of marital fertility
— post-partum amenorrhoea (C_i) and contraception (C_c) — for a whole
range of populations. One of the main sources of the variation in African
fertility is thus the pattern of marriage (or non-marriage). Particularly
distinctive are the marriage systems of a number of the pastoral and
agro-pastoral populations of the Sahel, represented in Table 2.2 by the
two Tamasheq populations of northern Mali.

Although there are many uncertainties because of missing or incomplete data, the overall fertility picture is clear. The most recent data
(see World Bank, 1986b, Table 20) indicate that the crude birth-rate in
sub-tropical Africa is above 45 per 1,000 in all but a few exceptional
countries — Cape Verde, Gabon, Lesotho and Mauritius among them.
Probably more interesting is the suggestion that fertility has risen
recently in several African countries, Kenya in particular, a trend that
would be in parallel with similar pre-transitional fertility increases
elsewhere (Henin *et al.* 1982; Dyson & Murphy, 1985). Certainly,
sterility levels in the past have been abnormally high in parts of
tropical Africa (Retel-Laurentin, 1974, 1979; Romaniuk, 1967, 1968;
and Frank, 1983) and several health interventions have reduced sterility and increased fertility in these areas (Romaniuk, 1980; Belsey,
1976 and 1979). More generally, however, behavioural changes affecting the other proximate determinants of fertility, such as curtailment
of breastfeeding, abandonment of traditionally long periods of post-
partum abstinence from sexual relations, and reduction in the incidence of polygyny have produced fertility increases amongst non-
contracepting populations elsewhere and most probably in sub-tropical
Africa too. Whilst there are very few long time-series on fertility levels
in sub-tropical Africa despite some new historical work (Edinburgh
Centre of African Studies, 1977 and 1981), it is somewhat easier
to detect changes in behaviour that affect fertility in a predictable
way through one or more of the proximate fertility determinants. We
consider the evidence on a few of these changes.

(a) Marriage

Until more representative statistical data on African marriages became
available, the pattern of marriage was generally described as 'early and
universal' (Aryee & Gaisie, 1982). While this statement was broadly
true over large parts of sub-Saharan Africa, there have always been
important exceptions, including the herding societies of the Sahel and
parts of southern Africa affected by migration (Lesthaeghe, Kaufmann
& Meekers, 1986; van de Walle and Kekovole, 1984; Randall, 1984).
Early in the colonial period, statisticians recognized the complexities

of African marriage systems and varied their definitions accordingly (van de Walle, 1968). Demographers have also adopted a more practical approach to marriage, separating out 'exposure' of couples to risk of conception from the notion of socially recognized stable unions. For the study of fertility, the former is clearly more important than the latter. None the less, there are difficulties in defining marital or extra-marital fertility and legitimate or illegitimate births, particularly since it appears that whilst mean ages at first marriage may be rising with modernization, fertility remains unaltered as young women, whether married or single, are continuing to bear a significant number of children (Lesthaeghe, Kaufmann & Meekers, 1986).

Without entering too deeply into the anthropological details of African marriage, it is clear that the bulk of African children are still born to couples living in a socially-recognized sexual union. In five recently surveyed African countries (Ghana, Kenya, Lesotho, Senegal and northern Sudan), the ratio of overall fertility to marital (recognized unions) fertility was between 0.74 (Lesotho) and 0.86 (Senegal). Very broadly, had it not been for some restriction of exposure to the risk of pregnancy by marriage rules and attitudes to extra-marital sex, realized fertility in these countries would have been between a quarter and a fifth higher (Casterline et al., 1984). Of course, divorce, separation of spouses and widowhood all reduce exposure, in addition to the age pattern of marriage and the proportions never marrying. In fact, interviews with women aged 15–49 have revealed that only a half to three-quarters of the women in nine sub-Saharan countries were still living in their first union at the time of interview (Smith, Carrasco & McDonald, 1984).

More interesting here is the direction of change of marriage in the rural areas. Unfortunately, there are very few longitudinal surveys that describe changing marriage patterns in a particular community, so most of the generalizing has to be based on rural–urban comparisons from cross-sectional surveys. Education, rather than rural or urban residence, is thought to be the key factor affecting the values of all the proximate determinants of fertility (Caldwell, 1982; Caldwell, Reddy & Caldwell, 1985), as it also appears to be for mortality (Caldwell, 1986). In Table 2.3, the ratios of total fertility to marital fertility are displayed for five African countries by both residence and education. In this table, the lower the ratio, the greater the effect of marriage in restraining fertility. Overall, both urban residence and formal schooling significantly reduce the value of this ratio because a proportionately smaller part of the woman's reproductive career is spent in marriage. Admittedly, some of the non-married women are in fact having children outside marriage, but these women have fewer children than their counterparts who live in recognized unions. The rather gross statistics on marriage in Africa conceal a large number of quite complex changes with partially compensating effects on fertility. These changes can be summarized as follows:

(i)   The better-educated women appear to be delaying their entry into first marriage (Lesthaeghe, Kaufmann & Meekers, 1986, Tables 5.17 and 5.18), although the fertility effects of such a change are partially offset by tolerance of pre-martial conceptions and births (Romaniuk, 1968; Adegbola & Page, 1982).

(ii)   Polygyny is probably becoming less widespread for both economic and cultural reasons, but is being replaced in some urban situations by forms of visiting unions, concubinage or resort to prostitutes. A side-effect of the change is a reduction in the male age at first marriage, producing a narrowing of the otherwise wide gap between the ages of husbands and wives (see Pison, 1983, for a good exposition of how polygyny produces large age differences between spouses).

(iii) Massive out-migration of males from the countries and homelands adjacent to South Africa has radically altered the traditional pattern of early and universal marriage. Marriage occurs later (20.1 years was the mean age at first marriage for women in Lesotho in 1981), widowhood and marital breakdown are quite common (McDonald, 1985), polygyny is declining and female-headed households are more common (Timaeus & Graham, forthcoming). Births to single, widowed and divorced women have become important in Botswana and Lesotho (ibid.), and probably elsewhere too.

Table 2.3 Ratios of total fertility rates to total marital fertility rates by residence and education in five African countries

	Residence			Schooling			
	Rural	Other Urban	Major Urban	None	1–3 yrs	4–6 yrs	7+ yrs
Ghana	0.84	0.79	0.77	0.94	0.78	0.81	0.76
Kenya	0.81	0.71	0.67	0.95	0.85	0.81	0.69
Lesotho	0.80	0.62	—	0.86	0.77	0.77	0.60
Senegal	0.92	0.76	0.74	0.95	0.88	0.73	0.51
Sudan (N)	0.79	0.76	0.67	0.83	0.74	0.70	0.60

Source: Casterline, Singh, Cleland & Ashurst (1984), Appendix C.

Regional differences in marriage in sub-Saharan Africa can still be recognized, with earlier female marriage and more polygyny in Islamic West Africa than elsewhere. Despite the major effects of urbanization and education, traditional rural marriage patterns appear to be changing slowly, and, where structural effects (i.e. unbalanced sex ratios arising

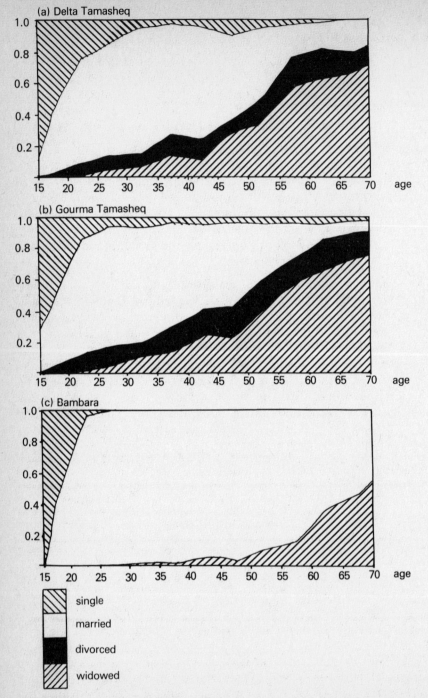

Figure 2.1   Proportions of women by marital status in three Sahalien population

Source: Randall (1984)

from male emigration) are important, other changes regarding attitudes to extra-marital births are occurring simultaneously. The net effect is to minimize the effects on overall fertility. It is instructive to conclude this section with an exception which helps in understanding the rule, for there are a few traditional African societies, mostly in the Sahel, with high ages of female first marriage and large proportions of 'non-exposed' women in the reproductive age groups. Figure 2.1 contrasts the marital status of Tamasheq and Bambara women in central Mali. As Randall (1984) and Randall & Winter (1985) show, consanguinous kin, the presence of subservient classes, a partially matrilineal inheritance system, and an enforced taboo on extra-marital sex result in low overall fertility among the noble Tamasheq, although their marital fertility is indistinguishable from that of the Bambara.

(b) The post-partum taboo on sexual intercourse

Schoenmakers *et al.* (1981) present a comprehensive review of the post-partum taboo in sub-Saharan Africa, along with some indications of change (in their Tables II and III). Without doubt, the tradition-ally long and widespread taboo is fast disappearing, with younger, well-educated, urban couples leading the way (Singh & Ferry, 1984). Table 2.4 shows average duration of post-partum abstinence positively correlated with age of women in several countries.

Table 2.4 Mean duration in months of the post-partum taboo by age of woman

	15-24	25–34	35	All
Benin (1981–82)	15.6	15.1	16.2	15.5
Cameroon (1978)	12.8	13.7	16.5	13.9
Ghana (1979–80)	9.4	9.6	11.7	10.0
Ivory Coast (1980–81)	11.4	14.0	16.0	13.1
Kenya (1977–78)	2.3	2.9	3.8	2.9
Lesotho (1977)	15.6	14.0	15.4	15.0
N. Sudan (1978–79)	2.5	2.6	2.8	2.6

Source: Singh & Ferry (1984), Table 7

Of course when post-partum amenorrhoea is long, as it still is in most sub-Saharan countries, whether the period of abstinence lasts one month or ten months its of little importance for fertility. The important finding is that the very long taboo, two years or more, is now very rare. In West Africa, the advance of Islam and the Islamic tenet of a forty-day taboo may be an important factor in changing attitudes and behaviour in this respect but the decline of polygyny and shorter periods of lactation are probably contributory factors. Although very long periods of abstinence may not have been so strictly observed as reported (see Monteil, 1924 and 1977, p. 215, for just one example), the net effect of their disappearance will be a rise in fertility, given that contraception is not widespread.

(c) Post-partum amenorrhoea

Again, the cross-sectional evidence is that mean durations of breast-feeding and hence of post-partum amenorrhoea are all becoming shorter among younger, educated, urban women (Singh & Ferry, 1984; Casterline *et al.*, 1984; Ferry & Smith, 1983). This alteration in the traditional pattern of infant feeding is the source of the pre-transition rise in natural fertility identified elsewhere (Dyson & Murphy, 1985 and 1986; Hill, 1983). Gaisie (1984) has illustrated the marked contrasts in the values of the post-partum variables by ethnic group rather than by residence in Ghana. Although there will be many more such contrasts elsewhere in Africa, the overall direction of change is clear, as are the positive effects on fertility.

(d) Contraception

As the World Fertility Survey and the Westinghouse Contraceptive Prevalence Surveys in Africa have shown, use of both modern methods of contraception remain extremely low in most sub-Saharan African countries. only a few countries report overall use rates over 10 per cent (Zimbabwe, Ghana, Benin), although some unsurveyed countries (e.g. Gabon) must have higher use rates (see Lapham & Mauldin, 1985 for a listing). Some recent results from southern Africa suggest that contraceptive use may be climbing steadily in a few sections of the population of Botswana, Kenya and Zimbabwe (Table 2.5). The pattern of use suggests that contraception is being used both to space and to limit the number of births. Despite these quite high overall use rates, fertility remains high, suggesting that compensating changes may be taking place involving alterations in post-partum behaviour or the replacement of traditional contraceptive methods with modern ones. With low rates of contraceptive use elsewhere, differentials by residence and education are not important except that they illustrate the concentration of users in particular socio-economic groups. In Kenya's major urban places, for example, contraceptive use rates were 17 per cent in 1977; 21 per cent amongst women with more than seven years schooling. Clearly, fertility will remain high until overall rates of contraceptive use rise significantly, bearing in mind that changes in both post-partum sexual abstinence and breastfeeding practice are affecting fertility in the opposite direction.

The broader research question for social scientists concerned with population increase and its effects must be the study of the social, economic and cultural changes that are clearly necessary if fertility is to fall. Here the debate is wide open and since the gist of the recent work cited above is that certain ineluctable changes are already under way (changing marriage, decline of traditional attitudes towards child rearing and the post-partum period), only one of which (wider contraceptive use) has restraining effect on fertility. The harvest of past work on fertility in sub-Saharan Africa is meagre; essentially, much of what we have learned is what can be regarded as lower priority for empirical and theoretical work in the future. The mechanics of fertility change are clear and the technology for restricting births is well-developed and relatively cheap. These discoveries at least reveal the need for some more holistic work on why African couples continue to desire and produce such large families, and the paucity of our existing theoretical explanations.

Table 2.5 Current contraceptive use by married women aged 15–49 for Botswana, Kenya and Zimbabwe by residence and number of living children

	Botswana (N = 2433)	Kenya (N = 4400)	Zimbabwe (N = 2127)
	Percentage currently using:		
Total (all methods)	27.8	17.0	38.4
Residence			
Urban	37.1	24.2	46.6
Modern	29.8	19.1	39.4
Traditional	7.3	5.1	7.2
Rural	24.9	16.0	34.0
Modern	14.9	8.4	19.9
Traditional	10.0	7.6	14.1
No.of living children			
0	8.6	3.7	7.1*
1	32.0	11.5	38.9*
2	30.9	13.5	N.A.
3	32.0	15.7	46.9†
4	36.4	16.7	N.A.
5	28.9	19.8	N.A.
≥6	25.5	22.7	39.0

Notes: N.A. = not available; *1–2 living children; † 3–5 living children
Source: Way, Cross and Kumar (1987), Table 1

Mortality

The statistical data on African mortality are far from complete but the overall picture is not in doubt (Hill& Kaufmann, 1987). Mortality, particularly infant and child mortality, remains higher in Africa than in all other less developed regions. In addition, the mortality of the under-fives improved more slowly from 1950–55 to 1980–85 than in all other regions of the world (UN, 1987; and see Table 2.6). More interesting are the differences between and within countries. Whilst the mortality rate of the under-fives is as high as anywhere in the world in certain West African countries such as The Gambia, Mali and Sierra Leone, the West African region as a whole has caught up with East Africa over the 1950-55 to 1980-85 period, although in both regions 20 per cent of children still die before their fifth birthday, compared with 12 per cent in southern Africa (Akoto, 1985; UN, 1987, Table A.1). Can we peer behind these rather large generalizations and obtain any useful insights into the factors responsible for mortality improvements, particularly in the rural areas?

The debate concerning the relative importance of rising living standards, medical care, improvements in sanitation and better education in reducing mortality rates is still very much alive (McKeown, 1967; Boulanger & Tabutin, 1980; Vallin & Lopez, 1985; Preston, 1975 and 1985; and Caldwell, 1986 amongst many others). Several detailed studies seem to indicate the varying role of the same factors in different circumstances. Work by Watterson (1986) in Britain and Masuy-Stroobant (1983) in Belgium has demonstrated the importance of cultural or regional factors and both studies have played down the role of medical care. Caldwell's 1986 article, based on a study of factors responsible for the exceptional mortality falls in states such as Kerala, Sri Lanka and Costa Rica, makes a powerful case for further investment in local health services and education. Secular education, Caldwell insists, will be most effective when couched in an ideological movement that stresses equality (particularly sexual equality) and the political involvement of communities in government. What sort of implications does such a conclusion hold for rural sub-Saharan Africa?

Table 2.6 Recent trends and forecasts of changes in the probability of dying by age 5 for major regions of Africa, 1950–2025

	Under-5 mortality rate per 1,000 births					
	1950–5	1960–5	1970–5	1980–5	1990-5	2000–5
Africa	322	280	233	182	147	118
Eastern Africa	286	249	222	204	170	136
Middle Africa	307	271	229	195	161	129
Northern Africa	326	271	219	152	107	73
Southern Africa	220	188	158	119	87	59
Western Africa	347	310	258	206	170	138

Source: UN (1987) Table A.1

Although high levels of child mortality in Africa can be partially explained in terms of the special risks associated with the tropical environment (Gourou, 1986; Woodruff, 1974), it is notable that on Caldwell's list of 'poor health achievers' — countries whose rankings for infant mortality were lower by at least twenty-five places than their per capita income rankings — three West African countries were represented (Caldwell, 1986, Table 1). For some time, it has been noted that the proportion of the budget spent on health care has been falling in many of the Sahelian countries affected by the drought-induced economic crises (see Hill & Graham, 1987 for some examples), but perhaps more serious is the suggestion that the 'classic' interventions supported by bodies such as UNICEF (immunization, oral rehydration, promotion of breastfeeding, and primary health care in general) may not be as effective as had been hoped in reducing high mortality rates. The evidence is still very scattered but there are certainly difficulties in explaining why in The Gambia, for example, infant mortality remains as high as 175 per 1,000 when vaccination coverage rates are as high as in Britain (Greenwood *et al.*, 1985; Gambia, 1985).

Caldwell's ideas about the central role of education in determining the pace of mortality decline are persuasive, although there may still be uncertainties about the exact nature of the causal chain (see Mosley & Chen, 1984, pp. 25–45, for a slightly different presentation). The difficulty is that the evidence from smaller-scale studies is always so complex and conditional that broad generalizations about the factors responsible for mortality change in rural areas are impossible. Thus, van Ginneken & Muller (1984) conclude their detailed study of a small area outside Nairobi with the conventional demand for more medical care. In central Mali, there is evidence that cultural attitudes related to social status are implicated (Hill & Randall, 1984; Hilderbrand *et al.*, 1985). Yet, in the same region, a recent study of mortality in two medium-sized towns, Mopti and Savaré, showed that, for most ethnic groups, families living in town displayed mortality levels approximately two-thirds lower than in the rural areas nearby. Since the educational levels and other socio-economic characteristics were virtually identical in both contexts, the suggestion is that provision of even a very elementary set of health services can prevent some premature deaths (Hill, 1986).

Several schemas of the 'proximate determinants of mortality' have been produced by demographers and epidemiologists in imitation of the proximate determinants' framework produced for fertility. Curiously, the sequence of events and processes ending in death has proved harder to model than for fertility; one problem is the lack of universal biological causes, as van Norren & van Vianen (1986) bring out in their presentation of the main factors in diagrammatic form (Figure 2.2). There we see plainly the important synergistic role of infection and malnutrition and the complex way in which health care and provision of health facilities affect morbidity and survival.

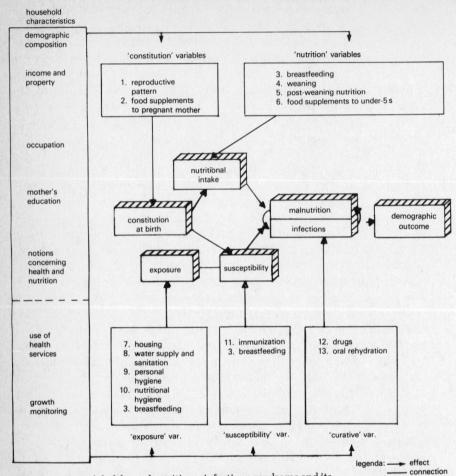

Figure 2.   A model of the malnutrition – infections syndrome and its demographic outcome in terms of the categories: risk factors, intermediate variables and household characteristics.

A much broader and more theoretical review of these issues is clearly necessary both to guide health policies and to answer key questions about the relationship of social change and economic development to mortality. At present, it is difficult to foresee much dramatic change in mortality in rural Africa with the exception of some possibly exceptional countries like Burkina Faso where some of Caldwell's requirements concerning political commitment to social development are probably being met. None the less, the United Nations projections for Africa as a whole, made on the basis of a continuation of present trends, indicate a 28 per cent reduction in under-five mortality between 1985 and the year 2000 (Table 2.6). In East and West Africa, the proportion dying by age 5 is foreseen as falling from 19 to 14 per cent; in middle Africa from 18 to 13 per cent; and in southern Africa from 10 to 6 per cent, (UN, 1987). These are substantial changes which will add significantly to the potential for future population growth, a problem that will be further exacerbated if exceptionally effective health measures are instituted. This should in no way retard the efforts to reduce mortality since the same sorts of changes in attitude and behaviour are probably implied when fertility as well as mortality is falling (see Caldwell, 1982 and 1986 for a longer discussion of this point).

Population growth and rural change

Whatever fertility assumptions are used in constructing African population projections, the absolute numbers of people are set to double at least in the next thirty or so years (UN, 1982). Whilst there is still some scope for international migration within Africa, the only major outlet for people in the rural areas without surplus land is rural-urban migration. From a development standpoint, the question is whether technological change can take place at a fast enough rate to permit more intensive use of existing physical and human resources in both rural and urban areas. Here the debate becomes strongly ideological, concerning those who see rapid population growth as a stimulus to economic growth (Simon, 1977; Thomas, 1973) and those who consider that population growth inhibits development overall (see US–NAS, 1971; Coale & Hoover, 1958; World Bank, 1981 and 1986).

Fortunately, there are now enough case studies in Africa where specific parts of these overall hypotheses could be examined in detail. Even highly traditional societies are not static, nor immune to external pressures. Essentially, the research needed now involves some evaluation of recent attempts to accelerate social change and the concomitant demographic transition with a view to deciding what level of intervention will prove most effective. There are those who believe that structural and institutional modifications are the precursors of social and hence demographic change (McNicoll, 1982); others who believe that meeting the 'unmet need' for family planning services through an efficient contraceptive delivery system can reduce fertility sooner (Pebley & Brackett, 1982; Lapham & Mauldin, 1984). This debate concerns more than just demographers or social scientists since the conclusions reached will affect the lives of millions and the disbursement of huge sums of money. The research agenda is large but the lessons from past work on population change in sub-tropical Africa will at least allow us to pose more apposite questions, now that the mechanical aspects of fertility change and mortality improvement are better understood.

References

Adegbola, O. & Page, H.J. (1982), 'Nuptiality and fertility in metropolitan Lagos: components and compensating mechanisms' in Ruzicka, L. (ed.) (1982), *Nuptiality and Fertility*, Liège, IUSSP, Ordina.

Akoto, E.M. (1985), *Mortalité infantile et juvénile en Afrique*, Louvain-la-Neuve, UCL, CIACO.

Aryee, A.F. & Gaisie, S.K. (1982), 'Fertility implicatioins of nuptiality in Ghana' in Ruzicka, op. cit.

Belsey, M.A. (1976), 'The epidemiology of infertility: a review with particular reference to sub-Saharan Africa', *WHO Bulletin*, **54** (3), Geneva.

— (1979), 'Biological factors other than nutrition and lactation which may influence natural fertility' in Léridon & Menken (eds) (1979), *Natural Fertility*, Leige, IUSSP, Ordina.

Bongaarts, J. & Potter, R.G. (1983), *Fertility, Biology and Behaviour*, New York and London, Academic Press.

— Frank, O. & Lesthaeghe, R. (1984), 'The proximate determinants of fertility in sub-Saharan Africa', *Population and Development Review*, **10** (3): 511–37.

Boulanger, P.-M. & Tabutin, D. (1980), *La mortalité des enfants dans le monde et dans l'histoire*, Liège, Ordina.

Brass, W., Coale, A.J., Demeny, P., Heisel, D.F., Lorimer, F., Romaniuk, A. & van de Walle., E. (1968), *The Demography of Tropical Africa*, Princeton University Press.

Caldwell, J.C. (1982), *Theory of Fertility Decline*, New York and London, Academic Press.

— (1986), 'Routes to low mortality in poor countries', *Population and Development Review*, **12** (2): 171–220.

— Reddy, P. & Caldwell, P. (1985), 'Educational transition in rural south India', *Population and Development Review*, **11** (1): 29–51.

Casterline, J., Singh S., Cleland, J. & Ashurst, H. (1984), 'The proximate determinants of fertility, *Comparative Studies* No. 39, London, WFS.

Coale, A.J. & Hoover, E.M. (1958), *Population Growth and Economic Development in Low-income Countries*, Princeton University Press.

Dyson, T. & Murphy, M. (1985), 'The onset of fertility transition', *Population and Development Review*, **11** (3): 399–440.

— (1986), 'On marriage trends and fertility transition in developing countries' in K. Srinivasan & S. Mukerji (eds), *Dynamics of Family Welfare*, Bombay, Himalayan Publishing House.

Edinburgh Centre of African Studies (1977 and 1981), *African Historical Demography*, Proceedings of two seminars held at the University of Edinburgh, 2 vols, Edinburgh.

Ferry, B. & Smith, D.P, (1983), 'Breastfeeding differentials', *Comparative Studies*, No. 23, London, WFS.

Frank, O. (1983), 'Infertility in sub-Saharan Africa: estimates and implications', *Population and Development Review*, 9 (1): 137-44.

Gaisie, S.K. (1984), 'The proximate determinants of fertility in Ghana', *Scientific Reports*, No. 53, London, WFS.

Gambia, Ministry of Health (1985), *Primary Health Care Review*, Banjul.

Gourou, P. (1966), *The Tropical World and its Social and Economic Conditions and its Future Status*, New York, Wiley.

Greenwood, B.M., Greenwood, A.M., Bradley, A.K., Tulloch, S., Hayes, R. & Oldfield, F.S.J. (1985), *Deaths in infancy and early childhood in a well-vaccinated rural, West African population*, The Gambia, Medical Research Council.

Henin, R.A. *et al.* (1982), 'Evaluation of birth histories: a case study of Kenya', *Scientific Reports*, No. 36, London, WFS.

Henry, L. (1953), 'Fondements théorétiques des mesures de la fécondité naturelle', *Revue de l'Institut international de la statisique*, 21 (3): 135-51.

Hilderbrand, K.A., Hill, A.G., Randall S. & van den Eerenbeemt, M-L. (1985), 'Child mortality and care of children in rural Mali' in Hill A.G. (1985), *Population, Health and Nutrition in the Sahel*, London, Kegan Paul International.

Hill, A.G. (1983), 'The Palestinian population of the Middle East', *Population and Development Review* 9 (2): 293–316.

— (1985), *Population, Health and Nutrition in the Sahel*, London, Kegan Paul International.

— (1986), 'Insights into mortality in the Sahel from some small-scale studies in Mali', *Fertility Determinants Research Notes*, New York, The Population Council.

— & Graham, W. (1987), 'A comparative review of the sources of mortality and morbidity data in four West African countries', *IDRC Technical Report*, Ottawa, IDRC.

— & Kaufmann, G. (1987), ' A review of materials and methods for the study of Infant and Child Mortality in Africa', *Centre for Population Studies*, Research Paper 87-1, London, London School of Hygiene & Tropical Medicine.

—— & Randall, S.C. (1984), 'Differences géographiques et sociales dans la mortalité infantile et juvénile au Mali', *Population*, 39 (6): 921–46.

Höhn, C. & Menken, J. (1979), *Natural Fertility*, Liège, Ordina.

Lapham, R.J. & Mauldin, W.P. (1984), 'Family planning programme effort and birth rate decline in developing countries', *International Family Planning Perspectives* 10 (4): 109-18.

— (1985), 'Contraceptive prevalence: the influence of organized programs', *Studies in Family Planning* 16 (3): 117-37.

Léridon, H. & Menken, J. (1979), *Natural Fertility* Liège, Ordina.

Lesthaeghe, R., Kaufmann, G. & Meekers, D. (1986), 'The Nuptiality Regimes in sub-Saharan Africa', Working Paper 1986-3, Inter-university Programme in Demography, Vrije Universiteit, Brussels.

— (ed.) (forthcoming), *Reproduction and Social Organisation in Tropical Africa*, University of California Press.

McDonald, P. (1985), 'Nuptiality and completed fertility. A study of starting, stopping and spacing behaviour', *Comparative Studies*, No. 35, London, WFS.

McKeown, T. (1967), *The Modern Rise in Population*, London, Arnold.

McNicoll, G. (1982), 'Institutional determinants of fertility change' in Höhn & Menken (eds), op. cit.

Masy-Stroobant, G. (1983), *Les déterminants individuels et régionaux de la mortalité infantile: la Belgique d'hier et d'aujourd 'hui*, Lovain-la-Neuve, UCL, CIACO.

Monteil, C. (1924 and 1977), *Les Bambara du Segou et du Kaarta*, Paris, Maisonneuve et Larose.

Mosley, W.H. & Chen, L. (1984), *Child Survival: Strategies for Research*, Cambridge, Cambridge University Press.

Page, H.J. & Lesthaeghe, R. (1981), *Child Spacing in Tropical Africa*, New York and London, Academic Press.

Pebley, A.R. & Brackett, J.W. (1982), 'The relationship of contraception availability to contraceptive use', *International Family Planning Perspectives*, **8** (3): 84–92.

Pison, G. (1983), *Dynamique d'une population traditionelle: les Peul Bandé (Sénégal oriental)*, Travaux et Documents, Cahier no. 99, Paris, INED, Presses Universitaires de France.

Preston, S.H. (1975), 'The changing relation between mortality and level of economic development', *Population Studies* **29** (2): 231–48.

— (1985), 'Resources, knowledge and child mortality: a comparison of the US in the late nineteenth century and developing countries today' in *International Population Conference*, Vol. 4, Florence, IUSSP, pp. 373–86.

Randall, S.C. (1984), *A Comparative Study of Three Sahelian Populations*, Unpublished PhD thesis, University of London.

— & Winter, M. (1985), 'The reluctant spouse and the illegitimate slave' in Hill (1985) op. cit.

Retel-Laurentin, A. (1974), *Infécondité en Afrique noire*, Paris, Masson.

— (1979), *Causes de l'infécondité dans la Volta Noire*, Cahier no. 87, Paris, Travaux et Documents, INED, Presses Universitaires de France.

Romaniuk, A. (1967), *Fécondité des populations congolaises*, The Hague, Mouton.

— (1980), 'Increase in natural fertility during the early stages of modernisation: evidence from an African case study — Zaire', *Population Studies*, **34** (2): 293-310.

— (1968), 'Infertility in tropical Africa' in *The Population of Tropical Africa*, J.C. Caldwell & C. Okonjo, (eds), London, Longman and the Population Council.

Ruzicka, L. (ed.) (1982), *Nuptiality and Fertility*, Liège, IUSSP, Ordina.

Schoenmakers, R., Shah, I.M., Lesthaeghe, R. & Tambashe, O. (1981), 'The child spacing tradition and the post-partum taboo in tropical Africa: anthropological evidence' in Page & Lesthaeghe, op. cit.

Simon, J. (1977), *The Economics of Population Growth*, Princeton University Press.

Singh, S. & Ferry, B. (1984), 'Biological and traditional factors that influence fertility: results from WFS surveys', *Comparative Studies*, No. 40, London, WFS.

Smith, D.P., Carrasco, E. & McDonald, P. (1984), 'Marriage dissolution and re-marriage', *Comparative Studies*, No. 34, London, WFS.

Thomas, B. (1973), *Migration and Economic Growth*, Cambridge, Cambridge University Press.

Timaeus, I. & Graham, W. (forthcoming), 'Labour circulation, marriage and fertility in southern Africa', Chap. 8 in Lesthaeghe, (forthcoming).

UN (1982), *Demographic Indicators of Countries: Estimates and Projections as Assessed in 1980*, New York.

UN (1987), *Mortality of children under age 5: World Estimates and Projections 1950-2025*, New York, Population Division, Dept. of International Economic and Social Affairs.

US National Academy of Sciences (1971), *Rapid Population Growth: Consequences and Policy Implications*, Vol. 2, Baltimore, Johns Hopkins Press.

Vallin, J. & Lopez, A. (eds) (1983), *La lutte contre la mort*, Travaux et Documents, Cahier no. 108, Paris, INED, Presses Universitaires de France.

van de Walle, E. (1968), 'Marriage in African censuses and enquiries' in W. Brass *et al.* (eds) (1968), op. cit.

—— & Kekevole, J. (1984), 'The recent evolution of African marriage and polygyny', Paper for Population Association of America, Annual Meeting, Minneapolis.

van Ginneken, J.K. & Muller, A.S. (1984), *Maternal and Child Health in Rural Kenya*, London, Croom Helm.

van Norren, B. & van Vianen, H.A.W. (1986), 'The malnutrition and infections syndrome and its demographic outcome in developing countries', *Publication No. 4 PCDR*, Department of Demography, State University, Groningen.

Watterson, P.A. (1986), 'Role of the environment in the decline of infant mortality: an analysis of the 1911 census of England & Wales', *Journal ·of Biosocial Science*, **18** (4): 457–70.

Way, A.A., Cross, A.R. & Kumar, S. (1987), 'Family planning in Botswana, Kenya and Zimbabwe', *International Family Planning Perspectives*, **13** (1): 7–11.

World Bank (1981), *Accelerated Development in Sub-Saharan Africa*, Washington DC, IBRD.

— (1986a), *World Development Report 1986*, Washington DC, IBRD.

— (1986b), *Population Growth and Policies in Sub-Saharan Africa*, Washington DC, IBRD.

Woodruff, A.W. (1974), *Medicine in the Tropics*, London, Churchill Livingston.

3 Anthropological Research in African Primary Health Care

C.P. MacCormack

Transformation in African health care: Sierra Leone case study

In the colonial period Sierra Leone had a serviceable skeleton national health service. A large public hospital was established in Freetown where Sierra Leonean doctors qualifying abroad could obtain practical clinical experience under good supervision before being posted to district hospitals. All twelve districts had hospitals; and dispensers with some curative skills and each with a small pharmacy were posted in many of the 146 chiefdom headquarters towns. This structure was augmented by military, mining and mission health services. Following independence, in a burst of national optimism, some of the non-government facilities were taken over by government. For example, the United Methodist Church (USA) hospital at Rotefunk, staffed by an expatriate missionary doctor and local staff, briefly became a government hospital. But when it was too expensive in staff and money to run, it was passed on to a team of doctors from the People's Republic of China. The Chinese, unlike the long-serving Dr Silver, the Methodist doctor, do not speak the local language, nor do they engage in community health activities. Other mission hospitals, notably at Serabu (Catholic) and Segbwema (Methodist) are still mission-supported and are in the forefront of community-based primary health care work.

Sr. Hilary Lyon, the nun-surgeon who headed Serabu Hospital, underwent a personal transformation when she realized one day that, in spite of the good curative services the Serabu hospital had been providing for decades, the infant mortality rate in the surrounding villages was as high as anywhere else in the country. At that point she stopped doing surgery and diverted her considerable energy into organizing the local chiefdoms to commence a truly participatory primary health set of preventive and curative activities (see Edwards & Lyon, 1983, for a description). This initiative stimulated the Ministry of Health to form a primary health care working party and there is now a comprehensive primary health care plan for the country. Its object is to organize village health committees, train village health workers, and link them with existing categories of government health workers (see MacCormack, 1984b, for a description).

Does this constitute a transformation in health care for Sierra Leone? National health expenditure as a proportion of total government expenditure has declined from 15.4 per cent in 1964, to 13.9 per cent in 1972, to 8.2 per cent in 1981 (based on Nickson, 1979). In 1971, the last year for which I could obtain figures, public and private expenditure for health amounted to only US $3.44 per person — for all preventive and curative services provided (Nickson, 1979). With that meagre amount, it is quite impossible for any but a privileged minority of children to be fully immunized, or for pregnant women to have ante-natal care, supervised delivery and post-natal care.

The alternative to a comprehensive primary health care service is special 'vertical' programmes funded by donors, such as the World Health Organization's Expanded Programme on Immunization. Special teams are trained and supplied to immunize children, but they do not have the skill or time to screen for current infections, teach methods of oral rehydration therapy for diarrhoea, give back-up training to village health workers, and so forth (see Mills, 1983; Rifkin & Walt, 1986). Another alternative to insufficient national funding is special integrated health and agricultural development programmes, as with the German GTZ funded programme in Bo and Pujahun districts, for example. In this programme, comprehensive primary health care is developing well; but will it collapse when the externally-funded programme ends and the government cannot take up the cost of recurrent expenditure?

With a low level of government expenditure, exacerbated by misman-agement of funds, the district, and even the urban Freetown hospitals, have run down to an alarming degree. They do not have drugs and dressings, and sometimes do not have electricity, water or food for patients. If, for example, a person cutting palm fruit or coconuts falls from a tree, but cannot pay for x-rays, blood typing, and other diagnostic procedures, the surgeon cannot proceed. If people with life-threatening infections cannot afford antibiotics, they cannot be treated. A woman with an obstructed labour, referred by the traditional midwife to a district hospital, may find the hospital without electricity and surgical supplies, the surgeon unable to do a Caesarean section. In functional terms, a primary health care system organized at the village level cannot function if district-level services have collapsed. There is no reliable service to which village health workers, taught to screen for high-risk cases, can refer people in acute need, nor is there petrol for district nurses to give back-up supervision to village-level health workers.

We must conclude that, except for externally-funded special health programmes, the health system in Sierra Leone has not been transformed into a more equitable and comprehensive system.

Social anthropology and health care research

Social anthropologists are drawn into research in Third World health care in many ways. Some have done broad-ranging anthropological research in a particular society and are asked to advise on a public health programme because of their knowledge of the social, political and economic organization of the area (see for example Paul & Miller, 1955; Leslie, 1976; Landy 1977). Some have particular links with a funding agency such as OXFAM or the Overseas Development Administration, and may be called upon to review project proposals or help with policy review, as well as doing field studies. Others begin with a medical or nursing qualification, then do a degree in social anthropology (see, for example, Frankel & Lehman, 1984; Littlewood & Lipsedge, 1982; Kleinman, 1980). On whichever side of the fence researchers have begun, they often do field studies in collaborative teams, and most planning and evaluation tasks in tropical public health require a minimum team of an epidemiologist, an anthropologist/sociologist and an economist.

Methods of investigation

Social anthropologists doing research in tropical public health use a range of methods, from intensive small-sample 'qualitative' methods of participant observation and open-ended interviews, to extensive large-scale 'quantitative' surveys. Ideally, both approaches are used. Intensive methods often constitute a pilot exercise to identify the nature of the problem, generate hypotheses, and understand the larger context in which cognitive patterns and social behaviour are expressed. Once problems, embedded in their cultural and social context, are understood and described, extensive survey methods might then be used to follow up hypotheses, allowing statistical conclusions to be reached. For example, in a large malaria chemosuppression programme along Lake Victoria that failed, open-ended conversations with children and their mothers about what they liked and did not like about the drug and its distribution generated hunches that we later confirmed statistically in a large-sample questionnaire (MacCormack & Lwihula, 1983). This anthropological investigation documented itching as a side effect of Chloroquine, something that had been known anecdotally by clinicians but not measured in a population. Following this anthropological study, the World Health Organization sponsored medical investigations into the nature of Chloroquine-induced itching.

Sometimes the research process begins at the other end, with a large survey. In its analysis, certain statistical associations are noted, but the investigators cannot explain, in cognitive and behavioural terms, why these associations exist. What do the associations mean in terms of what people actually think and do? Then, a small sample investigation, exploring the matter in some depth, might explain the phenomena and suggest aspects of policy.

One of the great advantages of the anthropological research traditions is that we are free to ask a wide range of questions: those amenable to statistical description and those that are not. We can count how many rural African women go to health centres for ante-natal care and childbirth, compared with how many use traditional midwives. We can also describe what childbirth means in terms of marriage and descent systems, household authority patterns, birth as an aspect of cosmology, and the role of traditional midwives as ritual specialists and social authority figures (see MacCormack, 1982). Both approaches, the quantitative and the qualitative, are useful in formulating a policy for training traditional midwives to be more effective village health workers (WHO, 1979). Or, a country can conduct a national fertility survey and discover that on average 98 per cent of women know about modern contraceptive methods, the country has excellent geographical coverage of family planning services, but most women end up with a larger completed family size than their ideal family size (Jamaica, 1979). By asking each of a relatively small sample of 268 women to draw her reproductive physiology as she visualizes her own body, and explain in terms of her drawing what she thinks the contraceptives are doing 'in there', we begin to understand some of the reasons why most women either have never used contraceptives or use them sporadically (MacCormack, 1985). For example, all women who had used or heard about the intra-uterine device draw it in the vagina, where it was thought to interfere with sexual pleasure, and they feared it might be pushed into the uterus where it could only be removed surgically. Should a woman become pregnant, it might become implanted in the growing foetus or obstruct the cervix at birth. In prompting questions which encouraged women to draw, we learned much about the cultural meanings of menstruation, and therefore about interpretations women gave to the IUD and other contraceptives that alter the time and/or the amount of menstrual flow. Policy recommendations included culturally appropriate health education that acknowledged folk concepts and fears, and a better quality of one-to-one interaction between family planning staff and clients.

In summary, social anthropologists use both large-sample surveys and small-sample intensive studies. The latter are sometimes done to help explain questionnaire survey results and to make specific policy recommendations. Whatever approach is taken, the hallmark of anthropological research is our concern for the quality of data collected, hence a tendency to prefer smaller samples exhaustively studied, and indirect data collection methods, especially where the topic of investigation is politically and socially sensitive, or conceptually complex and deeply embedded within the culture (see Hill, 1986, for a further discussion of methods).

Social anthropology and the primary health care strategy

By the late 1970s an international consensus acknowledged that many developing countries — especially those of Africa — will remain so poor that for decades to come they will not be able to provide their populations with the basic medical services of general practitioners and hospital back-up. In 1978 WHO and UNICEF therefore jointly declared a primary health care policy and strategy, which has subsequently been endorsed in virtually all nations. The strategy is summarized as 'essential health care based on practical, scientifically sound and socially acceptable methods and technology, made universally accessible to individuals and families in the community through their full participation and at a cost that the community and country can afford' (WHO–UNICEF, 1978). Since then anthropologists have carried out many studies of whole primary health care programmes, or have done detailed sub-studies (see, for example, Bloom & Reid, 1984). The WHO–UNICEF primary health care strategy can be subdivided into five guiding principles: (1) equitable distribution; 2) community involvement; 3) focus on prevention; 4) appropriate technology, and 5) a multi-sectoral approach.

Equitable distribution

The need to make health services more equally accessible, especially to rural populations, builds upon an extensive anthropological literature on the organization of rural societies, much of it explicitly analytical about social inequality (see, for example, Devitt, 1977; Elliott, 1975; Hill, 1977; Lewis, 1959; Parkin, 1972; Sahlins, 1974). There has not yet been an African study to match the quality of the Djurfeldt & Lindberg (1975) study in a Tamil area of India. The primary health care policy recommendations of those authors were supported by studies of income distribution and landholding related to nutritional status, morbidity, mortality, and the use of health services.

Community involvement

The primary health care strategy marks on official shift of emphasis from medical services provided *for* people, to health achieved *by* people (Newell, 1975), with all the liberating potential that community revitalization implies (Freire, 1967; Werner & Bower, 1982). The early literature rather romantically assumed that villages were cohesive moral communities, but anthropologists have described the way in which health may be a resource deployed in highly-charged political situations. Health workers may even be killed if they are too successful in stimulating village cohesion and local initiative and become a threat to the economic and political elite (Heggenhougen, 1984).

In rural Lesotho, clean drinking water projects sometimes became ensnared in contests of power between local chiefs and national party politicians. When the majority of villagers were not supporters of the ruling party, the chief often showed his strength against the kind of new leaders created by the central government by refusing to call public meetings, organize communal work, or even relay essential information. When projects were pushed forward anyway, they were sometimes actively sabotaged, or passively destroyed through lack of local maintenance (Cross, 1978, pp. 66–8). Anthropologists have attempted to lay down some guidelines for assessing the potential for community participation, and for stimulating the process in a culturally appropriate way (MacCormack, 1983).

Prevention

It is usually more cost-effective to prevent disease than to cure it, but preventive strategies such as digging latrines, which people may not want, must be linked with curative services that they do want. Anthropologists have systematically described the activities of women in breastfeeding, producing agricultural crops, managing child nutrition, water carrying, and cleaning and sweeping to maintain environmental hygiene (Elmandorf & Isely, 1981). Indeed, African women are often providers of health, not just consumers of curative services. Providers of health services can be analysed by social category, such as by gender, or by specific roles, such as traditional midwives or herbalists. A range of traditional practitioners has been offering primary preventive and curative services for centuries and they are obvious candidates for further training (Pillsbury, 1979). Additional training for traditional midwives, together with vaccination programmes, is the way to avoid as much as 20–40 per cent of infant deaths in Africa which result from the single cause of neonatal tetanus (Ross, 1986). The value of traditional practices is officially recognized in WHO publications (WHO, 1978; Bannerman et al., 1983), and advocated in primary health care planning (WHO–UNICEF, 1978). The implications of WHO's recommendation that traditional practitioners form themselves into a professional associations is thoroughly explored in a recent book sponsored by the International African Institute (Last & Chavunduka, 1986).

Appropriate technology

Traditional practices often incorporate effective local technologies which might be augmented through primary health care initiatives. With malaria, for example, there is a wide range of initiatives African people have taken to protect themselves, from burning pyrethrum in smoky fires to introducing larvivorous fish into water where Anopheles gambiae breeds (MacCormack, 1984a). Physical barriers against mosquito bites appear to reduce malaria morbidity in West Africa (Bradley et al., 1986). For centuries, in some areas of West Africa, people have slept under finely-woven mats or thick cotton cloths as an effective barrier to mosquito bites. More recently, rural African people have been purchasing manufactured bed net. Within a village, the dipping of bed nets in a residual insecticide appears to be a promising health care initiative, enhancing the protective efficacy of nets (Curtis & Lines, 1985). It is much more cost-effective than spraying whole houses with residual insecticides, and less damaging to the environment. But within the same economy and ecology, use of bed nets can vary remarkably by ethnicity, with 95 per cent of Mandinka but as few as 1–6 per cent of Wolof and Fula using them in Gambian villages. This difference can be explained anthropologically, and apparently be overcome in a programme where net use in Fula villages has been encouraged (MacCormack & Snow, 1985; MacCormack, 1987).

Multi-sectoral approach

The primary health care literature clearly recognizes that sickness and a high infant mortality rate are in a synergistic relationship with malnutrition and poor environmental hygiene. Therefore, close links must be made between health, agriculture, family planning, education, water and sanitation facilities. Chambers, Longhurst & Pacey have brought this synergism clearly into focus in their book on seasonality (1981). In The Gambia, for example, as the rains come on, food stores from the previous harvest run low and some grain must be used for seed. The body weight of everyone, including pregnant and lactating women, drops sharply. Because women work such long hours on the farms they wean children abruptly, and the latter are put at further risk of diarrhoea by eating infrequently and are often fed contaminated food left over from a previous meal because mothers are too busy in the fields to cook regularly. Water-washed pathogens pollute unprotected wells and ponds, further contributing to a peak of diarrhoea in the rainy season. Breeding conditions are optimal for *Anophelese gambiae* and malaria peaks in the rainy season, but people have no cash then to buy life-saving Chloroquine tablets. The policy implications are enormous (see Cham *et al.*, 1987).

Conclusions: the complementarity of anthropology and epidemiology

Sierra Leone, 'the white man's grave', is still a place of sickness and death for much of its African population. Its infant mortality rate is among the highest in the world, as is its fertility rate — a story of appalling human wastage (MacCormack, 1984b). Malaria is holoendemic, and to observe men and women farming under the stress of the rainy season is to witness courage. Other parts of Africa reel under drought, plagues of locusts and/or war. Where the health care need is so great, so obvious, why do research to plan primary health care?

The principal reason for doing research is because resources to meet needs are so limited in Africa, and every initiative must have a low cost-benefit ratio (see Robertson *et al.*, 1985). Epidemiologists conduct morbidity surveys, determine the prevailing diseases in the population, assess their debilitating or killing nature, and make judgements about the likely success of the control strategies available. They may then suggest that initial efforts should be concentrated on diseases that both affect many people and are relatively easy and cheap to control. Increasingly, the control strategies are not 'vertical' military-type campaigns against a single disease such as malaria, but 'horizontal' primary health care programmes involving village health workers, traditional practitioners and community action — all the complex organization outlined in the previous section of this chapter (see Mills, 1983). The control strategy has gone beyond the professional competence of epidemiologists and requires a collaborative team approach.

With community action as part of the control of diseases, we must work both with medical definitions and measurements of a disease and the people's own categories of disease and ideas of causation and cure (see Janzen & Prins, 1981). Immediately we are into the realm of cultural relativity. Bridges, often through metaphor, must be built between the biological universals of the European system of disease classification, cause and cure, and the culturally indigenous system if the community and health workers (and donor agency) have any hope of working together in concerted action.

Finally, although needs are indisputably great, whose needs matter? A delegation from the Ministry of Health of an African country came to the London School of Hygiene and Tropical Medicine in 1985 asking for assistance in research on the control of AIDS. It was presented as a disease that was killing the educated leadership of the country — the key political figures, who have many sexual partners. But no community-based surveys had been done to find out if it was a widespread disease in the rural countryside (as it is not in the United Kingdom). Should resources be diverted from children's immunization, malaria control and clean drinking water programmes for an AIDS programme? Such decisions require the combined wisdom of epidemiologists, social scientists, and all the wise elders of Africa.

References

Bannerman, R.H., Burton, J. & Wen-Chieh, Ch'en (eds) (1983), *Traditional Medicine and Health Care Coverage*, Geneva, World Health Organization.
Bloom, A.L. & Reid, J. (eds) (1984), 'Anthropology and primary health care in developing countries', special issue of *Social Science and Medicine*, **19**.
Bradley, A.K. *et al.* (1986), 'Bed-nets (mosquito nets) and morbidity from malaria', *The Lancet*, **2**: 204–7.
Cham, K., MacCormack, C., Touray, A. & Baldeh, S. (1987), 'Community assessment in primary health care: The Gambia,' *Health Policy and Planning*, **2** (in press).

Chambers, R., Longhurst, R. & Pacey, A. (eds) (1981), *Seasonal Dimensions to Rural Poverty*, London, Frances Pinter.

Cross, Piers, (1978), 'Village Institutions' in *Water, Health and Development*, Feachem, R. et al., (eds), pp. 65–80, London, Tri-Med Books Ltd.

Curtis, C.F. & Lines, J.D. (1985), 'Impregnated fabrics against malaria mosquitoes', *Parasitology Today*, **1**: 147.

Devitt, Paul, (1977), 'Notes on poverty-oriented rural development' in *Extension Planning and the Poor*. Agricultural Administration Unit Occasional Paper 2, London, Overseas Development Institute.

Djurfeldt, G. & Lindberg, S. (1975), *Pills Against Poverty: A Study of the Introduction of Western Medicine in a Tamil Village*, Copenhagen, Scandinavian Institute of Asian Studies, Mongraph 23.

Edwards, N. & Lyon, H. (1983), 'Community assessment: a tool for motivation in primary health care in Sierra Leone' in *Practising Health for All*, Moreley, D., Rohde J. & Williams, G. (eds) pp. 101–13, Oxford, Oxford University Press.

Elliot, Charles, (1975), *Patterns of Poverty in the Third World: A Study of Social and Economic Stratification*, New York, Praeger.

Elmandorf, M. & Isely, R. (1981), *The Role of Women as Participants and Beneficiaries in Water Supply and Sanitation Programs*, Arlington, Va., WASH Technical Report 11.

Frankel, S. & Lehmann, D. (1984), 'Oral rehydration therapy: combining anthropological and epidemiological approaches in the evaluation of a Papua New Guinea programme,' *Journal of Tropical Medicine and Hygiene*, **87**: 22–7.

Freire, P. (1967), *Educacão como prática da liberdade*, Rio de Janeiro, Paz e Terra.

Heggenhougen, H.K (1984), 'Will primary health care efforts be allowed to succeed?', *Social Science and Medicine*, **19**: 217–24.

Heggenhougen, H.K. & Shore, L. (1986), 'Cultural elements of behavioural epidemiology: implications for primary health care', *Social Science and medicine*, **22**: 1235–45.

Hill, Polly, (1977), *Population, Prosperity and Poverty: Rural Kano 1900 and 1970*, Cambridge, Cambridge University Press.

Hill, Polly, (1986), *Development Economics on Trial*, Cambridge, Cambridge University Press.

Jamaica, (1979) *Jamaica Fertility Survey*, Vols 1 and 2, Kingston, Department of Statistics.

Janzen, J. & Prins, G. (eds) (1981), 'Causality and classification in African medicine and health', special issue of *Social Science and Medicine*, 15B.

Kleinman, Arthur, (1980), *Patients and Healers in the Context of Culture: An Exploration of the Borderland between Anthropology, Medicine and Psychiatry*, Berkeley, University of California Press.

Landy, David (ed.), (1977), *Culture, Disease and Healing*, London, Macmillan.

Last, M. & Chavunduka, G. (eds), (1986), *The Professionalisation of African Medicine*, Manchester, University of Manchester Press.

Leslie, Charles (ed.), (1976), *Asian Medical Systems*, Berkeley, University of California Press.

Lewis, Oscar, (1959), *Five Families: Mexican Case Studies in the Culture of Poverty*, New York, Basic Books.

Littlewood, R. & Lipsedge, M., *Aliens and Alienists*, Harmondsworth, Penguin, 1982.

MacCormack, C.P. (ed.), (1982), *Ethnography of Fertility and Birth*, London, Academic Press.

MacCormack, C.P. (1983), 'Community participation in primary health care', *Tropical Doctor*, **13**: 51–4.

MacCormack, C.P. (1984a), 'Human behaviour and ecology in malaria control in Tropical Africa', *Bulletin of the World Health Organization*, supp. to Vol. **62**: 81–8.

MacCormack, C.P. (1984b), 'Primary health care in Sierra Leone', *Social Science and Medicine*, **19**: 199–208.

MacCormack, C.P. (1985), 'Lay concepts affecting utilization of family planning services in Jamaica', *Journal of Tropical Medicine and Hygiene*, **88**: 281–6.

MacCormack, C.P. (1987), 'Gambian cultural preferences in the use of insecticide-impregnated bed nets', *Journal of Tropical Medicine and Hygiene*, **90** (in press).

MacCormack, C.P. & Lwihula, G.K. (1983), 'Failure to participate in a malaria chemosuppression programme, North Mara, Tanazania', *Journal of Tropical Medicine and Hygiene*, **86**: 99–107.

MacCormack, C.P. & Snow, R.W (1985), 'What do people think of bed nets?', *Parasitology Today*, **1**: 147–8.

Mills, Anne, (1983), 'Vertical vs. horizontal health programmes in Africa: idealism, pragmatism, resources and efficiency', *Social Science and Medicine*, **17**: 1971–80.

Newell, Kenneth (ed.), (1975), *Health By the People*, Geneva, World Health Organization.

Nickson, R. (1979), *The Allocation of Public Health Resources in Sierra Leone*, paper, ECA/FAO/Sierra Leone Government Workshop, Njala, Sierra Leone.

Parkin. David, (1972), *Palms, Wine and Witnesses: Public Spirit and Private Gain in an African Farming Community*, London, Intertext Books.

Paul, B.J & Miller, W.B. (eds) (1955), *Health, Culture and Community: Case Studies of Public Reactions to Health Programmes*, New York, Russell Sage Foundation.

Pillsbury, Barbara, (1979), *Reaching the Rural Poor: Indigenous Health Practitioners Are There Already*, AID Program Evaluation Discussion Paper 1, Washington, AID.

Rifkin, S. & Walt, G. (1986), 'Why health improves: defining the issues concerning comprehensive PHC and selective PHC', *Social Science and Medicine*, **23** (6): 559–66.

Robertson, R.L., Foster, S.O., Hull, H.F. & Williams, P.J. (1985), 'Cost-effectiveness of immunization in the Gambia', *Journal of Tropical Medicine and Hygiene*, **88**: 343–51.

Ross, David A. (1986), 'Does training TBAs prevent neonatal tetanus?', *Journal of Health Policy and Planning*, **1**: 89–98.

Sahlins, Marshall, (1974), *Stone Age Economics*, London, Tavistock.

Werner, D. & Bower, B. (1982), *Helping Health Workers Learn*, Palo Alto, Hesperian Foundation.

World Health Organization, (1978), *The Promotion and Development of Traditional Medicine*, Technical Report Series 622, Geneva, WHO.

World Health Organization, (1979), *Traditional Birth Attendants: An Annotated Bibliography on their Training, Utilization and Evaluation*, Geneva, WHO.

WHO–UNICEF,(1978), *Primary Health Care*, Geneva, WHO.

4 Domestic Water Supply in Rural Africa

Sandy Cairncross

1 Objectives

What is a water supply, and what is it for? The question is not as naive as it sounds — certainly not in the context of rural Africa. The World Health Organization estimates that four out of five rural Africans are without reasonable access to safe water. In compiling that estimate very different definitions of what is 'reasonable' and what is 'safe' were used in different countries. The variation in definition is not the result of bureaucratic whims, but reflects the fact that the standard of adequacy for a water supply depends on the purpose it is intended to serve. At one extreme, every human community has a water source of some kind, for without one it could not survive; but at the other, the standard of service found in most of Europe, with a twenty-four hour supply of limitless quantities of chlorinated water to multiple taps and fittings inside the home, is enjoyed by a negligible number of rural Africans — as is likely to be the case well beyond the end of this century.

The purpose that is most commonly ascribed to better water supply is that of improved health. The relationship of water supply to human health is complex and frequently misunderstood; but those who pay for, build and operate rural water supplies often do so for other reasons, whether or not these are openly expressed.

Although the importance of water supply for the promotion of health has been well-known for the last 150 years, and the colonial powers in Africa were generally keen to maintain high sanitary standards in the settler cities, they rarely thought of health as a motive for building rural water supplies. It is symptomatic that a recent book on health in colonial Africa (Sabben-Clare et al., 1980) makes no mention at all of water supply as a health intervention. In those relatively infrequent cases where colonial administrations embarked on substantial rural water programmes, there was usually a link with settlement schemes. The aim was to make areas habitable and productive where previously human settlement, and particularly livestock farming, had been impractical, owing to the scarcity of water sources. This was the case, for example, with the wells built by the British administration in Anchau, Nigeria (Nash, 1948), and in the Chire valley, Malawi (Mitchell, 1956), by the French in the Baol-Saloum region of Senegal (Suret-Canale, 1976), and by the Portuguese in parts of Mozambique (Silva, 1956). The first and the last of these schemes aimed to control tsetse flies by encouraging human settlement. But the primary objective was economic: to open up new areas for production.

It was in the final years before independence, as internal self-government got under way, that water supply construction on any widespread scale began, as a response to political demand. Most of the rural water supplies built in colonial Tanganyika, for example, were built at the request of and with at least partial financing by the local Native Authorities (Tschannerl, 1979). In many countries, the local authorities were controlled by colonial administrators. This did not always make for equity. One observer (Brasseur, 1952, p. 44) noted that: 'Les dossiers abondent de requêtes émanant de personnages politiques ou religieux qu'on satisfait pour avoir la tranquillité; en même temps des besoins très urgents restent pendants.' In other cases, such as Basutoland, more enlightened colonial officials helped district councils to obtain funds for their rural water schemes in the belief that this would strengthen local democratic institutions.

However, it was only after independence that substantial expenditure on rural water began. In Kenya, the annual rate of investment in the sector increased from £48,000 to £654,000 between 1967 and 1971 (Carruthers, 1973, p. 9). The total sums involved were still small by comparison with other infrastructural investments, and too small to affect more than a minority of the population. In 1970, annual investment in rural water supply in Africa was little more than £8 million (Saunders & Warford, 1976, p. 10) At the costs prevailing at the time, this was enough to build water supplies for one million people a year, out of a rural population for the region of roughly 170 million. Over three times this sum was being spent on water supplies for the much smaller urban population.

Since then, the rate of investment in the sector has slowly increased, but still falls far short of what would be required to provide the same level of service to most of Africa's peasants. Moreover, awareness has gradually spread that simply to build water supplies is not enough, and that without adequate maintenance they break down (Cairncross & Feachem, 1977). In some countries they have been breaking down as fast as new ones are built.

The sector has come to depend increasingly on international aid and, as so often happens when aid donors are involved, it has suffered a fair amount of confusion of objectives. Aid agencies have often stressed the need for maintenance, but with few exceptions refused to contribute to the recurrent costs of the projects in which they have invested. A bilateral donor, while extolling the virtues of standardization and appropriate, locally-produced technology, will frequently press recipient governments to buy its own national brand of drilling rigs, handpumps or other equipment. The importance of institution-building is often emphasized, and yet there is an increasing tendency for a donor to bypass local institutions and set up its own parallel implementation system with a view to greater speed and efficiency.

Possibly the most muddled area is community participation, where the interests of both donors and recipients are served by keeping the concepts vague. This question has been trenchantly dissected by others (Feachem, 1980; White, 1983), and there is no need to add to a mountain of paper, beyond noting two often neglected points. First, setting up community institutions to participate in the construction and maintenance of rural water supplies is essentially the task of establishing local government. After all, local government in Europe began with institutions for the maintenance of community infrastructure, and that is still its main activity today. Conflict within the community, and also between it and the central government, can result, and political commitment at the highest level is therefore required. Second, community participation has a cost. Not only does it impose constraints on how the technical part of a water supply programme can be implemented — which will tend to make the programme more expensive — it also requires salaried community workers, vehicles and other inputs, the costs of which are rarely included when projects are appraised or evaluated.

Much confusion arises from reluctance to voice the real reasons for rural water programmes, which often underlie the vague statements of noble purpose. While local elites have long used village water supplies as instruments of patronage, the taboo on discussion of the political aspects is almost universal among the donors, and African governments are only too happy to help in the pretence that rural water supply is an untainted issue, like motherhood, which everyone must favour.

Whatever objective the aid agencies attribute to the rural water programmes they support, the political pressures at either end of the transaction generally arise from very different considerations. On the one hand, water supplies are attractive to the people who provide the aid agencies with funds, as they are more tangible and photogenic than many other forms of rural development activity and they can be completed within the span of a single aid agreement, providing the donor with visible evidence of his assistance in a short period of time. On the other hand, they are almost universally popular among their users, chiefly for their convenience and the saving in time that they can bring. They also involve minimal institutional conflict at village level and are much cheaper to maintain than schools or clinics. People with a water supply cannot be guaranteed to vote for the politician who facilitated it; but the *prospect* of water supply can be a strong inducement.

The political factor is not always electoral. For example, several African governments, such as those of Tanzania, Mozambique and the Congo, have tried to resettle their scattererd rural populations in villages. The rationale may be that concentration is necessary if infrastructural provision such as water supply is to be available in rural areas; but

(Feachem *et al.*, 1978, pp. 139–79; Young and Briscoe, 1986, Annex B) that the endemic paediatric diarrhoeas of poor communities are largely water-washed, as they are not substantially affected by water quality improvements when hygiene and access to water are unchanged. Moreover, one significant study in Nigeria (Tomkins *et al.*, 1978) showed that better access to water was associated with a benefit to children even more significant than freedom of diarrhoea, although possibly a result of it — namely, better nutritional status.

It should be stressed that measuring the health benefits of water supplies is extremely difficult. The incidence of a disease may easily be found to be lower in one community than another. But such a difference cannot easily be ascribed to the presence of a water supply, as can be seen from the data in Tables 4.1 and 4.2. If the figures in brackets were ignored, piped water would seem to give excellent protection against diarrhoea and typhoid; only the unusual circumstances of the two villages, by which not everyone drinks piped water in either, make it possible to see that there must be other factors at work.

Table 4.1 Children under 5 years having diarrhoea during previous week in two villages in Tanzania

Village	Piped water	Dug hole
Namabengo	15/216 = 7%	(5/70 = 7%)
Mkongo	(37/100 = 37%)	39/134 = 29%)
Total	52/316 = 16%	44/204 = 22%

Table 4.2 Children under 5 years with antibodies to typhoid fever in the same villages

Village	Piped water	Dug hole
Namabengo	4/216 = 1.9%	(1/70 = 1.4)
Mkongo	(7/100 = 7.0%)	12/133 = 9.0%
Total	11/316 = 3.5%	13/203 = 22%

Source: Prag JB, Balslev, K. Boesen, J,. Kapinga B.S., (1983) 'Water Master Plan for Iringa, Ruvuma and Mbeya Regions', *Tanzania*, Vol. 13, Ch. 11. Centre for Development Research, Copenhagen.

However, quite a few amateur epidemiologists have been undeterred by such difficulties (e.g. Gaddal *et al.*, 1986). Science is not well served when they publish their results and ascribe a spurious certainty to dubious data, especially when the authors have a personal interest in the project whose impact they claim to have measured.

One way around the problem of attributing a difference in disease incidence to the effect of water supplies is to consider many more than two villages; it can then be hoped that extraneous factors will cancel out. This becomes feasible with the case-control method (Briscoe *et al.*, 1985). Whereas conventional studies usually compare the incidence of diarrhoea in two communities (one with water supply and one without it), the case-control method compares the incidence of water supply between two groups of people; those with diarrhoea and those without it.

The method, which is still in an experimental stage of development, had its first trial in Malawi (Young & Briscoe, 1986). Africa is full of cases where laying on water supplies greatly improves access to water, and so probably the quantities used. Unfortunately, the study area in Malawi happened to be one where the taps of the water supply were no closer to users than the traditional water sources had been. In the circumstances it was to be expected that no significant difference in incidence would be found. The result only added more evidence to support the hypothesis that the endemic diarrhoeas of rural Africa are mainly water-washed.

Although the beneficial effects of water supply on the purely water-washed diseases such as trachoma have long been well-known, studies have only recently been published which measure them directly. Two of these studies were conducted in rural Africa (Keyran-Larijani *et al.*, in press; Cairncross & Cliff, 1987) and they have confirmed that the effects can be substantial.

Most health benefits, then, are likely to stem from use of increased quantities of water. How is this to be achieved? Health educators may rarely be deterred by failure, but they are unlikely to have much success in prompting by exhortation an increase in water use. Their efforts are likely to be dwarfed by the increases that occur spontaneously when access to water is significantly improved.

Table 4.3 compares the quantities used for various purposes in two comparable villages in Mozambique, one before and one after construction of a water supply. The journey to collect a bucket of water took over five hours for the unsupplied village, so the example is an extreme one; but it illustrates two points that may have general relevance.

First, a substantial proportion of the increased amount used in the supplied village was for personal hygiene. The bathing of adults and children and the washing of clothes represent 70 per cent of the total. In the other village, these items constitute less than half of a much smaller total. The most obvious aspect of this difference is the frequency with which children were bathed: every day in one village, but hardly ever in the other.

Table 4.3 Volumes of water used for different purposes, in litres per capita per day (l.c.d.), in two villages in Mozambique; one before and one after installing a water supply

	Before (90 person-days) Village A			After (95 person-days) Village B	
	lcd	%		lcd	%
Drinking	0.21	6		0.36	3
Cooking	0.67	21		1.93	16
Washing dishes and food	0.50	15		1.36	11
Bathing	0.80	25		4.75	39
Bathing children	0.04	1		1.23	10
Washing clothes	0.54	17		2.64	21
Other (animals, etc.)	0.48	15		0.03	0.3
Totals	3.24	100	12.30	100	

Source: Cairncross and Cliff, 'Water use and health'in Mueda, Mozambique, *Trans. Roy. Soc. Med. and Hygiene*, **81**: 51–4.

Also remarkable is the difference in the quantity used for cooking. Villagers sometimes claimed that they had cooked little food, and only once in the day, because of lack of water for cooking. Healthy adults may make up the difference with raw cassava, but small children and the elderly cannot. Water supply, it seems, can also affect people's health through their diet.

As the example shows, improved access to water can lead to greatly increased consumption. However, it does not always do so. Current knowledge of how domestic water consumption is related to access is based on few studies (White, G.F. *et al.*, 1972; Feachem et al., 1978; Cairncross & Cliff, 1987; Ministry of Health, Mozambique, 1981, Vol. 2, Tomo 2, p. 30; Warner, 1973, pp. 119–29), but all of them were conducted in rural Africa. The consensus from them gives a surprising relationship (Figure 4.1). As the time required to collect a bucket of water is reduced, water use increases progressively until it reaches a plateau at about thirty minutes, equivalent to a walking distance of 1 km each way, to and from the water source. Within this range, bringing the water source closer to the home does not lead to increased consumption.

Collection of water at a public standpipe, well or pump is therefore likely to cause increased water consumption only if the previous source of water was over a kilometre away. If health benefits are to be maximized, those whose source of water is further away than this should have priority in the allocation of water supplies. If, on the other hand, no-one lives so far away from a source of water, water supplies with house connections would be needed to increase consumption further.

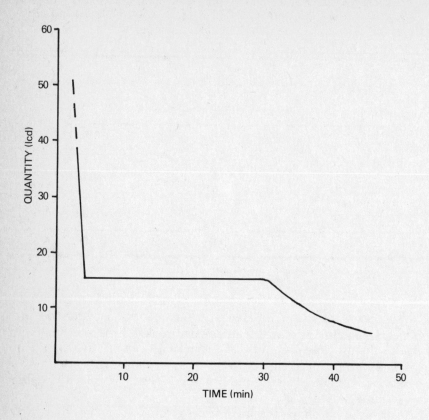

Figure 4.1   Schematic representation of the relationship between time taken to collect a bucket of water and the quantity used, in litres per capita per day (l.c.d.)

3   Time saving

The scant attention given this benefit by many writers on rural water supply in Africa (see, e.g., Roundy, 1985) may reflect a difference in perception between them and the users. Saunders & Warford, in their book (1976, pp. 72–3) which became a benchmark for World Bank policy on rural water supply over the subsequent decade, gave it only two pages. Significantly, the examples of water collection time which they mention are all from rural Africa.

Again, it was Bradley and his colleagues (White, G.F. et al.93–8) who pioneered the serious study of this aspect of water supply.

They measured the length of the water collection journey in various environments, and attempted to put a value on it by estimating the calories of energy consumed on the way, and the cost of enough food to provide those calories.

Others (e.g. Dalton & Parker, 1973), seeking a simpler solution, have asked women how they would spend the time saved if they had an improved water supply, and valued the time savings on the basis of the percentage that would be spent on productive work. There are two serious flaws in this approach.

First, very little confidence can be placed in the response to such hypothetical questions. Could the reader say what he or she would have done with the time that could have been saved by not reading this book? Observation is needed of what women actually do with their time if reliable conclusions are to be drawn.

Time-budget observation data of this kind were collected in connection with a evaluation of Lesotho's rural water programme in 1976 (Feachem *et al.*, 1976, pp. 187–92). The saving in time and the number of woman-days in the data collected were too small to estimate directly how time saved from water collection was reallocated. Instead, a comparison was made of the time-budgets of women among households having various numbers of other able women. In a household with two or more able women, the household tasks can be shared and the workload of each woman is reduced. Comparison of the different households shows how women use the time saved, not only from water collection, but from household chores as a whole.

The results are shown in Table 4.4. In the extreme case, a woman who is one of six in a household would be saved 250 minutes per day (more than four hours) of household duties, by comparison with a woman on her own. The figures in the table show that this time was very largely spent on social and leisure activities, not on agricultural work. Reading down the columns, it is clear that as women spent less time on household work they spent correspondingly more on social and leisure activities rather than on agriculture.

Table 4.4 Variation in Lesotho women's time-budgets with the number of able women in their household (minutes per day)

No. of women	Water collection	Other household work	Agricultural work	Rest, social, meals, etc.	Total	No. of women-days observed
1	33	537	34	238	842	5
2	10	478	70	291	849	14
3	15	375	44	376	810	18
6	·7	287	94	524	912	12

Source: Feachem *et al.*, (1978) *Water, Health and Development: an Interdisciplinary Evaluation*, Tri-Med Books.

In another study, in northern Mozambique (Cairncross & Cliff, 1987), I was able to make a direct comparison between the time-budgets of women using a traditional water source and those with access to a standpipe in their village. The saving in time was over five hours per water collection journey, and nearly two hours per woman per day (Table 4.5). Here again the time saved was not primarily re-allocated to agriculture, but to rest, social activity and other household work.

Table 4.5 Average time budgets of adult women (minutes per day) in two Mozambican villages, one before and one after installing a water supply

Activity	Before (110 women-days)	After (118 woman-days)	Difference
Fetching water	131	25	−106
Housework	126	161	+35
Grinding	84	98	+14
Agriculture	154	160	+6
Rest	385	433	+48
Totals	880	877	−3

Note: The standard deviation from each of the means given here was about 150 minutes. The standard error of each mean, therefore, is about ± 15 minutes.

One reason for this result would seem to be that there are often other constraints on an African peasant woman's production, such as her access to arable land, to traction for ploughing or to cash for inputs such as seeds or fertilizer. In the Lesotho case, women having a greater number of fields did spend more time tending them. When the Mozambican data were analysed in terms of the number of women in the households, it appeared that in households with many women, each woman spent more time in the fields, probably because polygamous men had more land as well as more female labour power at their disposal.

There is a second flaw in the method of valuing women's time on the basis of the amount they spend in farming. In addition to their agricultural production, peasant women provide a variety of unpaid services to their families, many of which are of undeniable value. Many household chores involve cleaning, sweeping, scrubbing and washing, and bring added health benefits in so far as they promote hygiene.

A meticulous study in Asia (Popkin & Solon, 1976) has shown how mothers with more free time raise children who are better nourished, because they can give more attention to food preparation and to feeding their children. This is certainly one possible explanation for the findings of the Nigeria study mentioned above (Tomkins *et al.*, 1978), and it may well be the most accurate one.

Moreover, an increase in women's free time constitutes a benefit in itself, however it is spent. It is a significant improvement in the quality of their lives, and a step towards their emancipation. That this benefit is perceived to be worth money is evident from the fact that households that are better-off financially often pay someone to collect water for them (Zaroff & Okun, 1984).

A striking feature of the time-budgets in Table 4.5 is the amount of time spent by the average woman in grinding, i.e. in pounding cereals with a large pestle. A similar result was found in another time-budget study (McSweeney, 1979) in a village in Burkina Faso, where the average woman spent 108 minutes a day pounding grain, compared with thirty-eight minutes collecting water. If the objective of water supplies is to free women's time from an onerous chore, the same objective might often be met more cheaply by providing a grain mill.

Nevertheless, the cost per minute of time saved by a water supply can be very low indeed (Cairncross *et al.*, 1980, p. 168). A typical water supply in rural Africa, costing £10 per head per year (including depreciation of capital and operation and maintenance costs) may save each adult woman an hour a day. This is equivalent to 146 hours per year per head, if women constitute 40 per cent of the total population. This puts the cost at 7p per hour saved. If the time saved were more than an hour a day, or if part of the cost were justified by health benefits, the cost per hour of the time-saving benefit would be cheaper still.

The cost per hour saved is typically less than the prevailing unskilled wage rate, which is quite a reasonable estimate of the value of that time to the beneficiaries. Observation of the behaviour of Americans paying to avoid a queue (Deacon & Sonstelie, 1985) has shown that their implicit estimates of the value of their time are quite similar to their after-tax wage rates. Rural Africans are probably just as rational.

The implications for rural water policy of setting time-saving as an objective are similar to those of using a health objective. Both objectives can be met most effectively by giving priority to those who live furthest from their present source of water, and to improving their access to water in quantity and convenience.

4 Future perspectives

If rural water supplies in Africa are to provide health improvements and time-savings, could these benefits be increased? Mention has already been made that water supplies are only being built for a tiny percentage of Africa's rural population each year, and that inadequate maintenance is an increasing problem.

The problem of maintenance is not essentially one of ignorance. In an African village of today one is quite likely to find at least a couple of inhabitants who know how to repair a motor vehicle or even a radio, and for them a broken pipe or handpump holds few mysteries.

Rather, the problem is one of institutional weakness and lack of material resources such as tools and spare parts. The weakness of

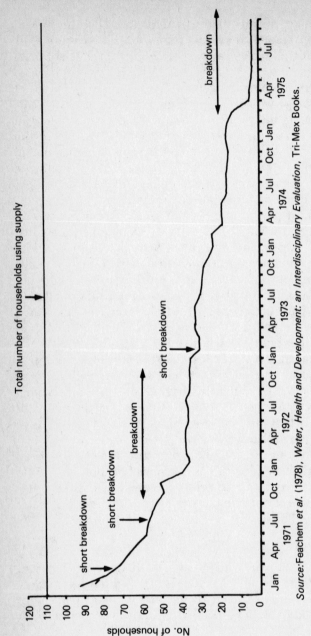

Figure 4.2 Number of households paying a nominal monthly subscription towards a diesel-pumped water supply in Lesotho. January 1971–July 1975. (Breakdowns of the supply are also shown.)

*Source:*Feachem et al. (1978), *Water, Health and Development: an Interdisciplinary Evaluation,* Tri-Mex Books.

village institutions contributes to the shortage of resources. In most countries in Africa a village is not a constituted body with legal powers to raise funds from its inhabitants. Without such powers and some form of sanction behind them, it is not possible to raise funds on a regular basis for the maintenance of water supplies or any other village infrastructure. Voluntary contributions in cash or labour may be easy enough to mobilize for a specific occasion such as the building of a new supply. But to maintain it on a voluntary basis does not work in the long term.

This failing is illustrated by the graph in Figure 4.2, showing the number of families in a village in Lesotho who contributed each month towards the diesel to operate their water pump. The steady decline in contributions was not a result of the occasional breakdowns in the supply; rather, families continued to contribute then, towards its repair. The defaulters simply noticed that their neighbours had already stopped contributing and that the village water committee was powerless to make them pay up.

Alastair White (1983) has argued cogently that the way to obtain wider coverage and more reliable functioning of rural water supplies is to choose cheaper interventions, in which the subsidy to the users is greatly reduced. The same budget could then serve more people, bringing most of the rural population to some minimal level of improvement in a few years, rather than leaving out most of them indefinitely, as at present.

A reduction in the subsidy would mean that the beneficiaries' contribution would be a more significant part of the total cost, and so give them more control over the process. It would also tend toward simpler technology, such as the windlass and the bucket rather than the pump, which would be easier for villagers to maintain (Wright, 1985; on the ingenious bucket pump, see Morgan & McPherson, 1985).

There is one health benefit which such minimal improvements can be more than adequate to achieve. Guinea worm is an excruciatingly painful parasitic disease found throughout much of the Sahel belt (World Health Organization, 1982). The victim is infected by drinking contaminated water, and the female worm emerges at the body surface under the skin one year later, causing an inflamed blister. The sufferer a feels strong desire to relieve the burning sensation by pouring water on the blister; this causes it to burst, releasing thousands of microscopic larvae of the worm. The process is repeated over several weeks, and if the larvae can reach a source of drinking water, the cycle can begin again.

Apart from the suffering it causes, the disease severely damages the rural economy, since the infection usually matures around the planting season, and pain in the affected limb greatly reduces the sufferer's ability to work (Belcher *et al.*, 1975). More than half the population may be affected, and many of them incapacitated for three months or longer. Schools sometimes have to close during the Guinea worm season (Nwosu *et al.*, 1982). There is evidence that increasing migration and dam construction are introducing the disease to new areas (Watts, 1984; Adekolu-John, 1983).

In many areas, unprotected springs and unlined wells are the principal or even the only focus of transmission. A simple spring box, or a parapet around a well to deflect spilt water away from the wellhead, can be enough to eradicate the disease in a year. Guinea worm is the only disease that can be completely eliminated by improved water supplies (US National Academy of Sciences, 1983). It has been suggested that its world eradication should be a goal of the World Water Decade. The Government of India, one of the few non-African countries affected, has taken up this challenge, and it is unfortunate that African governments seem not to share this enthusiasm.

Another simple improvement is the 'wet-season well' — a well which, though it may fail to provide water in the dry season, will at least provide it relatively close to home during the rains. It has been pointed out (Chambers *et al.*, 1979) that the wet season is the worst time of the year for many rural Africans; it is typically marked by a concurrence of food shortages, high demands for agricultural work, high exposure to infection — especially diarrhoea, malaria and skin diseases — loss of body weight, low birth weights, high neonatal mortality, poor child care, malnutrition, sickness and indebtedness. Women are among the most vulnerable at this time, and any lessening of their work burden by improved access to water is particularly valuable. Wet-season wells can often be built where perennial wells are not feasible. For example, they are used in parts of Shinyanga Region, Tanzania (DHV Consulting Engineers, 1978).

An alternative to the 'minimal improvement' policy, which has not received much attention in Africa, is to aim for a *higher* level of service, promoting as many private connections as possible. This is the policy followed in many Latin American countries, not all of which are much more developed than parts of tropical Africa. It has three important advantages.

First, the time-saving benefit is greater. A pioneering study by Tony Churchill of the World Bank (unfortunately still unpublished) has shown how, at typical costs and a value for time of US 10 cents per hour, the extra expense of a pumped water supply with private connections over a more rudimentary borehole and handpump system is justified by the value of the time saved from water carrying.

Second, it is through private connections that the greatest increase in water consumption occurs, and that health benefit is most likely. In the best-known documented cases of significant health benefits from rural water supplies, such as those quoted in the World Health Organization's manual on the subject (Wagner & Lanoix, 1959), this was the level of service provided. The greater the health benefit, the greater the externalities, and hence the stronger the case for meeting part of the cost of water supply from government subsidies.

Third, the institutional problem of collecting payment for the water supply is vastly simplified, as defaulters who have private connections can be disconnected. This simple sanction is enough to ensure an ample income for hundreds of rural water supplies in Latin America. USAID discovered its efficacy after the failure of two rural water supply projects in Thailand (Dworkin & Pillsbury, 1980), where people failed to make their contributions to the upkeep of the water supplies — hand pumps in the first project, and standpipes in the second. In the third project, house connections were allowed and the connecting households were required to pay the full operation and maintenance cost of the systems. A high proportion of families made the regular payments for this level of service, and the project was successful.

To entrust cost recovery to the private sector, as has been suggested by some writers (Lewis & Miller, 1987), neglects the arguments for at least a partial subsidy, and is likely to create more problems than it solves (Cairncross, 1987). House connections could increase the benefits of rural water supply, and might, by facilitating some recovery of cost, enable governments to widen coverage of this service.

There are few examples of this level of service in rural Africa. However, in our research in Lesotho (Feachem *et al.*, 1978) we were struck by the fact that the only village in the country with house connections was one of the tiny minority of villages with a surplus of funds for operation and maintenance — a very different story from that shown by Figure 4.2.

The extra cost of this higher service level need not be very great. Where gravity-piped systems are the type installed, as in much of Lesotho, Rwanda, Cameroon and Malawi, house connections could even be added to existing supplies. Pumped systems might be designed to run for only a few hours a day, as London's water supply did until the 1890s (Hardy, 1984), so avoiding the need for expensive storage.

My fellow engineers are notoriously conservative, and often unused to considering the broader issues related to their work. It will not be easy to persuade them to countenance the sweeping reappraisal of rural water technology and policy which these suggestions imply, and which modern rural Africa needs. Social scientists are well placed to try, if they are prepared to open the dialogue.

References

Adekolu-John, E.O. (1983), 'The impact of lake creation on Guinea worm transmission in Nigeria on the eastern side of Kainji Lake', *Int. J. Parasitol*, **13**, 5: 427–32.

Belcher, D.W., Wurapa, F.K., Ward, W.B., Lourie, I.M. (1975), 'Guinea worm in southern Ghana: its epidemiology and impact on agricultural productivity', *Am. J. Trop. Med. Hyg*, **24**, 2: 243–9.

Brasseur, G. (1952), 'Le problème de l'eau au Sénégal' (Saint-Louis, Centre IFAN.

Briscoe, J., Feachem, R.G., Rahaman, M.M. (1985), *Measuring the Impact of Water Supply and Sanitation Facilities on Diarrhoea Morbidity: Prospects for Case-control Methods*, WHO/CWS/85.3., Geneva, World Health Organization.

Cairncross, S. & Feachem, R.G. (1977), 'Operation and maintenance of rural water supplies', *EEC-ACP Courier*, **43**.

Cairncross, S., Carruthers, I., Curtis, D., Feachem, R., Bradley, D., Baldwin, G. (1980), *Evaluation for Village Water Supply Planning*, John Wiley & Sons.

Cairncross, S. (1987), 'The private sector and water supply in developing countries: partnership or profiteering?', *Health Policy and Planning*, **2**, 2: 180–2.

Cairncross, S. & Cliff, J. (1987), 'Water use and health in Mueda, Mozambique', *Trans. Roy. Soc. Trop. Med. and Hygiene*, **81**: 51–4.

Carruthers, I.D. (1973), 'Impact and economics of community water supply', London, Wye College.

Chambers, R., Longhurst, R., Bradley, D.J., Feachem, R.G. (1979), 'Seasonal dimensions to Rural Poverty: analysis and practical implications', *J. Trop. Med. Hyg.*, **82**, 8: 156–72.

Dalton, G.E. & Parker, R.N. (1973), *Agriculture in South East Ghana*, Vol. 2, Special Studies, University of Reading.

Deacon, R.T. & Sonstelie, J. (1985), 'Rationing by waiting and the value of time: results from a natural experiment', *Journal of Political Economy*, **93**, 4: 627–47.

D.H.V. Consulting Engineers, (1978), *Shallow Wells*, D.H.V. Consulting Engineers, p 15.

Dworkin D.M., Pillsbury, B.L.K. (1980), *The Potable Water Project in Rural Thailand*, USAID Project Impact Evaluation Report No. 3, USAID.

Feachem, R., Burns, E., Cairncross, S., Cronin, A., Cross, P., Curtis, D., Khan, M., Lamb, D., Southall, H. (1978), *Water, Health and Development: an Interdisciplinary Evaluation*, Tri-Med Books.

Feachem, R.G. (1980), 'Community participation in appropriate water supply and sanitation technologies: the mythology for the Decade', *Proc. Roy. Soc. London* B 209: 15–29.

Gaddal, A.A., Fenwick, A. & Tameem, O. (1986) 'Health aspects of water supply and sanitation', *Proceedings of the World Water '86 Conference*, Institution of Civil Engineers, pp. 97–100.

Hardy, A. (1984), 'Water and the search for public health in London in the eighteenth and nineteenth centuries', *Medical History*, **28**: 250–82.

Keyran-Larijani, E. et al. (in press), 'Epidemiology of trachoma in the lower Shire valley, Malawi', *Archives of Ophthalmology*.

Lewis, M.A., Miller, T.R. (1987), 'Public–private partnership in water supply and sanitation in Sub-Saharan Africa', *Health Policy and Planning*, **2**, 1.

McSweeney, B.G. (1979), 'Collection and analysis of data on rural women's time use', *Studies in Family Planning*, **10**, 11/12: 379–83.

Ministry of Health, Mozambique, (1981), *Projecto CSP/1-80*, Maputo.

Mitchell, J.C. (1956), *The Yao Village: a Study in the Social Structure of a Malawian People*, Manchester University Press.

Morgan, P.R. & McPherson, H.J. (1985), 'The Blair Laboratory's contributions to the Water Decade', *Waterlines*, **4**, 1: 9–12.

Nash, T.A.M. (1948), 'The Anchau Rural Development and Settlement Scheme', The Colonial Office.

Nwosu, A.B.C., Ifezulike, E.O., Anya, A.O. (1982), 'Endemic dracontiasis in Anambra State of Nigeria: geographical distribution, clinical features, epidemiology and socio-economic impact of the disease', *Ann. Trop. Med. Parasitol*, **75**: 187–200.

Popkin, B.S. & Solon, F.S. (1976), 'Income, time, the working mother and child nutriture', *Journal of Tropical Paediatrics and Environmental Child Health*, **22**: 156–66.

Roundy, R.W. (1985), 'Clean water provision in rural areas of less developed countries', *Social Science and Medicine*, **20** 3: 293–300.

Sabben-Clare, E.E., Bradley, D.J., Kirkwood, K. (eds) (1980), *Health in tropical Africa during the Colonial Period*, Oxford University Press.

Saunders, R.J. & Warford, J.J. (1976), *Village Water Supply: Economics and Policy in the Developing World*, Baltimore, Johns Hopkins University Press.

Silva, M.A. de A. (1956), 'A tse-tse em Mocambique', Lourenco Marques, Imprensa Nacional de Mocambique.

Suret-Canale, J. (1976), *French Colonialism in Tropical Africa, 1900-1945*, Heinemann.

Taylor, H.R., Velasco, F.M., Sommer, A. (1985), 'The ecology of trachoma: an epidemiological study in southern Mexico', *Bulletin of the WHO*, **63**, 3: 559–67.

Tomkins, A.M., Drasar, B.S., Bradley, A.K., Williamson, W.A. (1978), 'Water supply and nutritional status in rural Northern Nigeria', *Trans. Roy. Soc. Trop. Med. and Hygiene*, **72**, 3: 239–43.

Tschannerl, G. (1979), 'Rural water supply in Tanzania: is politics or technique in command?' in Coulson, A. (ed.), *African Socialism in Practice: the Tanzanian Experience*, Spokesman, pp. 86–105.

US National Academy of Sciences (1983), 'Opportunities for control of Dracunculiasis: report of a workshop', National Academy Press.

Wagner, E.J., Lanoix, J.N. (1959), *Water Supply for Rural Areas and Small Communities*, WHO monograph series No. 42, World Health Organization.

Warner, D. (1973), 'Evaluation of the development impact of rural water supply projects in East African villages', *Report EEP-50*, Stanford University.

Watts, S.J. (1984), 'Population mobility, urban development and Dracunculiasis in Kwara State, Nigeria', *Soc. Sci. Med.* **19**, 4: 471–3.

White, A. (1983), 'Community participation: the different determinants of ideology and practice', paper presented to the Linköping conference on Water for All, May/June 1983.

White, G.F., Bradley, D.J., White, A.U. (1972), *Drawers of Water; Domestic Water Use in East Africa*, Chicago University Press.

Wright, R. (1985), 'Unsealed wells: water quality implications', *Waterlines*, **3**, 3: 28–31.

World Health Organization, (1982), 'Dracunculiasis surveillance', *Weekly Epidemiological Record*, **57**, 9: 65–7.

Young, B.A., Briscoe, J. (1986), 'Water and health in rural Malawi: aspects of the performance, utilization and health impact of the Malawi self-help rural water supply project', report prepared for the USAID Mission to the Republic of Malawi, Contract CO-612-0000-5-50003, University of North Carolina at Chapel Hill.

Zaroff, B. & Okun, D.A. (1984), 'Water vending in developing countries', *Aqua*, **5**: 289–95.

5 Energy in Rural Africa: an Economist's Approach*

Walter Elkan

This chapter sets out to describe how energy is used in rural Africa by both households and industry. It looks in particular in some of the strategies that have been proposed for solving the problems created by the depletion of woodlands from which so much of the fuel used in rural areas is derived. What is described in the title as 'an economist's approach' could also be called an approach which views these strategies from the vantage point of the people who are supposed to benefit.

The energy used by both households and industry in most of rural Africa is derived largely from fuelwood. Fuelwood will therefore need to be the primary concern of this chapter. Other sources of energy play a part. For instance, kerosene (paraffin) is often used to provide light, and high hopes have been placed on electricity, on harnessing the sun and wind to provide energy and on using crop residues. Buses, lorries and cars use petrol. But, for a large majority of country dwellers, 'energy' is virtually synonymous with 'fuelwood'.

Uses of energy

Statistics of energy use in low-income countries are suspect because it is virtually impossible to make sensible estimates of the most important component of use, namely household consumption, especially for cooking. For whatever they may be worth, estimates may be cited of woodfuel as a ratio of total energy consumption ranging from 28 per cent in Zimbabwe, 35 per cent in Zambia and 46 per cent in the Ivory Coast to more than 70 per cent in Angola, Ghana, Guinea, Kenya, Mozambique and Sierra Leone, more than 80 per cent in Benin, Burundi, Cameroon, Madagascar, Niger, Nigeria and Sudan, and more

*This chapter draws heavily on the writings of Gerald Foley and Geoffrey Barnard of Earthscan, and on a conference paper by Simon Burne of the Intermediate Technology Development Group. The author would like to acknowledge how much of his own knowledge is derived from theirs, and also from having been privileged to participate in the World Bank's Zambia Energy Assessment Mission.

than 90 per cent in Burkina Faso, the Central African Republic, Chad, Ethiopia, Mali, Rwanda, Somalia and Tanzania (Hall *et al.*, 1982). These estimates are for countries as a whole, i.e. they include urban consumption where electricity, gas, kerosene and petrol are much more significant. The figures therefore underestimate the degree to which woodfuel dominates the rural scene.

Until a decade or two ago fuelwood was not a subject on which a great deal had been written, and certainly no-one had attempted to compile statistics on the subject. Here and there — especially in Lesotho — forestry departments and others expressed concern that it was difficult to plant trees to protect the soil from erosion because people immediately cut them down again to have fuel to cook with or to keep warm. If there was a concern about energy it focused on electricity. The question posed was how, and on what terms, one might provide electricity for rural areas since electricity was seen as a vital springboard for rural development — both agricultural and social.

Two developments have changed all that: first, the rise in oil prices which sharply focused attention on all aspects of energy in a desperate attempt to reduce the fuel import bill; second, a less dramatic but no less insistent recognition or belief that fuelwood, on which so many people depend in both countryside and towns, was becoming increasingly scarce. This increasing scarcity has been attributed to the rapid increase in populations, and the even more rapid growth of towns. The words 'deforestation' and 'desertification' came to be familiar to every television viewer, and new terms like biomass and non-conventional energy started to appear in the specialist literature. Fuelwood was classified as a renewable resource of energy to distinguish it from fossil fuels like coal and oil — an ironic use of language since the major question that this chapter will need to address is why in practice wood tends not to be renewed! Equally questionable is its classification as 'non-commercial', when in fact great quantities of it are sold, especially for urban consumption — another phenomenon posing a major problem.

Depletion of woodlands and household fuel

Despite the growing alarm at 'deforestation' there continues to be large parts of Africa where fuelwood consumption is still unconstrained by any locally perceived scarcity of wood. This is the case even in countries where the statistics suggest that natural wood cover is already seriously depleted. Even there people may still be able to obtain all the wood they want simply by collecting it (Foley, 1985, p. 32). Typically, where trees are thus plentiful and easily accessible, women go out to collect the wood they need, choosing species that burn well and are easy to split. Often it is only dead wood that is collected since it is lighter to carry, easier to cut and burns better. Though branches may be lopped off, whole trees are rarely felled merely to provide fuel. Where wood is collected in this way, a natural equilibrium is maintained; consumption does not deplete resources and no one has to plant trees to ensure a perpetuation of the status quo.

Much of the wood used for fuel in the countryside continues to be produced and consumed in this way. Where this is so, there is no scarcity and therefore no price; no money changes hands and wood used for fuel is automatically replenished, requiring no effort or investment. But, under pressure of growing populations, and rapidly expanding towns, the demand for fuelwood has in many places begun to exceed the natural replenishment. To what extent woodlands are being reduced as a result of an increasing demand for firewood is not easy to determine. There is evidence that around many major towns, with their geographically concentrated demand for fuel, woodlands are rapidly disappearing. But towns constitute markets for food as well as for the fuel with which to cook it, and it is plausible to argue that the disappearance of woodlands is better explained by the intensification and extension of agriculture than by the cutting down of vegetation to provide fuelwood. This is now generally accepted as the more tenable explanation, rather than the earlier view that fuelwood consumption was the principal culprit.

Land clearance for cultivation is not confined to the countryside surrounding towns, but occurs in many areas. Often the trees that are cut when land is cleared cannot even be readily sold as poles or firewood because the land clearance occurs in places where there is no one to sell them to, and they are then burnt simply to dispose of them. A diminishing resource is thus being wantonly wasted into the bargain. Society's interest not to let that happen is not matched by the interest of any one individual, and unfortunately there is no way in which government intervention could conceivably help.

Whether woodlands are cut down for fuelwood or land clearance, the effect is the same, namely that the areas from which 'free' firewood can be obtained are reduced. Even in a relatively well wooded country like Malawi, whose towns are still small by the standards of Lagos or Nairobi, consumption of wood is said greatly to exceed natural replenishment. Perhaps Malawi with its tobacco plantations, which account for 20 per cent of consumption, uses more wood than is common in most of Africa. But there is no reason to doubt that in many parts of Africa women are having to travel ever longer distances in search of wood and that stocks are diminishing. There is also evidence that urban supplies of charcoal and firewood are coming from increasingly further afield (Anderson & Fishwick, 1984, chap. 2; Courier, 1986, pp. 74–6). Increasing scarcity implies rising prices, but on the subject of prices and how they have changed in the course of time, the evidence is extraordinarily scanty

(Foley, 1985, p. 45). The World Bank's Ethiopian Energy Assessment Mission found that in Addis Ababa prices of wood/charcoal rose by an annual average of 9 per cent between 1970 and 1983, but Ethiopia is not a country one would wish to describe as typical. Despite the long history of eucalyptus plantations created specifically to provide the towns with firewood, fuelwood is in general a good deal scarcer there than in — say — Cameroon or Nigeria. Furthermore, neither in Ethiopia nor in most other African countries are prices likely to be determined purely by market forces. Where, as is commonly the case, governments attempt to control prices, the problem of finding accurate time-series data is compounded by the fact that what is recorded as information on changes in retail prices is likely to be the official fuelwood or charcoal prices rather than those acually charged. That may be one reason why none of the dozens of other World Bank Assessments contains any time-series for the price of wood; nor does the interesting World Bank Working Paper on Fuelwood Consumption & Deforestation in African Countries, (1984) by Denis Anderson and Robert Fishwick.

Perhaps, in a paper on rural energy, prices should not detain us since they principally concern urban consumers. But the urban damand for fuelwood and (more typically) charcoal affects availability to country dwellers and it also affects rural incomes since growing numbers of people sell 'free' wood for use in towns and thereby bring closer the day when it will no longer be 'free'.

The real worry about the gradual, or not so gradual, loss of trees and shrubs may not even be the disappearance of an accustomed fuel, since there are, after all, alternatives. In Europe people once cooked on wood, then moved to coal and now use predominantly electricity and gas. Some suffered hardship in the process but in the end all have become better-off. But in Africa a further worry is the consequential degradation of the environment. The loss of trees and shrubs introduces a break in the nutrient cycle of the affected areas and, worse, removes the protection they provide against soil erosion by rains and winds.

Industrial energy

It is not only households that face increased difficulty in procuring fuelwood. Industry, too, is a large consumer of fuelwood. We distinguish here between, on the one hand, large-scale and mostly agro-industries such as tobacco curing, tea processing, sugar milling, cotton ginning, and brick-making; and, on the other hand, the industries of small-scale entrepreneurs: brewing, drying fish, baking, metal working and roadside catering. In a number of countries, large-scale agro-industries use fuelwood because it is cheaper than any alternative, although they also sometimes use their own residues, especially bagasse. Where fuel-intensive agro-industry operates on the basis of outgrowers, it may also require its crop suppliers to grow and supply the fuelwood needed for processing. Kenyan tobacco is a case in point. Drying tobacco is very fuel-intensive. Since tobacco growing is geographically concentrated and there is no real alternative to using fuelwood for drying, it poses a serious threat to the supply of 'free' fuelwood. BAT (Kenya) Ltd have therefore made afforestation by the growers a condition of buying their tobacco. Since tobacco growing is comparatively profitable, farmers have readily complied. The trees provide fuelwood and increase soil productivity by augmenting its capacity to retain moisture. Furthermore, BAT provides credit on advantagous terms (Hughes-Scott, 1985, p. 25).

Much of the industrial use of fuelwood is by small-scale enterprises in the rural informal sector. It has been estimated that in some rural areas of Ghana as much as a quarter of fuelwood consumption is accounted for by informal sector industry — mainly producers of palm oil, sugar, beer, smoked fish and bread (Van der Plas, quoted by Simon Burne, 1986). As fuelwood becomes scarcer, these producers are increasingly having to buy their supplies with money instead of being able to treat fuelwood as a 'free good'. That affects their profitability. Some operators can switch to other fuels. In Kenya, women around Lake Victoria now smoke their fish with donkey dung rather than with wood, and use sorghum stalks as kindling. Potters in the Mauadi region of Niger have switched from wood to millet stalks; they buy them, but for less than the cost of wood (Burne, 1986). Other forms of switching to crop residues are sometimes possible, but often require the densification of the residues to be used, which may involve an outlay of capital that informal sector operators cannot afford.

Provision of credit to help in such cases is often advocated. But experience of giving credit to the poorer rural people has not been universally happy. Small loans are costly to administer, and borrowing has often been found easier than repaying! In general, having to pay for fuel that was previously free has faced many informal sector operators with a serious problem since they can rarely recoup their costs by raising the prices that they themselves charge. They operate under competitive conditions and sell to customers whose incomes may not be increasing. Consequently they are faced with the risk of declining incomes and ultimately with total loss of livelihood (Burne, 1986).

Increasing energy efficiency

Consumption of fuelwood is much influenced by the fact that it is perceived by a majority to be costless. How can one put off the day when fuelwood is no longer 'free'? Broadly, there are three ways. First, by using fuel more efficiently, in the sense of extracting more energy from the wood that is burnt or converted into charcoal. Second, by substituting other fuels. Third, by planting more trees. Much thought and money have gone into exploring ways of doing all three, and the number of projects and 'missions' to solve the fuelwood problem has by now run into hundreds if not thousands.

Taking energy efficiency first, there is no disputing the fact that fuelwood is very inefficiently used. In the countryside the customary fireplace consists of three stones. Well-designed stoves could greatly reduce the amount of wood needed to generate a given amount of 'useful energy' and much effort has gone into designing cheap and efficient models. Persuading people to use them has proved more difficult. Where it gets cool in the evening, the warmth of the open fire is missed. Open fires also provide light and keep insects away. Nor is it much fun to sit around a stove when one has been accustomed to sitting by the dying embers of an open fire. Stoves are also often far too expensive for villagers even when heavily subsidized. They may also be beyond villagers' technical ability to construct when there are no expatriate or other well-wishers around to help. Again, such stoves are only likely to appeal if the effort of collecting wood from ever further afield has really begun to reach breaking-point. Lastly, if the stoves have to be paid for, the outlay must compete with alternative uses for the funds. Making the task of women and children easier may be thought to produce a lower return than investments which yield a money income.

Converting timber into charcoal is another process in which much energy is wasted at present. Fuelwood destined for towns is most frequently made into charcoal, except in parts of West Africa (Foley et al., 1986, p. 74). The customary process of conversion using a pit is very inefficient. Its advantage is that it requires no capital outlay, in contrast to more efficient kilns. Most people who earn their living by making charcoal cannot afford to buy kilns. Besides, kilns are difficult to transport, and being able to move freely from place to place, wherever suitable wood is to hand, is an absolute prerequisite.

Another target for greater fuel efficiency is the charcoal stove commonly used in towns. These stoves are made very cheaply in the urban informal sector from old kerosene drums and other pieces of scrap metal. In Kenya they go by the name of *jiko*, in Senegal *fourneaux malagches*. Their energy efficiency is very low. Better models have been designed. There have been dozens of stove programmes in various parts of Africa, all initiated and pursued with great enthusiasm and often a good deal of foreign aid. In Kenya alone there were eight governmental and twenty-three non-governmental organizations engaged in developing and disseminating improved cooking stoves in 1983 (for a detailed account, see Egneus et al., 1985, pp. 65–7; see also Foley et al., 1984).

But the improved models have usually required methods of manufacture beyond the technical capacity of the informal sector, and their cost has therefore been high. This has reduced the numbers that can be sold.

In addition, there was no obvious method of marketing them. Failure to recognize the importance of marketing is commonplace in Africa.

It is only quite recently that there appears at last to have been a break-through — thanks largely to the pragmatic good sense of the Intermediate Technology Development Group which in Kenya found a way of making an 'improved' charcoal stove that was within the technical competence of informal sector manufacturers. This stove is now being made by large numbers of manufacturers and is becoming the standard model used in Kenyan towns (Foley et al., 1984, p. 70; Burne, 1985).

More fuel-efficient forms of energy production at low capital cost are to be found in small businesses as well as in households. Double-drum ovens for baking cost little, so long as there are empty oil drums to be had, and they are said to be much more efficient than traditional designs, provided they are properly used. But sometimes a new device will work only if people are prepared to adjust their accustomed work practices, and a new device for smoking fish that had been very successful in Ghana proved to be a failure in Benin for this reason (Burne, 1986). It is a familiar story in many fields of innovation and technology transfer, by no means peculiar to energy. To sum up: obtaining greater fuel efficiency as a means of conserving fuelwood almost always involves a cost.

Alternative sources of energy

The second option is to find alternative sources of energy. One obvious candidate is kerosene. Kerosene is already extensively used to provide light, in conjunction with appliances of varying degrees of sophistication and cost. At one end of the spectrum are imported Tilley (power) lamps, at the other, the so-called 'candles' made in the informal sector from empty oil cans, or simply a wick placed in an old glass jar. Kerosene is also used for cooking. Increasing numbers of people employ single kerosene burners to heat a pan of water. But kerosene has made little headway as a principal food for cooking. One reason is that food cooked on kerosene does not taste the same. But, so long as there is 'free' fuelwood to be had, that is, of course, the chief reason for preferring it, since kerosene has to be paid for, and, moreover, requires an appliance far more expensive than even an improved wood stove. Arguably, since oil has to be imported in most African countries, the deterrence of kerosene use is just as well. The cost of oil imports has been very high and until quite recently has absorbed a high proportion of many countries' export earnings. In 1981 this proportion was 77 per cent in Senegal, in Upper Volta 71 per cent, and even in Kenya and the Ivory Coast it was 23 and 21 per cent respectively (World Bank, 1984). These are high ratios for countries desperately plagued by balance of payments deficits which might be thought wise to avoid deliberately increasing their oil import bills by extending the use of kerosene. But the increase in the oil costs might be smaller than one would have guessed. On quite reasonable assumptions, Gerald Foley has shown that, if fuelwood and charcoal were totally replaced by kerosene and LPG, the foreign exchange cost would be the equivalent of only 11 per cent of total merchandise exports in Zimbabwe, and 14 per cent in Kenya. But it would be 73 per cent in Burundi and 91 per cent in Niger. His figures are not intended to be more than illustrative. Foley and Ms Van Buren have also explored the implications of using coal as a substitute in Senegal and Tanzania, but found that it was to all intents and purposes totally impracticable, even in the capital cities (Foley & Van Buren, 1980, Section 3).

Another alternative to fuelwood is electricity. Electrification has long been seen as the single most powerful instrument of rural transformation. Electricity is regarded by many as the very essence of modernity and is much beloved by visionaries with a weak grasp of economic realities. The idea of rural electrification as an essential element of economic transformation has had ardent advocates in both colonial and post-colonial governments since the end of World War II. It even goes back to Lenin's definition of communism as 'Soviet power plus the electrification of the whole country' and Roosevelt's New Deal in the 1930s. It comes almost into the category of truths to be taken as self-evident.

In post-war Africa, the Owen Falls Dam, the Zambesi power station, the Volta River Project and, most of all, the Aswan Dam were not built merely to provide energy for the urban industrial revolutions they were expected and failed to promote, but also to transform agriculture and to industrialize the countryside. They did neither, as we now know. In the words of one commentator, the Owen Falls Dam in Uganda achieved little more of consequence than to provide the well-to-do with cheap electricity and to light the streets at night for the residents of Kampala and Jinja, (Walker, 1958, pp. 99–100). Since 'peasants' could not be expected to increase agricultural output because they were deemed to be too 'backward' and altogether lacking in material ambition, the future was thought to lie in large irrigated agricultural projects — state farms in Zambia — which 'required' electricity to provide power for irrigation and for the associated processing plants. 'Countries of the Third World, often with the necessary support of external lenders, have invested thousand of millions of dollars in extending electricity grids to their rural areas' (Fluitman, 1983, p. 1). One might expect outlays of such magnitude to show evidence that the benefits associated with rural electrification do indeed occur — if not always and everywhere, at least in many cases. 'Alas', Fluitman continues (p.2), 'such evidence is rare, and, what is worse, a number of observers have begun to express serious doubts about the real benefits of rural electrification.' Some had these doubts a quarter of a century earlier (Elkan & Wilson, 1967). Rural electrification programmes continue, undeterred by such doubts, and are constrained only by difficulties in raising external finance.

Extending the grid from a hydro-electric or large thermal plant is the most expensive way of providing electricity in rural areas. Yet, taking Third World countries as a whole, 80 per cent of rural electricity is supplied in this way (World Bank, 1984, p. 18). Local oil-fired stations are cheaper even when oil prices are very high, though balance of payments constraints must normally rule them out. Electricity can also be generated by biomass and wind power, and sometimes purely local hydro-stations are technically feasible. Waste products from the processing of crops can sometimes be used to generate electricity for the processing plant, thus eliminating the need to buy fuel or to pay the cost of transmission.

Even in the late 1970s, Zambia's Development Plan for 1979–83 still showed no doubt that rural electrification would increase agricultural production, promote rural industries, bring about improvements in health, education, training and the standard of living in general, and generate employment opportunities that would reduce migration from the countryside to the towns (Zambia, 1979, p. 261). How and at what cost this was to be done was not explored, let alone whether previous attempts at extending the grid further into the countryside had resulted in these inestimable benefits. Zambia is a classic case of 'economic development with (what are mistakenly believed to be) unlimited supplies of power'. To pour scorn on the profligate way in which rural electrification has been advocated is not to deny that electricity is a very desirable amenity, even if it is used only for lighting, as in most electrified rural homes. Outside the towns, there are few in Africa who use electricity to cook on, let alone who have refrigerators, electric irons or television. Even in towns they are only a small minority. But who would not sooner have electric light than kerosene, especially when, because of subsidies, it might even turn out to be cheaper? Electricity is easier to use, it is cleaner, and it gives out a much better light. What is questioned, because it is more questionable, is whether rural electrification is the best use of scarce resources, from either an economic or a social vantage point.

The provision of motive power for pumps is often given as a prime example of the economic benefit of rural electrification: 'A penny's worth of electricity can provide as much water as a man at a hand pump all day'. But irrigation pumps can also be supplied with energy from a local diesel station, by gas, the sun or wind. One should therefore look at the relative cost of alternative ways of supplying the energy. But there is no other area of development that is so dominated by missionaries as that of energy. Each form of energy has its passionate advocates who are convinced that only their own horse can win. Studies of the relative costs of providing energy in different ways are therefore rare, and attempts to evaluate the relative social and economic effects of expenditure on energy and on alternative purposes are still more uncommon. To quote Fluitman once more:

The benefits of rural electrification, including the social benefits, tend to be overestimated and the costs understated. Multi-million dollar schemes, it appears, are repeatedly based on conventional wisdom fueled by extraneous motives rather than arithmetic. The role of subsidies is therefore debatable, particularly in countries yet unable to satisfy needs more basic than access to electricity. (Fluitman, 1983, p. 53).

Reafforestation

We come, lastly, to the attempts to solve the fuelwood problem by ensuring that enough trees are planted to maintain the existing stock and to allow for increases in fuelwood demand arising from an anticipated growth of population. Reafforestation can take the form either of plantations or of persuading small cultivators to plant woodlots on part of their land. Both methods have been strongly advocated by the World Bank and other foreign aid agencies. In the Sahel region, where the problem of deforestation is perhaps most acute, some $US 40 million of foreign aid has been spent over the last decade on establishing fuelwood plantations, and substantial investments have taken place in other parts Africa. Unfortunately, such projects have in general met with a notable lack of success. In the case of plantations, costs of production are high, given the long gestation period before the trees begin to yield a return. Even if the plantations can be adequately policed, they are not likely to pay their way so long as there is any indigenous wood left. They cannot hope to compete with wood which is virtually free to rural consumers and for which urban consumers pay little more than the cost of getting it to the towns.

David French has calculated for Malawi that, at the ruling prices for indigenous wood, the loss incurred by any government trying to grow wood for sale would be very large indeed. If it was grown on a sufficient scale to meet the prospective demand for wood, it would require a subsidy equivalent to about 10 per cent of Malawi's GNP (French, 1985).

Persuading farmers to set aside land for woodlots faces similar problems. The land is likely to compete with other uses in which the returns are higher and quicker. Crops are also easier to protect from people, who do not always recognize private property in fuelwood, and the returns from growing crops are therefore perceived as being more certain. Even fast-growing trees take at least five years to mature and, although a gestation period of five years did not stop Gold Coast farmers at the turn of the century from growing cocoa or Ugandan farmers after World War II from growing coffee (Szereszewski, 1966; Elkan, 1961), the prospective returns were very much higher than they appear to be for fuelwood or even wood poles. The reason for the much lower prospective return is that no one can anticipate the prices likely to obtain when supplies of 'free' wood are exhausted, and, until they are, their existence exerts a downward pressure on the price of planted wood. It might be a better strategy to suggest to farmers that they use the land to grow food or other crops that leave a woody residue; this would at least ensure a joint supply of fuel, assuming always that the residue can be burnt directly or that a really cheap technique of briquetting it becomes available. But it is unlikely that farmers will grow a particular crop just because it has a woody residue when another crop promises to be more profitable. The switch may happen eventually, but only when the cost of using fuelwood or other biomass fuel has risen to what it now costs to use electricity or LPG.

Manifestly, therefore, the fuelwood problem cannot be solved either by setting up plantations or by trying to encourage farmers to grow woodlots for fuelwood. But the stock of trees needs to be replenished for reasons besides producing fuelwood. Vegetation is needed to protect the soil, as Lesotho and the Sahel have demonstrated so dramatically. David French therefore argues that the best hope is to follow a strategy of persuading farmers to plant enough trees and the right species to protect the soil and to ensure that land does not dissolve into sand. The right species are likely to be those suitable for building poles, which fetch a higher price than, say, eucalyptus used for fuelwood.

Once indigenous wood is totally used up, the situation will be different. Commercially-grown timber will no longer have to compete with 'free' indigenous wood, the prices charged for it need then only be competitive with alternative fuels, and it will still have the advantage of not requiring expensive equipment to use. Whether it makes better sense to go for this solution rather than to switch earlier to alternative fuels is at present a largely open question.

Other sources of energy

We have said nothing about solar energy, wind power, or the production of ethanol from sugar cane to produce a substitute for petrol. All have attracted attention, research and foreign assistance, not to mention enthusiastic advocacy. Ethanol is produced from sugar cane at considerable expense which makes it no longer economic now that the price of oil has fallen so dramatically. Solar energy, which on the face of it must seem an obvious source in a sunny climate, does not live up to that expectation. Curiously, northern latitudes with long summer days and clearer skies are often better suited to harness solar energy than many parts of Africa (Dunkerley et al., 1981, pp. 164–6). Even where in principle solar energy could be used, it is better used to dry crops than to drive pumps for irrigation or to draw water. It is at its most useful as a way of heating water, but that has never been the greatest need in tropical countries where people are content to wash themselves and their clothes in 'unheated' (not necessarily 'cold'!) water. Some very simple solar heaters are to be found here and there, many of them introduced by Israelis, but, by and large, their impact on rural life has been slight. The same is true of wind power, which played such an important role, together with water-power, in North-West Europe right up to World War II. But the wind 'it bloweth where [and when] it listeth', and in many parts of Africa unfortunately too rarely to provide a dependable source of energy. Like solar power, it is, however, occasionally to be found in use.

In conclusion

We must conclude that these and other alternative sources of energy on which high hopes were placed ten years ago have failed so far to live up to expectations. But new ideas rarely catch on quickly unless, like the Green Revolution in South Asia, they are overwhelmingly advantageous, and the experience with charcoal stoves in Kenya points to the pay-off of being patient. If there is no future in cutting trees — there is none in cutting corners!

References

Anderson, D. & Fishwick, R. (1984), *Fuelwood Consumption & Deforestation in African Countries*, World Bank Staff Working Paper No. 704, Washington DC, World Bank.

Bauer, P.T. & Yamey, B.S. (1951), 'Economic progress and occupational distribution', *Economic Journal*, December: 741–55.

Burne, Simon (1985), *Charcoal Stove Developments in Kenya*, Rugby, Intermediate Technology Development Group.

Burne, Simon (1986), 'Rural industry and the commercialization of biomass', paper presented to Third World Energy Workshop, Reading University, April.

Courier (EEC), (1986), 'Woodfuel crisis', No. 95, January–February.

Dunkerley. Joy et al. (1981). *Energy Strategies for Developing Nations*, Baltimore, Johns Hopkins UP for Resources for the Future.

Egneus, H. et al. (eds) (1985), *Bioenergy 84: Volume V Bioenergy in Developing Countries*, London, Elsevier.

Elkan, W. (1961), *Economic Development of Uganda*, London, OUP.

Elkan, W. & Wilson, Gail (1967), 'Owen Falls hydroelectric dam: ten years experience', *Journal of Development Studies*, June.

Fluitman, F. (1983), *Socio-Economic Impact of Rural Electrification in Developing Countries: A Review of Evidence*, International Labour Office, Geneva Working Paper, November.

Foley, G. (1985), *Exploring the Impact of Conventional Fuel Substitution on Woodfuel Demand* (Working Paper), London, Earthscan, International Institute for Environment & Development.

Foley, G., Moss, P. & Timberlake, L. (1984), *Stoves & Trees*, London, Earthscan.

Foley, G. & Van Buren, A. (1980), *Coal Substitution & Other Approaches to Easing the Pressure on Woodfuel Resources: Senegal & Tanzania*, Rome, FAO Forestry Division, Technical Panel on fuelwood and charcoal, December.

French, D. (1985), 'Economics of bioenergy in developing countries' in Egneus, H. et al. (eds), *Bioenergy 84'*, Vol. 5, London, Elsevier, pp. 161–70.

Hall, D.O., Barnard, G.W. & Moss, P.A. (1982), *Biomass for Energy in Developing Countries*, Oxford, Pergamon Press.

Howes, Michael (1985), *Rural Energy Surveys in the Third World*, IDRC.

Hughes-Scott, Patricia (1985), 'Tobacco: the growing benefits', *African Technical Review*, October: 25–6.

O'Keefe, P. *et al.* (eds) (1984), *Energy Environment & Development in Africa: Kenya*, Stockholm, Beijer Institute & the Scandinavian Institute of African Studies.

Szereszewski, R.E. (1966), *Structural Changes in the Economy of Ghana, 1891–1911*, London, Weidenfeld & Nicolson.

Walker, D. (1958), 'Power in Uganda', *East African Economics Review*, Nairobi, January.

World Bank (1983), *Energy Transition in Developing Countries*, Washington DC.

World Bank (1984), *World Development Report 1984*.

Zambia (1979), *Third National Development Plan 1979–83*, Lusaka.

6 Rural–Urban Interaction and Rural Transformation in Tropical Africa

W.T.S Gould

Introduction

While it is not the objective of this chapter to demur at the view that critical research and policy issues in contemporary Africa lie in the area of rural transformation, it must be recognized that rural development cannot in any sense be independent of urban development. Extremely rapid urban growth throughout the continent, which has certainly created its own serious problems, undoubtedly allied to and exacerbated by the rural crisis, has intensified an essentially false dichotomy into 'rural' and 'urban' as spatial categories that are analytically convenient surrogates for economic, social and cultural differences. Langton and Hoppe have argued for medieval Europe that 'the conceptualizations of the process of development in Western Europe which incorporate self-contained rural and urban categories, whether these are considered separately or in some kind of opposition, are ... severely inadequate' (Langton & Hoppe, 1983, p. 9). And so for contemporary Africa. This chapter therefore attempts to place issues and debates on rural transformation in the specific context of rural–urban interaction. It does not directly address the dichotomy/continuum debate on the nature of the spatial categories, but identifies rather the complexity of interaction between them, and how interactions have a wide range of effects on rural areas that require adaptation of the wider structures of economic and social life. An understanding of these processes of rural transformation, it is argued, requires specific and not merely residual attention to the nature and extent of exchanges in both directions. Rural–urban interactions must be seen not merely as symptoms of the nature of rural and urban relations, but as features of major and positive significance in their own right in the processes of rural and urban change.

The study of rural–urban interaction, in Tropical Africa as elsewhere, has in the main been partial and indirect. Analysts and policy-makers have tended to assume and to act upon a rural–urban dichotomy. Major debates discussed in other chapters of this book, such as the role of market mechanisms as the primary organizing structure for rural transformation, or the nature and extent of urban bias as a feature of the underdevelopment of rural areas in Africa, must make explicit recognition of rural/urban interactions. In this respect African Studies have fallen behind scholarship in other parts of the world. Studies in East and South Asia have established basic conceptual models of these interactions. Michael Lipton's urban bias thesis, developed from Indian experience and ordered into what John Harriss has called 'a master metaphor rather than a well-substantiated theory' (Harriss, 1982, p. 40), is one model that needs to be examined in Africa on several scales (Lipton, 1977; Harriss & Moore, 1984). Using East Asian experience at first, but subsequently generalizing to all urbanizing societies, Dennis Rondinelli and associates have established a framework for the investigation of rural development through a focus on small towns (Rondinelli, 1983a and b; Rondinelli & Ruddle, 1978). While the Asian experience of rural development is certainly very different from that of Africa, not least, as Gordon White reminds us, in its dependence on the positive effects of state intervention (White, 1986), these models and planning assumptions provide valuable starting-points. Work in Latin America offers an analytical basis for further examination. David Preston (1975, 1978), working in the Andes, has used a five-fold classification of interactions that can equally be applied in Africa — exchanges of people, goods and capital, social interactions and administrative and service provision. Analysts in Africa have tended to examine each of these in relative isolation — witness the mountain of material on migration — but have not systematically viewed the totality of interaction, even though the whole is greater than the sum of the individual parts.

This chapter uses Preston's typology to summarize the nature and extent of rural–urban interaction in Africa. It is inevitably highly selective in its thematic and geographical coverage of such a large field, but it synthesizes the range of experience in an integrated view of rural–urban interaction that offers challenging prospects for new research directions on processes that affect the direction and intensity of the rural transformation.

Rural–urban interaction

Movement of people

Prima facie, the explosion of urbanization, and particularly the rapid growth of the primate capital cities of each African country, suggests a net transfer of people to urban areas that is associated with changing real and perceived economic opportunities between rural and urban sectors. Population mobility in this perspective is taken to be a principal symptom of the processes of development and underdevelopment, and to be also itself a cause of economic and social change, altering the distribution of the labour supply and therefore affecting both domestic and commercial activities in rural and in urban areas. This simplistic view requires qualification in five particular respects, each of which emphasizes the interaction perspective.

In the first place, not all mobility is rural–urban; indeed, rural destinations are likely to more important, at least in numbers of people involved, than urban destinations. Major moves to resettlement schemes, 'spontaneous' migration of individual farmers and their families, often to more marginal land and over short distances, flows of environmental and political refugees, all from rural areas, are themselves part of the process of rural transformation at both source and destination (Clarke & Kosinski, 1982; Clarke, Khogali & Kosinski, 1985).

Secondly, and more importantly in this context, mobility in Tropical Africa characteristically involves circulation rather than migration, premised on interaction between source and destination (Chapman & Prothero, 1985; Standing, 1985). Return to the rural source provides opportunity for the migrants' direct involvement in rural economy and society, apart from any contributions made in assets or capital. In neo-Marxian terms, it is the return and interaction that enable the reproduction of the labour force, as in the colonial economy through the development of labour reserves: 'the ideal reserve is a recruiting ground for labour, a place from which the able-bodied go out to work, returning occasionally to rest and beget the next generation of labourers' (M.A. Buxton, 1927, quoted in C.C. Wrigley, 1965, p. 246). That the migrant labour system has been and remains a major cause of rural underdevelopment is a widely-held view. Several governments have directed their attention to the problems of creating stable urban populations. In Zimbabwe, the creation of a larger urban proletariat is currently seen as one means of dealing with rural landlessness and some of the problems of reallocating land, since those families with access to an urban income will be ineligible for land allocations (Simon, 1986). However, it has the implication of aggravating an already economically serious and politically damaging cleavage between the peasantry and the proletariat (Simon, 1985). On the other hand, there is evidence everywhere that circular migration is attractive to individual families, that it may offer them long-term advantages, and should not be regarded as merely a temporary phase associated with capitalist exploitation and an articulation with the peasant mode of production (Elkan, 1976). Since rural–urban exchange of people is likely to remain a major feature in most countries in the foreseeable future, the debate about the directions as well as the level of these movements is of practical policy relevance.

A third qualification is that levels of mobility and the mix of the various dimensions of distance, direction and periodicity, including the relative importance of permanent and temporary moves, are spatially selective within each country. The forms and extent of population movement are affected by local economic circumstances, on and off the farm, and by local social relationships. Generally, out-migration is lowest from areas with a vigorous local economy and highest from lagging and peripheral regions. In West Africa this is apparent on an international scale (Zachiariah & Conde, 1981). Levels of circulation and return migration may be similarly affected, with greatest return to areas in which migrants are able to retain access to economically viable plots, and least to areas of crippling impoverishment, landlessness and lowest off-farm incomes (Lipton, 1980). Largely because of analytical difficulties connected with cluster sampling techniques in national surveys, systematic regional and local comparisons of migration systems have proved elusive.

Fourthly, population mobility is known to be socially and economically selective at its source. It is not usually the poorest who migrate; their living is often too precarious and they have neither the education nor the capital to be able to benefit from or run the risk of migration. Wealthier peasants, on the other hand, have a surplus to support migration by some members of the household. They tend to live in more accessible areas, such as in roadside locations, and they can afford more education for their children. Collier & Lal (1984) have argued for Kenya that, through that differential pattern of migration and access to urban income, the effects of migrants' remittances and of their return tend to exacerbate intra-rural inequality.

Finally, it must be borne in mind that not all those involved in migration and in rural–urban interaction are labour migrants. Many are dependants of these migrants, principally wives and children, who may even move periodically between an urban and a rural household of the same extended or polygamous family, as vividly described for Kenya by Ross & Wisner (1977). Others may move between country and town to visit relatives or cement social relationships, or simply to experience the 'bright lights' of the city, if only for a short period.

Much has been written and will continue to be written about each of these features of population exchange between town and country as serious theoretical and empirical controversies in the study of population mobility continue (Gould, in press). It is sufficient here to note that demand-based explanatory models of migration, mostly in economics, that see the level and form of mobility principally as a response to conditions in the urban employment market are seriously flawed, and economists too have recognized the importance of the supply side (Knight, 1972; Rimmer, 1984, pp. 87–95). A recognition of the importance and persistence of a wider migration *system*, as identified by Akin Mabogunje (1970), in which the rural context is afforded equal prominence and in which 'rural' and 'urban', conceptually separated, are analytically integrated through rural–urban interaction, offers a more realistic approach. Increased levels of population mobility, associated with cheaper and more widely available transport and greater integration into commercial market systems, must in themselves be major factors in rural transformation, but the form and complexity of that mobility and its social and spatial selectivities have precluded satisfactory generalization about its impact.

Movement of goods

The most immediately apparent economic exchanges between rural and urban areas are of goods: rural produce to urban centres and through a hierarchy of centres upwards to the capital city and perhaps thence for export; imports and urban manufactures downwards to smaller towns and outwards to rural consumers. However, just as all population movement is not rural–urban and vice versa, so too with movement of goods. Trade within rural areas is everywhere important. A practical implication of viewing such exchanges as a process of development would be policies that accelerate them, as regions or whole colonies and countries are progressively brought into wider systems of exchange. But the processes of exchange are not neutral; some areas and countries benefit more than others and perhaps even at the expense of others. The questions that arise in the present context are the extent to which rural impoverishment may be attributed to the exchange of goods between rural and urban areas and to the terms on which trade is conducted, and, if impoverishment can be so attributed, the mechanisms by which exchange may be organized to alter the balance of advantage and disadvantage.

The range of goods involved in this exchange, their relative values and the predominant direction of movement vary. A common pattern is the export of primary agricultural produce from peasant farms and plantations, not only providing income to farmers, labourers and traders, but also generating export tax revenues. Rural areas, whether engaged in agriculture, mining or even tourism have been a main source of public receipts of foreign exchange. In all countries dominated by primary production there seems to be a net transfer out of rural areas, for governments will expend the revenues on general services and provision in both rural and urban areas. The key variables in the balance of rural and urban benefits are the prices received by producers and the extent to which governments use export crop revenues for urban-based development purposes — issues raised several decades ago when colonial marketing boards were perceived to have become instruments of rural taxation.

With the rapid growth in urban populations, the matter of urban food supply from rural areas has assumed considerable importance, but has been strangely ignored by scholars working in English-speaking countries. It has been studied more in Francophone countries, where *approvisionnement* of towns has been shown to have created a complex structure extending over wide areas. According to Vennetier (1976, chap. 10), the principal beneficiaries are not the producers, but either the trading middlemen, in countries with little government involvement in distribution and pricing, or the urban consumers in states with strong government involvement in setting price levels, usually in an attempt to subsidize consumers for political reasons. In Tanzania, the massively greater demands of the much increased and richer urban population, rather than rural production declines, have been shown to be primarily responsible for the increase in food imports (Bryceson, 1985). In Dar es Salaam the rural–urban movement of fresh foodstuffs has grown rapidly, but has failed to match population growth, and the shortfall has not in this case been met by increased production of food on small plots within the urban areas itself or on its immediate fringes (Sporrek, 1985). As Swindell discusses elsewhere in this book (Chapter 7), the fringes of West African towns are apparently more productive.

Increased urban demands on rural primary produce are also felt in energy supplies, particularly in wood fuel, including the semi-refined form of charcoal. Here the exchange may be particularly disadvantageous to rural areas unless there is direct management of the wood resource, either commercially, as in imperial Addis Ababa within the forest belt planted round the city (Horvath, 1969), or by official control of destruction of forest and its replacement. In eastern Africa supply of fuelwood to urban areas has been shown to be operated as a classic 'robber' economy by urban entrepreneurs, seriously depleting the resources available to rural dwellers and, in the medium term, to the nation as a whole, as natural or managed regeneration is exceeded by consumption (O'Keefe *et al.*, 1984). In West Africa, on the other hand, there are traditional energy supply structures of longer standing and greater viability, for example in the exchange of firewood for manure round Kano (Mortimore, 1970), but they too are strained by the joint pressure of urban growth and environmental deterioration (see also Elkan, Chapter 5).

The predominant flow of goods from urban to rural areas comprises urban manufactures. Demand may continue even with stagnant or falling rural incomes, if they are products for which there are no ready substitutes, notably cloth and some manufactured foodstuffs, or if the manufactured product has captured the market of the traditional rural product by competition in price or quality, for example the substitution of moulded plastic or enamel products for household utensils in traditional materials, or of manufactured roofing material, window frames and bricks for traditional building materials. Rural–urban interaction may spread a growing range of urban products into rural areas and extend the market for manufactures while undermining rural craft industries or forcing adaptation upon them.

These exchanges, taken as a whole, need to be examined by the terms of trade. This is a complex issue, for it involves not only questions about the benefits of specialization and of observing Ricardian comparative advantage, but also practical difficulties of measurement. Furthermore, it is an essentially dynamic concept, since exchanges occur over time and their terms vary over time. Hence the paucity of empirical studies of rural–urban terms of trade. The most prominent of recent studies, however partial, are in Tanzania, where, despite the socialist rhetoric and explicit rural bias of government policies, there was throughout the 1970s an adverse trend in terms of trade against agricultural produce (Ellis, 1984). A similar pattern was identified earlier for Zambia (Miambo & Fry, 1971; Fry, 1975). In Kenya, on the other hand, recent evidence on agricultural prices is contradictory. Sharpley (1981) believes that incentives for farmers were so low in the 1970s that there was a net flow of capital out of estate and peasant agriculture; Jabara (1985), by contrast, uses price data from the early 1970s to 1982/3 to show an increase of 13 per cent in barter terms of trade for export and domestic crops, and concludes that in the aggregate there is no great evidence for a widening rural–urban income gap in Kenya. Such a controversy raises as many questions about data and methods as about the conclusions. What is clearly needed is further disaggregation by type of farm and by region, given the wide range of economic and ecological circumstances in Kenyan agriculture.

Movement of capital and income

Spatial patterns of income generation are not necessarily or even usually similar to spatial patterns of expenditure. Income may be moved from urban to rural areas or vice versa in the form of cash or in kind. These transfers create further difficulties for the measurement and assessment of the impact of rural–urban interaction on rural areas, difficulties that are rooted in some of the complexity of circulation and continuous interaction noted above.

At the scale of the individual and the household, redistribution of income occurs through remittances in cash or, less commonly, in goods. The very nature of population mobility facilitates remittance directly (though postal remittances are also important and widely used). Probably more important for the totality of rural–urban interaction, remittances can ensure that the main focus of a household remains in the rural area. The culture of migrancy has maintained the remittance imperative in most parts of Africa, though the relative importance of remittances is probably less now than earlier, as the rising cost of living in town and relative stagnation of money-wages, especially at lower levels of the occupational hierarchy, have reduced the proportions of urban incomes available to be remitted. However, the poor still remit larger proportions of their incomes than the rich (Knowles & Anker, 1981). Recent estimates suggest that about 6 per cent of urban incomes in Kenya are remitted to relatives, mostly to rural areas (Mukras, Oucho & Bamberger, 1985), though it is known that remittances in Kenya, as elsewhere, may also be rural–rural (i.e. from workers in rural areas) and, in much smaller amounts, rural–urban to support family members temporarily looking for work in towns.

Remittances continue because, in Africa, unlike Latin America, there is considerable reluctance among migrants to make permanent investment in towns, particularly in housing. Much low-income housing is rented, illegally built or made of semi-permanent materials, particularly in East and Central Africa. In those areas of West Africa with an indigenous urban tradition, the urban compound can absorb rural migrants, and men and women may seek investment opportunities in trade. Opportunities for and levels of urban investment of urban incomes are therefore higher than elsewhere. But the low levels of private long-term investment by Africans in African cities remains a significant general feature.

As far as the rural transformation is concerned, a crucial issue is to examine how remittances are spent, and here again there is likely to be a wide range of experience related to local economic prospects. Many migrants invest in additional land to provide for a growing family. In areas of a vigorous commercial economy, for example in Central Province, Kenya, in eastern Zimbabwe, or in Ivory Coast, they may spend on seeds, fertilizers or tractors or on hiring labour at peak periods to increase farm productivity. In areas of limited opportunities for investment in the rural economy, whether in new land or in raising output from land already available, remittances may be invested in people themselves in the form of paying school fees, to acquire educational qualifications that will perpetuate the cultural and economic bases of urban migration (Martin, 1982). Whether investment is in land or people may depend critically on prevailing systems of land tenure and the extent to which individual tenure has replaced traditional arrangements.

In many cases, remittances are not used for productive purposes. At one level these are evident in the beer halls and increased personal consumption of food of the immigrant when he or she returns to the rural area and in purchase of consumer durables — radios, watches, etc, — at another, in housing in the rural source area, which, although an investment, can be essentially non-realizable and for immediate personal or family satisfaction in the improvement of existing housing or, more commonly, the building of a new house of modern materials and design. In such cases of rural investment, levels of rural production may not benefit directly, or even indirectly, since these expenditures in rural areas tend to be on urban products, and the greater the expenditure, the more likely the shift to urban preferences in foods (e.g. to wheat flour products, to modern beer rather than traditional brews) and household durables.

At a community level, remittances are often made through and by ethnic associations to provide facilities such as school or health centres in a home village. This aspect of remittance is particularly strong in Nigeria. It not only maintains redistribution from urban to rural areas, but also strengthens the awareness of the essential complementarity between urban and rural members of a community. Similarly, in Kenya, remittances for *harambee* communal facilities are solicited by ethnic organizations, as in the case of the Ramogi Institute for Advanced Technology in Kisumu, though in that case the net direction is more evidently urban–urban (Mukras, Oucho & Bamberger, 1985, p. 419). Individual incomes earned in urban areas are used to support rural communities as a whole as well as individual families within it, but the division of remittances between communal and individual benefit will vary greatly from community to community.

The effect of individual remittances on socio-economic stratification in the rural areas may be the greatest single impact of rural–urban interaction, for there is mounting evidence that access to an urban income and the remittances associated with it is one of the main factors in rural differentiation (Collier & Lal, 1984; 1986, Chap. 8). Since it is the relatively well-off rather than the relatively poor who tend to migrate, it is the relatively well-off who remit most and thus make investments or increase consumption in rural areas. Furthermore, rural credit through commercial and official channels has gone disproportionately to the already better-off people and better-off areas. In Kenya, for example, a study of lending to farmers by the Kenya Commercial Bank has shown that, while credit is being extended to a farm-dependent clientèle not reached by other financial institutions, loans tend to go to those with businesses and incomes other than farming (David, 1981).

Social transactions

Many interactions do not have direct economic motivation, but nevertheless cement economic relationships. The extended family offers social cohesion with spatial separation in which economic exchange is implicit. The example of a polygamous man having wives and households in rural and urban areas, with social as well as economic obligations in each, provides an ideal case of how social and economic transactions are analytically related (Lux, 1972). The widespread practice of child fostering with rural relatives in West Africa also maintains rural and urban kinship links (Isugo-Abanihe, 1985). Such exchanges are associated with patterns of reciprocity in gift-giving that are probably dominated by urban–rural transfers for school fees, wedding or funeral expenses or other ceremonies. The flows may also be reversed as rural societies cement the social system by contributing to urban life. Susan Watts, for example, records the preference of many women in Ilorin, Nigeria, for seeking a marriage partner in town, since a wife has greater opportunities for independent trade from an urban compound than in a rural area (Watts, 1983). But in this case and others (e.g. Peel, 1983) the particular economic geography of Yoruba society and its distinctive rural–urban relationships may set it apart.

At a wider level, social transactions can involve urban political brokerage of rural interests. Figures of influence, 'big men' locally or nationally, usually have an urban life style and an urban base, even when their political strength depends on a rural constituency. This may be no less true in countries without representative democracy than in those where elections are held. These big men maintain their prestige through patronage — the extension of the economic and political fruits of urban life to their rural clients, whether by finding a job for a migrant or supporting a school or individual pupils in school with fees or donations, paying hospital expenses or financially supporting a local football team or dance troupe. In return the rural clients provide support in business or politics and possibly votes at an election, and the rural voice is expected to be heard when decisions are made by public or private agencies (e.g. Vincent, 1971;1979). The net political effects of such brokerage may be to exacerbate intra-rural and rural–urban inequalities. If, for example, the middle peasantry reaps most benefit from schooling and the effect of schooling is to ensure that more young people seek an urban future, the patronage of an urban-based politician in ensuring the provision of a school in his constituency may strengthen his authority and prestige without benefiting the rural community as a whole, though individuals and families will benefit. Never the less, such social and political transactions maintain the complementarity of rural and urban areas.

Administrative and service provision

It might be held that one of the main roles of the state in contemporary Africa is to redistribute to rural populations the benefits of a development that seems to occur chiefly in urban areas. There is some generally weak redistribution of economic opportunities, as a result of regional policies and investment decisions controlled by the state. There is a spread of social provision in health care and clean drinking water. However, choices need to be made since universal provision cannot be achieved in the short term, and the evidence everywhere is for urban areas to receive priority in social as well as economic investments. Undoubtedly the spatial bias is mitigated somewhat by the political brokerage mentioned above, but, in the absence of strong central control to achieve a different allocation, inter-rural as well as rural–urban inequalities have increased as facilities are built in or allocated to those areas with most political influence or having most resources of their own, including remittances from migrants. In Kenya and Malawi, for example, where much store was placed on local self-help initiatives, the richer rural areas moved rapidly ahead of the poorer, peripheral areas in the years immediately after independence. Lagging areas may now have caught up in facilities, such as primary schools, which were built in the early phase, but may now be lagging in provision of higher threshold facilities such as secondary schools.

This differential impact of state allocations does not occur merely by default. It may be deliberate in mutually reinforcing policy decisions, as has recently been illustrated in three papers on Sierra Leone by Riddell (1985a, b and c). He argues, with several telling examples of state activity, that a clear urban bias in allocations and policy impacts is due in no small measure to the actions of an urban-based bureaucracy acting in its own interests. Far from acting as an agent for diffusion of development and innovation, public officials have, in a period of severe national economic decline, acted against the interests of rural people and rural areas. Rural services have been cut back and producer prices have fallen, but urban consumers and wages have been relatively protected, more so in Freetown than elsewhere.

Discussion

This chapter has thus far described five forms of rural–urban interaction and has suggested how each may affect the processes of rural transformation in contemporary Africa. Each of the five is of major importance in its own right and the subject of considerable research and policy concern. However, the main thrust of the argument presented here is that rural–urban interaction needs to be seen as an integrated whole, and that further and better insights into its role in rural transformation in Africa are most likely to be forthcoming where they are grouped in an holistic rather than sectoral conceptualization.

This analytical framework, first identified by David Preston, may be complemented in some respects. Riddell identified five specific mechanisms of interaction in his analyses of urban bias in post-colonial Sierra Leone. Systematic urban bias was demonstrated by case studies of food policy, intensification of rural production, purchase of agricultural exports, rural development programmes and land tenure. Clearly these cases are not comprehensive, since, for example, they make no reference to population mobility as a factor in rural underdevelopment, though Riddell has much to say on that subject elsewhere, making out a structuralist case that migration flows reflect and reinforce inequalities in West Africa generally (Riddell, 1981). An alternative approach is to adopt a more behaviouralist perception focusing on the actors in the process of exchange — migrants, households, traders, capitalists and public functionaries (Funnell, 1987; Swindell, 1979). Here again, however, only a partial view is possible and it is subject to the analytical difficulties (e.g. inferring general cases from small samples; differentiating perceived and real causation) of using behavioural approaches in the analysis of macro-processes. The Preston classification offers a more general prospect that is at once flexible in scale, amenable to aggregate and to individual approaches, and comprehensive in its basic typology.

As a framework of analysis, this classification can be related to Lipton's hypothesis of urban bias. This hypothesis has not been systematically tested in an Africa context, and, given the complementarities between rural and urban areas discussed above, it needs seriously to be questioned. However, it provides a context from which the relationships between rural and urban areas and thus the issues of rural change cannot realistically be separated.

Within the conceptual context set by Lipton and the empirical context set by Preston, the earlier sections of this discussion have identified some research findings and achievements in Africa. This concluding section uses these findings to examine three areas where further work is urgently required if there are to be significant advances in understanding the role of rural–urban interaction in rural change. Each of the three — the role of small town, the role of household exchange, the issue of regional variations — invokes the holistic approach advocated above, and, while each is worthy of further investigation in its own right, all three can be related to each other.

The role of small towns

Although the role of small towns in rural development has been a recurring issue in Third World studies for several decades, it has been the focus more of ideological and polemical than of empirical discussion, with the result that most controversies remain unresolved. Aidan Southall's 'Introduction' to a collection of preliminary papers on small towns in Africa adopts a distinctly negative tone:

Small towns appear as the lowest rungs of systems for the oppression and exploitation of rural peoples; it is obvious that most small towns are less likely to be innovative local centres of stimulus for rural development than pawns in a larger contrary game [Southall, 1979, p. 213].

For small towns to play a positive role, he argues, requires a decentralized and participatory political structure, such as is not found in any real sense in Africa. Small towns are in most circumstances an extension of the apparatus of the state that can only affect rural areas to the advantage of the urban-based state. Small towns exacerbate rural underdevelopment. Several of the case studies in the Southall study confirm this view: in Sudan 'the role of the centre has been to draw its surroundings into active participation in the national and international economy ... exploitative relations under the merchant and tribal elite [are] gaining dominance' (Ahmed & Rahman, 1979, p. 270); in Mali and Tunisia 'Kita (Mali) extracted rural surplus through trade: while Testour (Tunisia) did it through property and wages' (Hopkins, 1979, p. 237).

An opposite, diffusionist view, associated particularly with Dennis Rondinelli and his colleagues, sees the strengthening of the urban hierarchy, particularly at its lower levels, as a necessary component of rural development. This view is that many rural areas, especially those with dispersed settlement patterns, suffer because of the lack of lower-order service and exchange settlements; promoting these centres is an essential mechanism for bringing rural production into the national market economy. While Rondinelli does admit that there may be some exploitation of rural areas, he also argues

that towns and small cities are not necessarily parasitic ... towns and small cities can and do perform beneficial functions for rural residents; ... The linkages between towns and small cities are the primary channels through which populations derive income [Rondinelli, 1983b, p. 392].

Most of the evidence for this view is adduced from Asia and Latin America (including extensive use of Preston's study of rural–urban interaction in Bolivia), and African evidence is weak and partial. The growth of lower-order settlements needs to be encouraged to deflect flows of migrants and produce away from increasingly primate capital cities, and thus to create a more diverse distribution of population and economic activity, as well as ensuring a more direct effect on rural change *per se*:

Policies encouraging more widespread distribution of population in secondary cities and towns and policies promoting investment in physical infrastructure, marketing, small-scale manufacturing, and agro-processing in secondary cities and town can provide a stronger base for both rural and urban development in many African countries in the future [Rondinelli, 1985, p. 173].

There is an assumption here of the beneficial power of trickle-down development strategies: a small towns policy, with centres well distributed throughout the country, is both efficient and equitable and will accelerate the rural transformation.

Such a belief is implicit in settlement policies developed in several African countries where one objective is to have a 'balanced' settlement hierarchy as part of a 'top-down' development strategy. In Kenya, for example, the Fourth National Development Plan sought to strengthen the urban hierarchy at the lowest level, primarily in order to extend the market economy:

[Support elements] will include a centre where basis inputs [for agriculture] can be purchased, a credit and information centre where information on agricultural prices and markets and where either credit or information on how to obtain it is available. There will also be a transportation centre which provides quick access to markets [Kenya Government, 1979, para. 6. 130, p. 250].

This policy may be defended on the assumption that both the rural producers and the small towns benefit and there is not gross exploitation of one by the other. However, as we have seen, terms of trade may have moved adversely and to exacerbate rather than reduce the rural–urban income differential. But Rondinelli therefore suggests additional requirements for successful implementation for a small towns strategy. These include changes in trading and credit structures to accompany the strengthening of the hierarchy, notably improving prices for rural produce, perhaps even selective regional closure to protect some local production from the competition of cheaper substitutes from other regions or towns. It may also require an element of bottom-up as well as top-down economic management to promote local decision-making. These are issues also identified by Southall. Clearly in these circumstances the role of small towns cannot be seen in isolation, but should be related to particular economic and political objectives. A blanket strategy of small town development and a strengthening of rural links with lower orders of the urban hierarchy as a means of rural transformation need to be qualified by local circumstances and local experience.

Studies of the range of circumstances and experience have been distinctly patchy. Jan Lundqvist's (1975) study of local and central impulses for change and development in Morogoro District, Tanzania, in the early 1970s identified the strength of these impulses coming more in cash crop production and adult education from Morogoro Town than from elsewhere in Tanzania, but showed that an important factor was the diligence and enthusiasm of local agricultural extension officers and adult education officers. Joan Vincent's studies of Teso District, Uganda, also identify the importance of individuals — the 'big men' — in the scale and substance of urban–rural transfers (Vincent, 1979). Hjort's (1979) study of Isiolo, Kenya, confirms the importance of small-scale exchange of people, goods and services both for the town and for the economy of the surrounding rural population: rural households need cash from urban occupations, often casual and very short-term; in Isiolo the small-scale formal and informal economy needs a constant flow of labourers and rural produce. But these studies, like many others elsewhere in Africa, do not begin to tackle the problems of systematic analysis of the exchanges as a whole, identifying the reciprocities rather than measuring the value of exchanges between town and country.

In other contexts the relationship between town and country is not conditioned by distance but by cultural and historical factors that would suggest a general policy of promoting small towns as likely to prove ineffective. The traditional spatial relationships between Yoruba towns and the countryside or between Kano and the Kano close-settled zone create their own specific forms of exchange — of men, women and children in different ways, of rural and urban produce and capital — that defy generalization. My own research in Tiriki, western Kenya, has shown how, in the 1970s, despite the population and functional growth of several secondary towns within 100 km of the field area (including Eldoret, Kisumu and Kakamega), continuous interaction with Nairobi, 400 km away, remained dominant. The spatial patterns of migration, employment and remittance in this overcrowded and impoverished former 'reserve' remain in the 1980s much as they did in the 1960s (Gould, 1985). In that area, and the same would apply to neighbouring areas in the south of Kakamega District such as Maragoli and Bunyore, local opportunities on and off the farm are so limited and long-distance labour migration so common that a vigorous policy of strengthening lower-order settlements may not be felt to be immediately relevant to the development of the area.

We need to examine more systematically the range of experiences with small towns. Under what conditions are mutually beneficial exchanges between town and country more prominent than mutually reinforcing inequalities? How, at the local level, can exchanges be measured? What are the conditions under which small towns can exercise a positive effect on rural transformation? We are nowhere near to resolving these questions in Africa, but again we can look at the Indian experience, particularly in the rich study by John and Barbara Harriss of Arni, Tamil Nadu, a small town which has had a major and generally deleterious effect on its rural hinterland through control of trading and credit. Here the specific circumstances of exchange of various types have been considered in considerable detail and over a long period of time as the primary focus of an interdisciplinary research effort (Harriss & Harriss, 1984). No similarly intensive and comprehensive study exists for any African town.

The role of household exchange

Scholars are now much more aware than they have ever been of the importance of the rural household as an economic unit, but at the same time they are also aware of conceptual and empirical difficulties in getting to grips with relationships within and between households: 'A focus on households is both exciting and dangerous' (Guyer & Peters, 1987, p., 209). In the context of rural–urban interaction, the spatial separation of different members of the family is crucial: at the rural 'home'; in other rural areas as independent farmers, tenants or labourers; in urban areas in waged jobs or looking for work. Each may be individual components of an integrated network of exchange of people, goods and money. Walter Elkan (1976) made particular use of Ross & Wisner's work in Kenya to elaborate the rationale of circular mobility through spatial separation, often of wives of a polygamous husband, in rural and urban households of the same family. Studies like his describe particular flows within households, but there is a need also to measure and systematically analyse the overall patterns of exchange and to relate them to changes over time or in the life cycle of the household.

The Kenya Rural Household Survey data, 1974–75, have been used to show how remittances have been a prime factor in differentiation among rural households, since access to remittances from urban income has been used to overcome allocative inefficiencies in the rural land market (Collier & Lal, 1986). Collier & Lal take an explicitly anti-Lipton stance in arguing 'Why poor people get rich' and they conclude that 'rural–urban interactions are benign' (p. 1010). Theirs is a challenging paper, not least because it incorporates the remittance component in analysis of rural incomes, and thereby raises quite fundamental issues about the impact of income transfers that their data cannot answer. How are these transfers allocated and used within the household; for what (agricultural investment, household goods, school fees) and by whom (wives, children, other relatives); and what are the economic and social circumstances that affect this mix in each case? These questions lead easily on to wider questions in rural Africa, such as gender conflicts, the role of women in the rural transformation, and inter-generational wealth transfers as a factor affecting the fertility transition — the Caldwell hypothesis (Caldwell, 1978).

Inter-household exchanges comprise not only income transfers, important as these may be, but flows of people and household products. As noted above, patterns of marriage migration round Ilorin, Nigeria illustrate how rural women seek urban husbands to pursue better trading opportunities. Are such marriages then followed by a redistribution of children to the rural areas through fostering arrangements? Rural produce is sent to support relatives and households in town, where food is generally very expensive, and may be a significant direct contribution to the urban household economy. Remittances of goods purchased in urban areas, rather than cash *per se*, are certainly important and substantial; they are carried to rural areas through a network of individual contacts, as anyone who has spent any time in an urban bus station or lorry park would testify.

Flows of resources of labour, land and capital within the extended household are everywhere important, but households vary over time in the extent of their spatial disaggregation. Flows between individuals and sub-groups within the household, especially rural–urban flows in both directions, are important for the household directly, as well as for their specific effects on the rural transformation. One possible avenue for further progress on the analysis of changing household structures, identified by Donald Funnell (1987), is a Chayanovian approach, as used in southern Africa to examine the relationships between family labour on and off the farm as they change with the structure of the household (Low, 1982).

Regional variations

Students of rural change are mostly well aware of regional variations in its nature, rapidity, causes and effects. National generalizations need to be tempered with spatial disaggregation at various levels, whether provincial or within local administrative units. What is less widely recognized is how the complexity of rural–urban interactions and their impacts in rural areas also vary to the extent that a simple rural–urban analysis seems grossly inadequate. Regional circumstances vary so much that the resulting mosaic of interactions invites region-specific consideration. Moore has identified the problem in his critique of Lipton and others:

They simply divide countries into an urban space or sector and a rural space or sector. Variations among rural areas in access to cities are not dealt with at all; the perspective of economic and political geography is totally absent. [Moore, 1984a, p. 17].

He goes on to operationalize this general criticism with reference to Sri Lanka where 'the permeability of the rural–urban divide' renders the dichotomy unoperational.

Intra-rural variations in population density, occupation, access to services, cropping patterns and farm structure form a spatial pattern which can relatively easily be fitted into a core-periphery framework: their political consequences can be analysed in tandem with purely spatial considerations. The 'fit' of this core-periphery framework is in large degree the consequence of factors peculiar to Sri Lanka. [Moore, 1984b, p. 120].

Scepticism of the validity of the rural–urban dichotomy and the recognition of the necessity of a finer regional perspective are as valid for any African country, and I have recently explored them in the particular case of Kenya, using some of the evidence identified earlier in this chapter (Gould, 1987). In terms of population movements, remittances, agricultural production and other interactions there is a range of circumstances differentiating region-specific flows. The nature of exchanges between Central Province and Nairobi is different from that of exchanges between Western Province and Nairobi, and both are different again from that between Coast or North-Eastern Province and Nairobi. These differences are not merely a matter of degree, but may be a large factor in the net direction of flows as well as in their impacts at source and destination. It can be argued, with Collier & Lal, that in dynamic regions such as Central Province the interactions have a positive impact on rural production, probably at the expense of exacerbating intra-rural inequalities. But in lagging or 'downward transitional' regions, such as part of Western or Nyanza Provinces, where opportunities for productive investment in the rural economy are more limited, the survival of rural households is increasingly dependent on urban incomes for basic subsistence. Between these extremes there may be a range of intermediate regional circumstances with different mixes of interactions and their effects.

Major consequences for further studies of the ways in which rural economies can adapt and have adapted to rural–urban interactions are readily apparent. Research requires not only a clearer sense of regional identity and economy, a recognition that 'rural' is itself a summary for a wide range of circumstances, but it also requires more appropriate spatial frameworks for official and non-official data collection. Better data collection would recognize the need to identify, for example, regional terms of trade and regional patterns of remittances and their use; it would therefore require more carefully constructed samples, that permit statistically valid inter-regional comparison and are rooted in a better appreciation of the character of each region as an integrated and unique system. The extent to which regions are open systems and the mechanisms of interaction through which that openness operates command our immediate attention.

Conclusion

Rural transformation in any society cannot be structured in isolation from the interactions between rural and urban areas that are associated with the workings of the rural system. In Africa the range and extent of these interactions call into question any simplistic categorization of a rural–urban dichotomy and easy identification of urban bias. Research has not adequately grasped the totality of interaction, preferring partial studies of migration, or terms of trade, or whatever, and, as a result, policies towards rural transformation have been ill-served by the range and quality of evidence of the overall effects of rural–urban exchanges. Furthermore, since rural–urban interactions are continually becoming more complex, they are becoming increasingly significant for rural transformation. Recent evidence has tended to confirm the spatial and economic complexities of interaction, but also to suggest that interactions have highly differentiated effects, both socially and spatially. Some people benefit from them more than others; some areas benefit more than others. The processes by which social and spatial differentiation are generated by rural–urban interaction and the extent to which these spatial and social processes are interlinked require full investigation in a wide range of economic and environmental circumstances, within and between countries. Armed with the results from such research, policies can be formulated on a firmer basis than the broad, two-sector models on which they are currently based in many African states. Until we know much more about the conditions under which rural–urban and inter-regional interactions can facilitate rural change, and what are the various effects of interactions, our understanding of rural systems and rural transformations in Africa will remain woefully inadequate.

References

Ahmed, A.G.M. & Rahman, M.A. (1979), 'Small urban centres: vanguards of exploitation. Two cases from Sudan', *Africa*, **49** (3): 258–71.

Bryceson, D. (1985), 'Food and urban purchasing power: the case of Dar es Salaam', *African Affairs*, **84** (337): 449–522.

Caldwell, J.C. (1978), 'A theory of fertility: from high plateau to destabilization,

Population and Development Review, **4** (4): 553–77.

Chapman, M. & Prothero, R.M. (eds) (1985), *Circulation in Third World Countries*, Routledge & Kegan Paul.

Clarke, J.I., Khogali, M. & Kosinski, L.A. (eds) (1985), *Population and Development Projects in Africa*, Cambridge, Cambridge University Press.

Clarke, J.I. & Kosinski, L.A. (eds) (1982), *Redistribution of Population in Africa*, Heinemann.

Collier, P. & Lal, D. (1984), 'Why poor people get rich: Kenya, 1960–79', *World Development*, **12** (10): 1007–18.

Collier, P. & Lal, D. (1986), *Labour and Poverty in Kenya 1900–1980*, Oxford University Press.

David, M. (1981), 'The transition in small holder banking in Kenya: evidence from rural branch loans', *Journal of Developing Areas*, **16** (1): 71–86.

Elkan, W. (1976), 'Is a proletariat emerging in Nairobi?', *Economic Development and Cultural Change*, **24** (4): 95–106.

Ellis, F. (1984), 'Agricultural price policy in Tanzania', *World Development*, **10** (4): 263–83.

Fry, J. (1975), 'Rural–urban terms of trade in Zambia, 1960-73', *African Social Research*, **19**.

Funnell, D. (1987), 'Rural–urban linkages: research themes and directions' in C. Dixon (ed.), *The rural–urban interface*, Institute of British Geographers, Developing Area Research Group, Monograph 4.

Gould, W.T.S. (1985), 'Migration and development in Western Kenya, 1971–82: a retrospective analysis of primary school leavers', *Africa*, **55** (3): 262–85.

Gould, W.T.S. (1987), ''Urban bias and regional differentiation: the role of rural–urban interaction in Kenya', in C. Dixon (ed.), *The rural-urban interface*, Institute of British Geographers, Development Area Research Group, Monograph 4.

Gould, W.T.S. (in press), 'Population mobility' in M.B. Gleave (ed.), *Tropical African Development: Geographical Perspectives*, Longman.

Guyer, J.I. & Peters, P. (1987), 'Conceptualizing the household: issues of theory and policy in Africa, *Development and Change*, **18** (2).

Harriss, B. & Harriss, J. (1984), 'Generative or parasitic urbanism? Some observations on the recent history of a South Indian market town, *Jnl. of Development Studies*, **20** (3): 82–101.

Harriss, J. (ed.) (1982), *Rural Development: Theories of Peasant Economy and Agrarian Change*, Hutchinson.

Harriss, J. & Moore, M. (eds) (1984), Development and the Rural–Urban Divide (Frank Cass), Special issue of *The Journal of Development Studies*, **20** (3).

Hjort, A. (1979), *Savanna Town: Rural Ties and Urban Opportunities in Northern Kenya*, Stockholm Studies in Social Anthropology.

Hopkins, N.J. (1979), 'The small urban centre in rural development: Kitu (Mali) and Testour (Tunisia)', *Africa*, **49** (3): 314–28.

Horvath, R.J. (1969), 'Von Thunen's isolated state and the area round Addis Ababa, Ethopia', *Economic Geography*, **59** (3): 308–23.

Isugo-Abanihe, U.C. (1985), 'Child fosterage in West Africa', *Population and Development Review*, **11** (1): 53–65.

Jabara, C.L. (1985), 'Agricultural pricing policy in Kenya', *World Development*, **13** (5): 611–26.

Kenya Government (1979), *Development Plan, 1979–1983*, Nairobi, Ministry of Planning and Economic Development.

Knight, J.B. (1972), 'Rural–urban income comparisons and migration in Ghana', *Bulletin of the Oxford Institute of Economics and Statistics*, **34** (2): 199–228.

Knowles, J.C. & Anker, R. (1981), 'An analysis of income transfers in a developing country', *Jnl. of Development Economics*, **8** (2): 205–36.

Langton, J. & Hoppe, G. (1983), *Town and Country in the Development of Early Modern Europe*, Historical Geography Research Series, No. 1, Norwich, Geo books.

Lipton, M. (1977), *Why Poor People Stay Poor: a Study of Urban Bias in World Development*, Temple Smith.

Lipton, M. (1980), 'Migration from rural areas of poor countries: the impact on rural productivity and income distribution', *World Development*, **8** (1): 1–24.

Low, A.R.C. (1982), *Farm Household Theory and Rural Development in Swaziland*, University of Reading, Dept. of Economics and Management, Development Study, No. 23.

Lundqvist, J. (1975), *Local and Central Impulses for Change and Development: a Case Study of Morogoro District, Tanzania*, Ad Novas, Norwegian Geographical Studies, No. 12.

Lux, A. (1972), 'Gift exchange and income redistribution between Yombe rural wage-earners and their kinsfolk in Western Zaire', *Africa*, **42** (3): 173–91.

Mabogunje, M. (1970), 'Systems approach to the theory of migration', *Geographical Analysis*, **2** (1): 1–18.

Martin, C.J. (1982), 'Education and consumption in Maragoli (Kenya): households' educational strategies', *Comparative Education*, **18** (2): 139–55.

Miambo, F. & Fry, J. (1971), 'An investigation into the changes in the terms of trade between rural and urban sectors in Zambia', *African Social Research*, **12**: 95–110.

Moore, M. (1984a), 'Political economy and the rural–urban divide, 1767–1981', *Jnl. of Development Studies*, **20** (3): 5–27.

Moore, M. (1984b), 'Categorizing space: rural–urban or core-periphery in Sri Lanka', *Jnl. of Development Studies*, **20** (3): 102–22.

Mortimore, M. (1970), 'Population densities and rural economies in the Kano close-settled zone, Nigeria' in W. Zelinsky, L.A. Kosinski & R.M. Prothero (eds), *Geography and a Crowding World*, Oxford University Press, 380–88.

Mukras, M.S., Oucho, J.O. & Bamberger, M. (1985), 'Resource mobilization and the household economy in Kenya', *Canadian Jnl. of African Studies*, **19** (2): 409–21.

O'Keefe, P. et al. (9184), *Energy and Development in Kenya: Constraints and Opportunities*, Stockholm, Beijer Institute.

Peel, J.D.Y. (1983), *Ijeshas and Nigerians: the incorporation of a Yoruba Kingdom, 1890s-1970s*, Cambridge University Press.

Preston, D.A. (1975), 'Rural–urban and inter-settlement interaction; theory and analytical structure', *Area*, **7** (3): 171–4.

Preston, D.A. (1978), *Farmers and Towns: Rural–Urban Relations in Highland Bolivia*, Norwich, Geobooks.

Riddell, J.B. (1981), 'Beyond the description of spatial pattern: the process of proletarianization as a factor in population migration in West Africa', *Progress in Human Geography*, **5** (4): 370–92.

Riddell, J.B. (1985a), 'Beyond the geography of modernization: the state as a redistributive mechanism in independent Sierra Leone', *Canadian Jnl. of African Studies*, **19** (4): 529–45.

Riddell, J.B. (1985b), 'Urban bias in underdevelopment: appropriation from the countryside in post-colonial Sierra Leone', *Tijd. v. Econ. en Soc. Geografie*, **76** (5): 374–83.

Riddell, J.B. (1985c), 'Internal and external forces acting upon disparities in Sierra Leone', *Jnl. Modern Af. Studies*, **23** (3): 389–406.

Rimmer, D. (1984), *The Economies of West Africa*, Weidenfeld & Nicolson.

Rondinelli, D.A. (1983a), *Secondary Cities in Developing Countries: Policies for Diffusing Urbanization*, Beverly Hills, Sage.

Rondinelli, D.A. (1983b), 'Small towns and cities in developing countries', *Geographical Review*, **73** (4): 379–95.

Rondinelli, D.A. (1985), 'Population distribution and economic development in Africa: the need for urbanization policies', *Population Research and Policy Review*, **4** (2): 173–96.

Rondinelli, D.A. & Ruddle, K. (1978), *Urbanization and Rural Development: a Spatial Policy for Equitable Growth*, New York, Praeger.

Ross, M.J. & Wisner, T.S. (1977), 'The rural–urban migrant network in Kenya: some general implications', *American Ethnologist*, **4** (3): 359–75.

Sharpley, J. (1981), 'Resource transfers between agricultural and non-agricultural sectors 1964-77' in T. Killick (ed.), *Papers on the Kenyan Economy, Performance, Problems and Policies*, Heinemann: 311–19.

Simon, D. (1985), 'Agrarian policy and migration in Zimbabwe and Southern Africa: reform or transformation?', *Review of African Political Economy*, **34**: 82–9.

Simon, D. (1986), 'Migration, regional inequality and development in the Third World', *Tijd. v. Econ. en. Soc. Geografie*, **77** (1): 7–17.

Southall, A (1979), 'Introduction: results and implications of the preliminary inquiry (into Small Towns in Africa)', *Africa*, **49** (3): 213–27.

Sporrek, A. (1985), *Food Marketing and Urban Growth in Dar es Salaam*, Lund Studies in Geography, Series B, No. 51.

Standing, G. (ed.) (1985), *Labour Circulation and the Labour Process*, London, Croom Helm.

Swindell, K. (1979), 'Labour migration in underdeveloped countries: the case of West Africa', *Progress in Human Geography*, **3** (2): 239–60.

Vennetier, D. (1976), *Les villes d'Afrique tropicale*, Paris, Masson.

Vincent, J. (1971), *African Elite: the Big Men of a Small Town*, Columbia University Press.

Vincent, J. (1979), 'Room for manoevre: the political role of small towns in Uganda' in J. Owusu & M. Fortes (eds), *Colonialism and Change: Essays Presented to Lucy Mair*, London, Mouton, pp. 115–44.

Watts, S. (1983), 'Marriage migration, a neglected form of long-term mobility: a case study from Ilorin, Nigeria', *International Migration Review*, **17** (4): 682–98.

White, G. (1986), 'Developmental states and African agriculture', *IDS Bulletin*, **17** (1): 1–11.

Wrigley, C.C. (1965) 'Kenya: patterns of economic life, 1902–45' in V. Harlow & E.M. Chilver (eds), *History of East Africa: Vol. 2*, Oxford University Press, pp. 209–64.

Zachariah, K.C. & Condé, J. (1981), *Migration in West Africa: Demographic Aspects*, Oxford University Press for World Bank/OECD.

7 Agrarian Change and Peri-Urban Fringes in Tropical Africa

Ken Swindell

The urban fringes and hinterlands of African towns display a wide range of crops and diverse methods of production, yet surprisingly little attention has been paid to the transformation of agriculture which is taking place in these areas. The best accounts of agriculture in urban fringes come from French research in Central and West Africa (Champaud, 1983; Franqueville, 1972; Jeannin, 1972; Kayser et al., 1971; Laserre, 1958; Morriniére, 1972; Prioul, 1969; Sirven, 1969; Vennetier, 1961 and 1972), while a limited number of studies have been made in Anglophone Africa (Hill, 1977; Lubeck, 1977; Mortimore & Wilson, 1965; Amerena, 1982; Sutherland, 1985; Van den Berg, 1984). These studies indicate that even towns of modest size (20,000) are surrounded by intensively cultivated land, while larger towns (100,000) have conspicuous inner and outer zones where foodstuffs are being cultivated commercially together with market garden crops. Farming in the urban fringes embraces both urban and rural-based farmers and is a reflection of the increased demand for foodstuffs and their costs. In addition, urban fringes are an area where the advantages of combining farm and non-farm work can be maximized.

Around major town one finds a spectrum of production relations that range from household subsistence farming to large-scale capitalist production. The upward surge in food prices has led many of the urban unemployed and under-employed to look for land that can be used to supplement their feeding. On the other hand, the survival of small and poor farmers in rural areas adjacent to towns depends on casual urban employment. Both these groups fit what have been described as 'semi-peasants' or 'proto-proletarians'. In contrast are capitalist farmers, based either rurally or in towns, who are investing in land in the urban fringes and who rely on hired labour to produce for the very profitable urban markets. An intermediate group is the small commodity farmers whose production is also geared towards the urban food market, and who themselves buy food. The continued success of these farmers is often linked to one or more of their households being in non-farm employment in the city, although the dependence on this source of income renders them particularly vulnerable.

Thus, urban sub-regions are characterized by a mosaic of production and exchange relations with considerable connectivity between urban and rural areas expressed in two-way flows of goods, labour and money. If this is the case, the notion of an urban–rural divide and the impoverishment of rural people by a privileged class of urban dwellers seems open to question, or at least in need of modification. While the urban–rural division may identify spatial differences in wealth, it also obscures important interrelationships between town and countryside. Also, there is considerable heterogeneity and economic differentiation within rural populations, especially in fringe areas, and there must be doubt as to whether differences between urban and rural areas are always much greater than those found within either category. More importantly, concern with the subordination of rural to urban interests ignores the power of the state favourably to influence the fortunes of farmers; appropriation of land by the state for institutional use or for redistribution to its clients, and the legitimation of individual tenure, are much in evidence in urban fringes and hinterlands.

The primary concern of this chapter is not an assessment of the urban–rural divide, but the identification of urban fringes as an interface where urban and rural interests meet in diverse forms of agricultural production and exchange. Upon this interface there is an accelerating shift towards commodity and capitalist production, a process that involves the marginalization of both the urban and rural poor as significant shifts in land ownership and employment take place. But it is important to stress that towns and their sub-regions are both geographic and historic-specific. For example, there is much difference in the development of urban fringes and hinterlands between the colonial cities of Central Africa and the Islamic emirate cities of Hausaland. Colonial towns were frequently established in areas of relatively low population density where tracts of empty bush provided niches for urban farmers (in many instances Europeans). Here the urban–rural divide was and is quite sharp. On the other hand, the pre-colonial cities of Africa have a long history of urban food production and they have been the foci of political power and trading networks which integrated urban and rural populations.

The definition and delimitation of peri-urban fringes and hinterlands are not easy, although a number of methods have been suggested, using criteria such as land use, population density, the catchment area for food staples and the distance travelled to work (see Franqueville, 1972, Mortimore, 1975, and Van den Berg, 1984). Around African towns there is a 'gradient' of urban influence that is shaped by past and present socio-economic forces, while in recent years access to urban markets and services by rural people has been substantially altered by the spread of motor transport. The following discussion makes a distinction concerning agrarian change in the fringes and hinterlands between recent colonial and pre-colonial towns, and emphasizes that in both cases these areas are cultivated by both urban and rural people. Urban sub-regions embrace much of interest to theorists of agrarian change.

They are also areas worthy of consideration by regional and national planners, particularly in view of the current debate about urban food supply and food imports.

Urban household food production

Many urban households, and not necessarily only the poorest, grow a substantial proportion of their food requirements. Studies of Brazzaville (Jeannin, 1972, pp. 70–82), Pointe Noire (Vennetier, 1961), Libreville (Lasserre, 1958), Bangui (Prioul, 1969), Yaoundé (Morrinière, 1972), and villages near Bouaké (Sirven, 1969) indicate the presence of intensively cultivated peripheral zones that have developed since the 1930s, extend outwards for some 10 km and are cultivated partly by urban households. All of these accounts show the importance of women farmers: between 30 and 80 per cent of all urban households surveyed had one or more adult women farmers, with the highest percentage recorded for the Makélékélé quarter Brazzaville (420,000) investigated by Jeannin. In every case, women were almost exclusively concerned with food-staple production, while market garden crops and fruit were grown by men. While employment opportunities for women in cities are limited, the studies cited above show that women are playing a significant role in the reproduction of their households by providing substantial amounts of food. The differences and inequalities between men and women observable in many rural areas where commercial crops are grown seem to obtain here too: men are concerned with market gardening which yields cash income, while women produce food for domestic consumption.

In the Makélékélé quarter of Brazzaville investigated by Jeannin there was a preponderance of women farmers who belonged to households headed by relatively affluent salaried bureaucrats; 63 per cent of the women interviewed belonged to households headed by such men. Jeannin suggests several reasons why these women farm: they are carrying on doing what their mothers did (or do) in the villages from which they came not so long ago; they remain responsible for feeding their families in a situation where food prices are high and rising; they do not have the same levels of education as their husbands; and, as with poorer women, their opportunities of employment are few.

The principal crop grown by poor and rich women alike in Brazzaville was the long-established staple, manioc, of which there are some twenty-five varieties. Three or four varieties were grown on the same plot and farmers were constantly experimenting with new varieties, some of which were used for bread-making. Jeannin estimated that in 1970 the Makélékélé quarter needed about 600 ha under manioc to meet its food-staple intake, but in fact there were some 700 ha, indicating sale of surpluses by some farmers. Although manioc was grown by women right across the socio-economic spectrum, market gardening was generally done by poorer or unemployed men who were farming salad crops bought by better-off households, hotels and restaurants.

Urban capitalist farmers

Around some towns, richer urban-dwellers have been involved in much more capitalistic ventures than those described in Makélékélé. In the periphery of Kinshasa (2.2 million), the capital of Zaire, there is considerable pressure on land for speculative building and farming, and the laws of 1963 and 1973 which sought to prevent the sale of communally-held land have been largely ignored. A zone of intensive cultivation now stretches into Lower Zaire in what otherwise is an area of relatively low population density and bush-fallowing. The first stages of development occured when urban bureaucrats bought up blocks of farm-bush and forest in lots of between 50 and 200 ha; these were than stripped for firewood which fetched good prices in the town market. Once the land was cleared, the next stage was the cultivation of fruit and cassava for the Kinshasa market, using young unemployed or under-employed labourers recruited in the city (Kayser *et al.*, 1981). Communal landholdings and small farms had already been reduced during the colonial period when land was appropriated for sugar plantations, and more recently cattle ranches have been established by urban entrepreneurs.

The use of unemployed school-leavers, under-employed male migrants and women as agricultural labourers can be observed in many urban peripheries; this labour reserve, which spans both town and countryside, has many advantages for the employer since it is cheap and may be easily controllable. For example, the recruitment of casual or 'by-day' labour was an important part of the development of capitalist mechanized rice farming around Tamale (80,000) in Ghana, where farmers were either big traders or civil servants who bought up machinery cheaply after the break-up of state farms in the early 1970s. According to Van Hear (1982), these farmers contrived to mobilize ever-cheaper labour, as they moved through a succession of groups — first northern migrants, then women, and finally unemployed school-leavers. In Sierra Leone, Binns (1981) noted that urban-based farmers recruited gangs of daily-paid labourers from the unemployed in towns, and then transported them by lorry to work on surrounding rice farms, returning them after each day's work.

This relatively large-scale capitalist farming involves a tightening grip on the means of production in the rural periphery by urban bureaucrats and politicians who have recently entered farming. Their exploitation of labour and expropriation of land aggravate inequalities in both urban and rural situations. At least two levels of inequality can be recognized. The first is between the urban poor, who shift between casual employment in town and farm jobs, and their employers who are steadily acquiring farmland on the periphery and profiting from rising food prices in town markets. Second, there is inequality between these urban-based farmers and the small peasant farmers in the peripheral villages who are being squeezed by the bigger town farmers as they compete for land and labour.

In addition to capitalist farmers, there are speculators who acquire tracts of land in both the inner and outer fringes of towns, and hold the land as an asset which they may either develop in the future or sell when the market rises. Such land accumulation is part of a general pattern of acquisition by those in government, who see it as a reward of office, and one better secured when the going is good, given their frequently uncertain futures. Land acquired by such influential people may be temporarily rented to small farmers, especially to migrants newly arriving in the orbit of the city.

The conclusion that might be drawn from the above accounts is that in some urban peripheries there are increasing numbers of capitalist farmers and an emergent agrarian proletariat. But several caveats need to be entered. The mobilization of labour is one thing, but proletarianization also involves control and management. The management of farm labour can be difficult, and farm workers are not easily subjected to labour discipline so long as many of them have some land and are not entirely separated from the means of production. This is why many urban and rural-based employers prefer migrant workers, or urban school-leavers: they are easier to control than older men recruited from within the periphery who have some access to land, and who will not hesitate to return to their own farms, albeit briefly. Many private contractors in Nigeria during the 1970s preferred to employ long-distance migrants (for example from Ghana) for precisely these reasons. The alternative to migrant labour is the recruitment of young men in peripheral villages who may have farms but who lack control over the product of their labour, and they, together with the urban under-employed and school-leavers, comprise a floating reserve of labour, which has a rapid turnover rate.

Peri-urban migrants

Urban peripheries attract some migrants who do not become town dwellers but instead inhabit or create peripheral villages which provide them with a base from which they engage in similar strategies to their counterparts, the urban poor. Households became involved in farming for subsistence and producing occasional surpluses for urban markets, while one or more members may be employed casually or permanently in the town. Around Bangui (300,000) in the Central African Republic, there is a belt of market gardening developed on marshland which allows cultivation to continue throughout the dry season, from December to February. These market gardens are run by immigrants who are of diverse ethnic origins, but have generally come from areas where commercial farming is less developed, or where the agricultural potential is poor. Alongside the farms of these migrants are some operated by large commercial firms using hired labour, as well as government schemes using tenant farmers (Prioul, 1969).

Peri-urban farming by migrant communities is also a feature of Free town (214,000) in Sierra Leone, one of the oldest colonial settlements in West Africa. In the late nineteenth and early twentieth centuries there was plenty of land in the interstices between the several settlements that had grown up around the core of Freetown, and this allowed the continuation of farming by urban migrants. In a study of the Safroko Limba, Moseley (1987) shows that these people moved outwards as the town expanded, in order to preserve their interests in palm-tapping and market gardening, and sometimes joined earlier Limba migrants in the mountain villages around Freetown who were also engaged in those occupations, as well as in wood cutting and charcoal burning. The Safroko–Limba were residentially and occupationally marginal groups. They had entered the urban job market at its base as casual labourers, and agriculture remained important to them as a 'fall-back'. Moseley's account takes note of cultural segmentation of the job market in Freetown and he observes that the social history of the town lies very much in the competition for an appropriation of different types of employment. Even today, ethnic segmentation has not disappeared: it is a reminder of the heterogeneity of urban occupations and opportunities, well removed from any simple urban–rural distinction.

One of the problems encountered in studying households, whether urban or rural-based, which combine farm and non-farm work, is that of assessing accurately the total of their several sources of income. Of particular interest here is the analysis by Kitching (1980) of farm and household incomes obtained through surveys conducted in Kenya during the 1960s. The survey carried out in Central Province (1963–64) gives information about on-farm consumption of agricultural produce (imputed value), sales of produce, and other sources of income such as off-farm jobs and trading. In the context of the present discussion, Central province is sufficiently close to Nairobi to experience the city's influence in labour and product markets. All households in Central Province were heavily reliant on off-farm sources of income, which were principally from wages and salaries, comprising between one-quarter and one-third of total household income. This suggests a substantial transfer of income from town to countryside. These earnings were double the amount received from the sale of agricultural produce. The proportion of total income derived from off-farm sources was greatest for the lowest income groups (up to 1,000 shillings per annum) and for the highest group (over 5,000 shillings). The imputed value of agricultural products consumed on-farm ('subsistence') was 46 per cent of total income for the poorest groups, compared with only 14 per cent for the top-income groups. Off-farm work for poorer farmers was a necessity, while for the richer it was part of the process of financing investment in land and the creation of bigger farms, using income from good non-farm jobs or successful trading.

Pre-Colonial towns and peri-urban farming: northern Nigeria

The pre-colonial towns of Africa, such as those in the central and western Sudan, were centres of government, religion and industry, and were integrated into regional economies by long-distance trade routes. The Hausa-Fulani towns in northern Nigeria have long been surrounded by areas of intensively cultivated land with high population densities. In particular, Kano and Sokoto are set amidst close-settled zones where population densities reach three hundred per square kilometre, extending over several hundreds of square kilometres. Permanent fields with annual cultivation account for 80 per cent of the cultivated area, while the river bottom floodlands (*fadamas*) support dry-season irrigated farming. These urban peripheries and hinterlands contain myriad rural households with rights to farmland, together with the farms of urban dwellers, especially of descendants of traditional rulers and office-holders. In addition there are the farms of city traders and modern bureaucrats and politicians.

The farms around towns such as Kano, Katsina and Zaria have been cultivated for hundreds of years and have been continuously improved by animal dung and refuse, a good proportion of which is brought out from town compounds. The huge allegiant rural populations of the emirate cities were integrated by a complex network of economic and political factors contained within the over-arching framework of Islam. The city has an important role in the Islamic world as the place where Islamic law and practice are consolidated and disseminated. On the other hand, when Islamic practice has become debased, reforming influences have from time to time sprung from the countryside, especially from the ranks of pastoralists. Therefore, the town and the village are integrated through a shared faith and its organization and practice, which also underwrite local and regional trading networks.

Peripheral villages of Hausa towns have long histories of food-staple production, especially of millets, sorghums and onions for sale in central and rural markets, as means of redistributing natural surpluses and paying the taxes of both colonial and pre-colonial states or acquiring surplus cash. Today food production for the town continues, but new production relations obtain and large amounts of wage-labour are used.

Also, many villagers are heavily involved in urban non-farm jobs which differ from the traditional artisan, trading and craft work which characterized Hausaland. Non-farm work may provide a substantial proportion of household income and be either a necessary condition of household reproduction or part of a process of investment in and expansion of commercial farming aimed at the urban market. Many rural people now commute daily to town jobs, and escape the high accommodation and food costs of their urban counterparts.

Non-farm work in the town removes people from the farm labour force, and they may have temporarily to be replaced by hired labour, or their absence compensated by those who remain on the farm working longer and by the increased use of women and the elderly. Hired labour is an essential part of big farming businesses. Villages in the periphery of Hausa-Fulani towns now contain heterogeneous populations — people who are part-peasants, traders, artisans, small commodity producers and capitalist farmers. Features of these villages are involvement in the urban-food market, a high proportion of non-farm employment, substantial agricultural wage-labour forces and a burgeoning land market.

The urban food market

Food-staple production for urban markets in Nigeria became increasingly attractive in the 1970s as export crops such as groundnuts fetched relatively less, and drought and urban expansion drove prices upwards. The benefits to rural farmers from these price increases are difficult to determine, and it is generally assumed that urban-based traders and forestallers were the beneficiaries. This assumption needs to be treated with caution, or at least qualified. The prices received by farmers may be influenced in several ways: first by season, second by the efficiency of rural marketing systems and the competition among traders in the urban hinterland, third by relative distance from the urban market, fourth the financial resources of the rural farmers and their access to transport, and fifth the type of produce.

Seasonal variations in the price of food staples are common throughout tropical Africa and reflect the alternation of wet and dry seasons and the predominance of rainfed cultivation. Prices before the harvest may be two, three or even four times greater than afterwards. The problem for many small farmers is their lack of storage, a situation that can be exacerbated after bumper harvests. In northern Nigeria after the good harvests of 1985, prices of millet were pushed down to very low levels, as farmers emptied their granaries of the grain they had put by in the event of a repeat of the poor years preceding 1985. Seasonal and annual variations in the supply and price of grains are advantageous for both urban and rural-base merchants, and the larger ones move food staples from one region to another.

In the ares around many of the newer colonial towns with low population densities, rural markets may still be rudimentary and here the power of an urban-based trader or merchant may be considerable. For example, around Yaoundé in southern Cameroon, rural markets were colonial innovations designed to facilitate urban food supply, and in fact there is no word for market in the local Beti language (Franqueville, 1972). This situation contrasts strongly with the densely-settled rural area of southern and northern Nigeria, with their sophisticated and long-established periodic markets operating on ring cycles. These markets embrace local traders who bulk produce, itinerant merchants operating inter-regionally and urban-based merchants as well as local sellers and buyers.

Depending on their proximity to urban markets and the means of transport at their disposal, rural producers may be able to by-pass traders and take their produce into central markets themselves. In this respect it is important to distinguish between the inner and outer agricultural fringes. For example, in a study of Ilorin it was found that within a zone of some 11 km many farmers were headloading their produce into the market (Mortimore, 1979). The alternative to spending time transporting produce into market is to sell to forestallers; this may be the only option for smaller and poorer farmers who cannot afford to spend their labour time on transporting and who have only small surpluses for sale. For the richer and larger farmer who has a small truck and hired labourers, there is greater flexibility since he can shift produce around over a wide area to take advantage of price differentials, and he may become a small trader himself. It would not be surprising, however, to find the small farmers, whose time may be worth less, by-passing the middlemen (as in Mortimore's study of Ilorin) while the large farmers, whose time is worth more, use trading intermediaries.

The price that producers receive and the retail prices that obtain vary considerably according to the size and location of towns and rural markets. In November/December 1985, producers were receiving N40.00 per 100 kg bag of millet in a village in the south of Sokoto State, Nigeria, close by the town of Gusau (80,000). In the local rural periodic market, the same amount was retailed at N44.00, while in Gusau town the price was N46.00. (One naira (N1.00) was equivalent to £0.80 at the official rate of exchange).

As to the type of produce, a basic distinction must be made between market-garden produce and food staples such as grains and roots. The perishability of market-garden produce and fruit requires visits to markets every day or every other day — something that can be accomplished by small farmers on foot or by taxis if they live within the inner fringes. Not only must perishable produce be shifted quickly, but small farmers also need a continuous flow of cash for wages, as most market gardening requires irrigation and intensive labour inputs. It is for these reasons that market gardening is concentrated within the inner zones around most towns. In the case of densely-populated urban hinterlands such as those in northern Nigeria, market gardening and grain production are carried on up to the edges of the built-up area, and their relative importance alternates between wet and dry seasons. Where irrigation schemes have been set up beyond the inner fringes of urban areas, such as the Kano River Project to the south of that city, small farmers who grow vegetables as part of the scheme may be subject to exploitation by urban merchants. Farmers on the Kano River scheme were encouraged to grow tomatoes in the dry season for the urban market but were not given adequate marketing facilities, and because of the perishability of their produce they had to accept the prices paid by Kano merchants who came out in lorries to buy tomatoes.

Because of its high value in relation to its bulk, market-garden produce can be marketed daily by small farmers, but grains are a different matter. There is no advantage in selling small bundles of grain that can be stored; consequently, different marketing methods are used. Interesting studies by Clough (1981, 1985) of Hausa farmers and traders in a grain surplus area in Katsina emirate expose the complexities of the trade in guinea corn (and cotton). Clough identifies big farmers who are involved in inter-village trade and thereby expand their landholdings, buy cattle and hire labour; farmers who produce modest surpluses; and poor farmers whose landholdings and grain production are insufficient to meet household requirements. The big farmers who are inter-village grain traders become clients of urban merchants and receive advances that allow them to secure grain for their patrons. Inter-village traders also sell to local authorities and state governments and they act as money-lenders. In subsidiary hamlets there exists a lower tier of traders, who are clients of and recipients of advances from inter-village traders. Clough concludes that the crucial difference among farmers is between those who trade and those who do not; it is not between those who hire and those who perform labour. Clough sees the employment of labour as rooted in local culture, and in the periodic needs imposed by the family life cycle where traditional complex joint-production units (*gandaye*) continue as the basis of production relations.

In the case of villages in urban peripheries one is aware of traders in grains and the investment of rural and urban merchant capital in farming. But the involvement in non-farm jobs, especially in the town, and the kind of jobs to which access is obtained, are what mainly separate richer and poorer farmers. Clough's observations about the interplay between traditional and modern forms of political power are relevant in connection with jobs in government and in food contracting to institutions such as schools. However, Clough's stress on the traditional complex joint-production units and their ability to provide labour is less pertinent since they have been very much eroded in peripheral villages and the hinterlands of large towns. For example, Sutherland (1985), in a study of four villages close by Sokoto, found that some 70 per cent of households comprised simple units, most commonly of a man,, his wives and dependent children, and that this figure increased to 85 per cent in the dry season.

For many farmers, the hiring of labour allows a combination of farm and non-farm work, but for big farmers it is an essential part of the process of agricultural expansion and the response to urban food demand. In particular, dry-season irrigated farming is extremely labour-intensive, and requires substantial inputs if it is to be more than a supplement to upland grain farming; also it is, and always has been, commercial farming. It is also worth noting that non-farm employment may be the means whereby small traders acquire capital, and is an alternative to becoming clients of larger merchants.

Non-farm work in fringe villages

In a study of two villages near Kano, Amerena (1982) found that 31 and 34 per cent of farmers participated in non-farm occupations in both wet and dry seasons, and that 64 per cent of these farmers in one village and 90 per cent in the other put non-farm work as their chief source of cash income. These farmers had become semi-peasants who relied on their wives and younger members of the household to run their farms as they became involved in non-farm work, principally in Kano. An examination of PAYE returns showed that about one-third of those employed in both villages were in the large-scale commercial and industrial sector. Thus, household reproduction in many households had become split into two: household subsistence and food were the responsibility of women, and cash earning through urban wage-employment that of male heads and seniors. These villages contained big farmers, who were also involved in trade or urban employment and who relied on hired labour to run their farms. A distinction has to be made between those farmers who take up low-grade non-farm employment to maintain their stake in a village society in which their farming interest is dwindling, and those with secure and well-paid jobs or trading activities, who are net hirers of labour and who are expanding their holdings in rural areas as part of a process of accumulation.

However striking the extent of non-farm employment may be, it is necessary to place it within a historical context. Among the Hausa–Fulani there is a long history of trading, and the social division of labour was well developed in pre-colonial society. The Hausa have a comprehensive range of occupations which are ranked in order of status and which may be engaged in singly or in combination with farming. M.G. Smith's work in Zaria in 1949 showed a diverse range of non-farm jobs, which a man would often do within a week, or even a single day. At that time there was only a small amount of modern sector employment and jobs were often done at home, not at a separate place of work (Smith, 1955). In addition to localized non-farm work, northern Nigeria has been notable for the annual dry-season exodous of migrants who looked for work in the larger towns and the commercial agricultural zones of the south. These dry-season migrations developed in the twentieth century, but by the 1980s their volume and scale had been greatly reduced (Prothero, 1957; Swindell, 1984, pp. 3-11: Abdu, 1983).

In the late 1970s the employment situation began to change as a result of the creation of many additional urban job opportunities. Many men in urban peripheries became commuters and the overlap between non-farm work and income-earning at home was small; fractionalized work patterns such as Smith encountered in Zaria in 1949 were less possible, as the modern sector (government or private) demanded regular hours and labour discipline. Also, very few farmers had more than one non-farm job. But if farmers spend so much time on their other jobs, how is farming maintained? Partly through the intensification of household labour, and partly through hiring: Amerena suggests for her Kano villages that women work longer and older people are doing more farmwork than hitherto, while wealthy farmers rely increasingly on hired workers. The hiring of non-household labour is important in urban peripheries, and reveals the differences between the richer and ordinary farmers in a village.

Land

The emergence of small commodity producers and capitalist farmers is related to increasing land sales, and the emergence of 'land-poor' (if not 'landless') farmers, especially in densely populated areas around large towns such as one finds in Hausaland. In 1967–68 Goddard *et al.* found that between 19 and 29 per cent of land had been acquired by purchase in the three villages they studied on the periphery of Sokoto (Goddard *et al.*, 1971). Near Kano, Hill (1977) estimated that 44 per cent of the land of rich farmers had been purchased. Similar observations have been made in the areas around Zaira and Katsina. Land sales were stimulated by the oil boom of the 1970s. There is now considerable pressure on access to the peri-urban land, as private investment and speculation by both urban and rural dwellers have increased together with public-sector purchases for schools, universities, administrative buildings and government housing. In the densely-populated areas that fringe these large towns, land sales are accelerating, leading to an increased polarization between rich and poor farmers, their access to resources and incomes and the way they manage their farms.

Lubeck (1977) pointed out that urban expansion around towns such as Kano was frequently associated with state interventions, as land was acquired for public buildings and industrial estates. For example, on the fringes of Sokoto and Kano, 17,000 and 14,000 acres respectively have been acquired for university development. In other words, it is state rather than urban or private interest that is at work. When peasants' land is absorbed, compensation is paid, but not at the market price. The encroachment of the city into the densely populated rural fringe forces villagers to seek urban employment or move into petty trading, and produces what Lubeck describes as 'proletarianized' villages. In one village he investigated in 1970–72 he found that about one-half of adult males were employed in the urban modern sector. Villages were either absorbed into the urban area, or they lost able-bodied sons to town jobs, and often through permanent emigration into Kano. In more distant villages, a division of labour occured whereby the father and eldest son were traders, the second son was engaged in factory work, and the remaining sons managed small plots of land.

In 1978 the military regime issued a Land Use Decree that was aimed at extending to the whole of Nigeria the principle that ultimate ownership of land was vested in the state, while preserving customary use rights and offering statutory occupancy on long leases, which could be bought or sold. It also reaffirmed the right of compulsory purchase by the state, subject to compensation. But the decree also contained a clause which sought to halt land speculation, whereby areas of undeveloped land in excess of half an hectare were to be taken over by the state governments. Rather than eliminating speculation, the decree made property rights subject to bureaucratic power. The avenues of speculation have merely altered; land acquisition is mediated through a bureaucracy, as undeveloped land is forfeited or land appropriated by compulsory purchase. The abuse of power is all too plain. As Lubeck (1977) has pointed out, in peri-urban Kano the state appropriates land for urban expansion, peasant owners are compensated not at market value but for loss of trees and crops, and then land is allocated to individuals by officials who are rewarded by the purchasers.

Villages nearby large towns have many short-run advantages related to urban food markets and employment opportunities, but they may also be more vulnerable in the longer run. These villages at the inner edge of the periphery are susceptible to the loss of their land by urban expansion, while they may be dependent on income from town jobs, which are precarious (Watts, 1983). However, the incidence of economic fluctuations in the job market does not fall equally on all households or classes.

Summary

Urban fringes and hinterlands contain areas of intensive and varied agriculture, which rests on a multiplicity of urban–rural relationships.

Both pre-colonial and colonial cities have had a transforming influence on agricultural practice and production, an influence that appears to strengthen as urbanization spreads and intensifies. Peri-urban areas and hinterlands contain much of intrinsic interest to students of agrarian change and urban–rural relations, and they present practical issues for those involved in the management and planning of local and national economies. By way of summary, attention is drawn to the several kinds of farmers and farming in urban fringes, together with some of the problems and issues raised by the competition for resources in these areas.

First, fringe farming includes marginalized people, both urban and rural, whose household reproduction depends on farming small plots of land, together with their earnings from casual wage labour. For the town-dweller, especially for one at the bottom of the job hierarchy, farming or farm labouring may be a 'fall-back' when urban employment is uncertain. Among rural dwellers, casual work in towns or for neighbours may allow the land-poor or landless to maintain a stake in their villages. These men and women, together with unemployed school-leavers, can form an important labour reserve, on which both urban and rural capitalists and small commodity producers draw when faced with seasonal or fluctuating labour demands. This labour pool is sometimes joined by people from villages further away from the town, who move into its orbit for several days or weeks. Whatever reservations one might have about the social and economic position of these farmers, there is no doubt that on the one hand those who remain in their villages slows the pace of urban drift, while on the other peripheral farming can lessen the difficulties of the urban underemployed and unemployed.

Second, within the fringe there are numerous small commodity producers and semi-capitalist farmers who use the labour described above, together with family labour, to produce surplus grains, tubers and vegetables for the urban market. Such farmers usually have customary rights to land and they may be increasing their holdings as the market in land develops; the key to accumulation is often their town jobs or trading ventures. Local chiefs and office-holders may also be extending their traditional farming base by becoming agents or clients of local and national political parties, thus gaining access to useful non-farm jobs and agricultural services located in the town. Even so, there are successful commercial farmers who have succeeded largely through their own economic enterprise and efforts; usually they began as petty traders or casual labourers, before becoming farmers for the urban market.

Third, there are conspicuous capitalist farmers who rely almost exclusively on hired labour, and who are buying land in peri-urban fringes and hinterlands, usually along major roads, to supply the urban food markets. The size and nature of their holdings depends on the degree to which land surrounding the urban centre is populated by an established peasantry and small commodity farmers, having traditional rights to land. The capitalist farmers of the fringe comprise politicians and officials of the modern state and its agencies, together with urban and rural-based merchants and traditional rulers. These individuals use salaries, graft, profits from trading and privileged information about future urban plans and schemes to further the process of accumulation. One of the issues for planners and those in favour of government intervention is whether the formation of larger farms, by either private capital or the state, should be encouraged with a view to creating greater surpluses to supply the towns. The alternative is to provide incentives and to secure the co-operation of the small commodity producers, who, it can be argued, are more efficient and adaptable as producers of food for the urban market.

Arguments about the shift towards capitalist relations of production in Africa have cut a fairly well-worn track through the academic literature. Over much of tropical Africa the control of labour, not land, was — and to a large extent still is — the means of differentiating agrarian people. The evidence from urban fringes and hinterlands is that capitalist farmers and agricultural labourers are to found alongside many small commodity and household producers. In most fringes one can discern a significant number of capitalist farmers, but this does not mean that capitalist relations of production are widely established. While a landlord or *rentier* class in tropical Africa remains limited, within urban fringes and hinterlands there appears a growing market for land and a shift towards capitalist farming.

The theme of this paper is that agrarian change around medium and large towns is rapid: if a researcher is looking for landless or land-poor people and their exploitation by a rising class of capitalist farmers, urban peripheries and hinterlands may be better places to look than where Green Revolutions are taking place. Rapid urbanization and the rising market for foodstuffs have given a considerable fillip to agriculture, and this is reflected not only in prices of produce, but in land values and sometimes in agricultural wages. Land is being purchased and labour hired by both urban and rural employers. In addition, the rise of landless (or more often land-poor) people results from the acquisition of peripheral land by the state — frequently on unfavourable terms to its former users — for the expansion of public services, such as education. The abstraction for institutional use of large amounts of farmland near or adjacent to urban areas sometimes seems little short of prodigal. A more efficient management of resources can be achieved by careful site selection and the exercise of restraint on the amounts of land acquired.

The initial means whereby land is bought and labour hired are commonly found from income earned in non-farm jobs, or from the profits of trade or contracting. Government and its patronage are therefore important. African states are among the principal employers of salaried labour. Civilian and military regimes alike dispense patronage in the form of jobs and contracts, and political or official patronage is enjoyed not only by big men, but extends down a hierarchy that allows some of those at the base to purchase a little land, hire some labour and indulge in small-scale accumulation. Nor is this process confined to urban dwellers, but spreads into the countryside, although it is true that the state and political apparatus are located firmly within an urban setting.

While towns and expanding urban markets have clearly been important in reshaping agriculture within their orbit, due weight should be given to the historic and geographic specificity of towns and their agricultural fringes. The colonial towns of central Africa, set amidst areas of low population density, have quite different historic roots from the towns of the central Sudan of West Africa; and this historical difference continues to affect patterns of development in the peri-urban fringes. The proportions of different classes of farmers and the types of farming and non-farm jobs are affected by the distance of villages from the edges of towns and by their proximity to roads. Urban–rural dichotomies are not clear-cut either in spatial, economic or social terms. The movements of goods, people and services are not unidirectional, and there are significant levels of social and economic differentiation within villages, as well as between town and countryside. There is a lack of small-scale and sub-regional information on these matters.

The people who inhabit peripheral villages are conscious of widening gaps among levels of well-being within their communities, as well as between themselves and their urban neighbours. Resentment and conflict between competing interests and classes are expressed in various ways. Local politicking over the succession of traditional chiefs, alliances with particular national parties and religious factionalism may reflect the changing balance of power and new production relations. As for those who become agricultural labourers, their dissatisfaction may take the form not of organized protest but of continuous bickering about how wages and working time are calculated and about the provision of food. Absenteeism or withdrawal from the labour force are other options.

Two of the most important issues facing small farmers in urban fringes are land and the prices received for their produce. The appropriation of land by state and private interests is frequently unjust, and there is little hope of improvement without efficient and cheap registration of both statutory and customary land rights. The loss of land by small farmers undercuts their livelihoods and contributes to the increased numbers of urban migrants. It can be argued that the removal of small farmers to make way for larger-scale enterprises may be the necessary price of creating an agriculture more suited to supply the urban food market. But this does not excuse the alienation of excessive blocks of land for institutional use, nor land being left idle by speculators. Also, there is not much evidence that large farms, either private or state-owned, are more efficient food producers. State farms are badly managed, while many large capitalist farmers are not real risk-takers since their links with politicians and bureaucracies underwrite their failures. Poor harvests, lost crops and stock and mismanagement can be offset by continued access to government funds, either by legal or illegal means. There are exceptions, but the bulk of locally-produced foodstuffs for urban markets is provided by small farmers.

The extent to which small farmers benefit from the opportunities provided by urban food markets varies among rural households and their access to resources and to those markets. The question of producer prices and how they are affected by merchants and middlemen is one of some complexity. Much depends on the development of local marketing networks, which may be better around the older towns. Also, some farmers near to roads and the inner fringes can bypass merchants. When state buying agencies have been introduced to lessen the exploitation of small producers, the results have been less than encouraging and the situation has often been exacerbated rather than improved.

In the short run, in the absence of either efficient state or capitalist large-scale farming, some attention might be given to supporting small farmers through co-operative marketing ventures. The truth of the matter is that we need to know much more about the marketing of urban foodstuffs and the kinds of buyers and sellers according to the type of crops they are marketing. Urban peripheries and hinterlands comprise such a varied mosaic of conflicting interests, production relations, systems of exchange and land use, that they demand closer analysis for the sake of the theoretical and practical insights they offer for an understanding of agrarian change.

References

Abdu, P. (1983), 'Further investigation of population movement in rural Sokoto, Nigeria', Ph.D. thesis, University of Liverpool.

Amerena, P.M. (1982), 'Farmers' participation in the cash economy: case studies of two settlements in the Kano close-settled zone of Nigeria', Ph.D. thesis, University of London.

Barth, H. (1965), *Travels and Discoveries in North and Central Africa, 1849–55*, London, Cass.

Berry, S.S. (1983), 'Work, migration, and class in Western Nigeria' in *Struggle for the City* F. Cooper, (ed.), London, Sage.

Binns, J.A. (1981), 'The dynamics of Third World food production systems: an evaluation of changes in the rural economy of Sierra Leone', Ph.D. thesis, University of Birmingham.

Bird, A. (1983), 'The land issue and large-scale irrigation projects: some problems from Northern Nigeria' in W.M. Adams & A.T. Grove (eds), *Irrigation in Tropical Africa: Problems and Problem Solving*, Cambridge African Monographs 3, Cambridge, African Studies Centre.

Champaud, J. (1983), *Villes et campagnes du Cameroun de l'ouest*, Paris, ORSTOM.

Clough, P. (1981), 'Farmers and traders in Hausaland', *Development and Change*, **12**: 273–92.

Clough, P. (1985), 'The social relation of grain marketing in northern Nigeria', *Review of African Political Economy*, **34**: 16–34.

Ellis, F. (1983), 'Agricultural marketing and peasant state transfers in Tanzania', *Journal of Peasant Studies*, **10** (4).

Francis, P. (1984), 'Nigeria's land use decree', *Africa*, **54** (3): 5–28.

Franqueville, A. (1972), 'Les relations ville-compagne sur la route au Nord de Yaoundé', Cahiers ORSTOM, series sciences humaines, **9**, No. 3: 337–87.

Funnell, D. (1985), 'Rural–urban linkages: research themes or directions', Oxford, Development Studies Association, Regional Development and Planning Study Group Meeting.

Goddard, A.D., Fine, J.G. & Norman, D.W. (1971), *A Socio-Economic Survey of Three Villages in the Sokoto Close-Settled Zone*, Samaru, Nigeria, Institute of Agricultural Research.

Hill, P. (1977), *Population, Prosperity and Poverty: Rural Kano 1900 and 1970*, Cambridge, Cambridge University Press.

Iliffe, J. (1983), *The Emergence of African Capitalism*, London, Macmillan.

Jeannin, M. (1972), 'L'Agriculture et les habitants Makélékélé' in *Dix études sur l'approvisionnement des villes*, Bordeaux, CEGET, pp. 19–46.

Kayser, B. *et al.* (1971), 'Cherté du manioc et pauvrete paysann', *Cah. d'Outre Mer*, **134**: 97–110.

Kitching, G. (1980), *Class and Economic Change in Kenya: The Making of an African Petit Bourgoisie, 1905–1970*, New Haven, Yale University Press.

Lasserre, G. (1958), *Libreville, la ville et sa région*, Paris, GELIN.

Lubeck, P. (1977), 'Contrasts and continuity in a dependent city: Kano, Nigeria' in J. Abu-Lughod & R. Hay (eds) *Third World Urbanization*, London, Methuen, pp. 281–9.

Main, H.A.C. (1982), 'Time–space study of daily activity in urban Sokoto, Nigeria', Ph.D. thesis, University of Liverpool.

Morrinière, J.-L. (1972), 'La région maraîchère intra et péri-urbaine de Yaounde' in *Dix études sur l'approvisionnement des villes*, Bordeaux, CEGET, pp. 49–80.

Mortimore, M.J. (1975), 'Peri-urban pressures' in R.P. Moss & J.A.R. Rathbone (eds), *The Population Factor in Africa Studies*, London, University of London Press.

Mortimore, M.J. (1979), 'The supply of urban foodstuffs in Northern Nigeria' in J.T. Coppock (ed.), *Agriculture and Food Supply in Developing Countries*, Department of Geograhpy, University of Edinburgh, pp. 45–65.

Mortimore, M.J. & Wilson J. (1965), 'Land and people in the Kano close-settled zone', Occasional Paper 1, Zaire, Dept. of Geography, Ahmadu Bello University.

Moseley, K.P. (1987), 'The Safroko Limba of Freetown', *Africana Research Bulletin*.

Prioul, C. (1969), 'Les cultures maraîchères à Bangui', *Cah. d'Outre Mer*, **82**: 191–202.

Prothero, R.M. (1957), 'Migratory labour from North–Western Nigeria', *Africa*, **27**: 251–61.

Sirven, P. (1969), 'L'évolution des villages suburbaines de Bouaké', thèse 3ᵉ cycle, Bordeaux.

Smith, M.G. (1955), *The Economy of Hausa Communities of Zaria*, London, H.M.S.O.

Sutherland, A.M.D. (1985), *The Organization and Redistribution of Labour in Peri-Urban Sokoto*, Ph.D. thesis, University of Birmingham.

Swindell, K. (1984), 'Farmers, traders and labourers: dry season migration from North-West Nigeria', 1900–33, *Africa*, **54** (1): 3–19.

Van den Berg, L.M. (1984), 'Anticipation urban growth in Africa: land use and land values in the urban fringe of Lusaka, Zambia', Zambian Geographical Association, Occasional Study No. 13.

Van Hear, N. (1982), *Northern Labour and the Development of Capitalist Agriculture in Ghana*, Ph.D. thesis, University of Birmingham.

Vennetier, P. (1961), 'La vie agricole urbaine à Pointe Noire', *Cah. d'Outre Mer*, **14**: 60–84.

Vennetier, P. (1972), 'Réflexions sur l'approvisionnement des villes en Afrique Noire' in *Dix études sur l'approvisionnement des villes*, Bordeaux, CEGET, pp. 1–13.

Watts, M. (1983), *Silent Violence: Food, Famine and Peasantry in Northern Nigeria*, Berkeley, University of California Press.

8 Farmers and the State

Richard C. Cook

Introduction

The purpose of this paper is to survey recent work, published principally in the 1980s, on relations between the sub-Saharan African states and the agrarian societies and economies they dominate. One outstanding feature of this literature is the renewed emphasis, especially by economists, on the significance of 'political factors' in explaining the mostly negative assessments of agricultural development that are now being made. The state is said to be crucial, in its impact on markets and prices, the institutions of agricultural development, and the structure of agrarian production; but its centrality is predominantly of a destructive kind — an 'incubus' on economic growth (Rimmer, 1984). To review the literature of the 1980s is, therefore, a uniquely depressing experience; the tone ranges from, at best, cautious pessimism, to nothing short of savage despair. It is even more sobering to notice that the essentials of the political analysis — the unreality of technocratic approaches in states characterized by patrimonialism — were apparent in standard texts and articles a decade or more ago (Leys, 1971; Schaffer, 1969). Current literature, however, does not content itself with 'taking account' of political realities.

One trend is to argue that the state systematically and 'rationally' (i.e. in response to particular interests) pursues policies that are generally harmful to agriculture (interpreted as peasant farmers). Bates (1981 and 1983) uses collective choice theory to explain why governments systematically favour economically inefficient policies and structures. This is an advance on the popular 'urban bias' theory (Lipton, 1977). Others cast doubt on the rational choice approach by arguing that the state bureaucracy is not pursuing — and is not capable of pursuing — any interests other than its own. What appears to be ignorance about agriculture, incompetence and corruption are exactly that: not really a rationally planned transfer of resources but the self-defeating behaviour of office-holders aiming to extract and appropriate the benefits of office.

Underlying and often coupled with the assertion of systematic harmfulness is another argument, now fully developed in the literature, concerning the capacity of the state. The state, it is said, has been over-ambitious. Managerial competence and discipline are simply not up to the tasks of marketing export crops, maintaining large-scale projects, delivering inputs or administering prices. The pressures of parallel markets and bureaucratic bottlenecks — familiar to those who have studied India's 'permit Raj' (Kochanek, 1985) — are bound, in this view, to vitiate attempts to run an 'administered' economy.

The above arguments — a systematic and politically rational anti-agricultural bias, and the incompetence of a corrupt, patrimonial state — have been combined (although they are not necessarily compatible) to support the currently popular call to roll back the frontiers of the state. The state must either withdraw on all fronts, but particularly from economic management and agricultural development, or it must be by-passed, either by international agencies and aid workers or, for neo-populists, by peasant-based revolutions. The dominant voice is in favour of restoring the 'market', both international and domestic, allowing market incentives to work freely on both peasant and capitalist farming.

In the analysis that follows it is argued, with some support from the literature, that the issue of state capacity and efficiency remains central and cannot be ducked in any discussion that purports to be relevant to policy. Neither peasant farmers nor would-be capitalists can develop in the context of a declining and chaotic state. It is not sufficient for those who advocate a privatization strategy (e.g. Berg, 1985) to contend that the state should restrict itself to functions such as providing a stable and efficient macro-economic environment, since it cannot be assumed that the state is capable even of this limited role. Study of successful cases of agricultural development and consideration of the problems of marketing boards show that prices and the market are not necessarily the determining factors. In other words, assertion of the centrality of 'politics' is not just a truism but rather an argument about the importance of 'non-price' factors, including the institutional capacity of the state. Given the kinds of agrarian economies that exist (the export orientation in particular) and the kinds of political imperatives that flow from state–society relations in Africa, the state is, and is likely to continue to be, involved more intimately in the articulations between agrarian society and the market than a *laissez-faire* model of its functions allows. What is needed is a better understanding of how this relationship has been developed more effectively and benignly in some countries than in others. The variety of environments and outcomes in tropical African countries warrants more genuinely comparative analysis, and should deter single-factor sloganizing.

The state as systematically anti-agriculture

The Berg Report of 1981 (World Bank, 1981) was undoubtedly intended to set the agenda for debate in the 1980s, and in this respect it has achieved its objective. Its attack on government policies which 'distort' markets — over-valued currencies, import controls and protection, subsidies, price controls — and on institutions such as marketing boards which exploit monopsony powers to reduce farmers' incomes, their productive efficiency and ultimately their incentive to market their crops, hardly needs any recapitulation here. Most of the major studies published since 1981 have either followed its lead or entered into debate with it. Indeed, its message expressed as an Orwellian slogan — 'peasant farmers good, state bad' — can be discerned in a remarkably wide spectrum of opinion, from the 'new right' to the 'revolutionary left'!

Bates' contribution was to develop a model of how government intervention works through three inter-connected markets: the market for farm produce — sub-divided into export crops and domestic crops — the market for consumer goods, and the market for farm inputs and factors of production (seeds, fertilizers, labour, land). In the first market, governments systematically hold down prices. For export crops, marketing boards expropriate the surplus represented by the difference between world prices and producer prices, most of which is used by the state as transfers to other social groups or for investment. Producer prices for food crops and for local agri-business inputs are also contained, either administratively or by the competition of imports artificially cheapened by an over-valued currency; the excess demand for imports is controlled by licensing, thus generating rents for those given access to such imports. In the second market, Bates argues, prices are generally driven up by measures in support of import-substituting industrialization, including protection against imports and monopolies to inward investors. Cheap loans to and direct state investment in manufacturing projects are also financed partly at the expense of rural producers' incomes. In the third market prices may be reduced by subsidy but the benefits are again allocated selectively; the state engages directly in large-scale production schemes (usually loss-making), or it allocates scarce resources, including land and water, to favoured groups — for example big commercial farmers — or pet projects (Bates, 1983, p. 118 and 1981, p. 39).

Bates then asks the question that the World Bank had naturally tended to avoid: why do governments persist with such policies when their effects on agricultural production become obviously negative? The answer requires some conception of the nature or character of the state and Bates makes it clear that he regards the state as 'an agency for aggregating private demands' (Bates, 1983, p. 121). The policy outcomes described above are therefore 'an expected result of a political process in which private interests, behaving rationally, seek economic rewards through their influence over public policy' (ibid., p. 125). The interests that succeed in gaining such influence are predominantly urban: workers, employers (amongst which the government itself is typically one of the largest) and the educated middle classes. In so far as these interests are in most African states a minority of the population, there is an additional consideration — how to maintain political control. Here again agricultural policies are argued by Bates to be rational ways of organizing support in the countryside; indeed, that is their prime justification. In such economies, the state both extracts and allocates its revenues from the peasant economy by regulating markets. Administratively-generated rents are the most powerful weapons in the political armoury of the bureaucracy, and this is so, argues Bates, whether the governments call themselves capitalist or socialist. All are driven by the same logic, even if they (supposedly) allocate access to the benefits to different groups of clients. another reason why these policies are tolerated is that those who might be supposed to suffer from them pursue such private solutions as circumventing official markets or even withdrawing altogether from commercial activity — another familiar feature of the current crisis.

The policy conclusions that Bates draws from his analysis are sombre. Governments do have a vested interest in economic inefficiency, and the reactions of individual farmers, bureaucrats and other actors on the African scene do little to disturb it. A rational choice model does, however, point to ways out of the dilemma, in so far as it assumes government in contemporary African states to be a 'going concern'. In countries such as the Ivory Coast and Kenya, commercial farmers have been brought into the ruling coalition. Although exceptional historical conditions prevailed in these cases, Bates argues that if larger numbers of the ruling elite in other countries invest in commercial farming themselves, the general interests of the farming community will be less frequently ignored; in spite of differences of interest between large and small farmers, improvements in prices will benefit all. Alternatively, ruling interests can be persuaded to see that the pursuit of short-run political advantage is destroying their own economic bases and that it would be in their longer-term interests to 'evoke co-operation by sharing joint gains.' (Bates, 1981, pp. 95 and 132). (It can be argued that the current attempt to revive the cocoa industry in Ghana is an example of this kind of realization.)

Some parts of Bates' analysis have gained more general acceptance than others. The idea that peasant farmers will respond to market incentives receives almost universal assent (Lofchie, 1985, p. 180; Hart, 1982, p. 119). This idea echoes an older debate between 'substantivists' and 'formalists' (see Jones, 1960; Hopkins, 1973; Bond, 1983; Bates, 1983, p. 139 and 1984), with perhaps only Hyden amongst current writers arguing that there is a distinctive 'peasant economy', the principles of which are derived from the ecologically precarious nature of African farming and supremacy of familial and social obligations over the cash nexus (Hyden, 1980 and 1985). Others, whilst not accepting Hyden fully, would emphasize that, in the highly imperfect markets that obtain in African economies, there is little point in calling 'perverse' peasant responses to price incentives which do not conform to neo-classical expectations (Colclough, 1985, p. 27). Nevertheless, the World Bank continues to call for market solutions in which the state would facilitate the pursuit of private interests by withdrawing from its attempts to intervene in the three markets of Bates' model (World Bank, 1983), a call echoed by De Wilde in his recent survey of agricultural marketing in seven countries (De Wilde, 1984). Berg and others now assert even more strongly that private traders are the only solution to the problems of agricultural marketing and that peasant smallholders can, given the right incentive, create 'rapid agricultural transformation' (Berg, 1985, p. 143; Filippi-Wilhelm, 1985: Good, 1986, p. 265). The fullest development of the approach is to be found in the work of economists such as Rimmer and Teal. Rimmer gives an economic analysis of the consequences of ignoring the potential gains to be had from exploiting comparative advantage in international trade. Like Bates, he argues that governments can become an interest systematically opposed to economic growth, but he eschews speculation as to how this barrier might be overcome (Rimmer, 1984, p. 264; Teal, 1986).

Difficulties with and objections to the Bates model have emerged in the literature in three main areas: (1) doubts concerning the appropriateness of a rational choice model of the state; (2) the issue of withdrawal of the state and its relation to peasant-based strategies for improving agricultural performance; (3) empirical analyses and case studies which show that food prices can rise without benefiting farmers or that marketing boards do not necessarily transfer resources away from agriculture.

Patrimonialism and state capacity

In the field of political analysis some of the most important recent books have stressed that the African state is best characterized as a 'neo-patrimonial bureaucracy' which is not responsive in any coherent way to social or economic 'interests'. The essence of patrimonialism (Joseph uses the term 'prebendalism') is that state offices are appropriated by office-holders and their benefits distributed to followers or clients. In the absence of an indigenous bourgeois class, and, indeed, of any other well-articulated classes, the state controls accumulation, breeding parasitic mercantile groups whose relationship to state power is organized through ethno-clientelism rather than class (Sandbrook, 1985; Callaghy, 1984a and 1984b; Jackson & Rosberg, 1982 and 1985; Young 1984; Kasfir 1984; Joseph, 1984; Clapham, 1982; Randall & Theobald, 1985). In so far as the accumulation of wealth is not associated with the development of new forms of production, the state, in this theory, is a factionalized arena for the often fiercely contested allocations from the surplus of the trading economy — hence the frequent resort to analogies with mercantilism (Callaghy, 1979; Crook, 1983). The political or bureaucratic elite is self-serving, yet driven by the need to finance its clientelist networks. For this reason, its levels of extraction, however ruinous, have no rational limit — unless they are exposed to the disciplines of a productive group, which the literature implies to be uncommon, with terms such as 'non-bourgeois', 'non-productive', a 'larcenous conspiracy' (Callaghy, 1984b, p. 64; Hart, 1982). Even a centralizing patrimonial bureaucracy such as Callaghy describes in Zaire — and is perhaps also developing in Nigeria (Joseph, 1984) — is compared unfavourably to that of seventeenth-century France. 'Extraction is a full-time and often brutal business'; yet the Mobutu state lacks even a 'national' concept and has to use foreign military power when its extractions provoke resistance (Callaghy, 1984a, p. 419).

Some Marxist analysts, on the other hand, have suggested that, however irrational and economically destructive the depredations of the Zairean or Nigerian states may appear, a process of 'primitive accumulation' is occurring in which state officials are the core of a new bourgeois class. This perspective is based partially on the evidence of extensive land appropriation by elites in those two countries, an uncommon development in Tropical Africa outside Kenya (Brett, 1986; Newbury, 1984; p. 113; Schoepf, 1984, p. 89; Watts & Shenton, 1984). The objection to such a view is that these appropriations do not in fact seem to be leading to new forms of production by an established capitalist class but are either another form of wasteful consumption by the 'predator' elite (in so far as the land is not utilized efficiently) (Young, 1984; Hyden, 1985), or a subsidy to local parasitic or foreign capitalist clients (Forrest, 1981). Similarly, Saul's concept of a 'bureaucratic bourgeoisie' appears in essence little different from the neo-patrimonial approach, since it fails to link the alleged bourgeoisie to any specific set of productive relations (Saul, 1979). The orthodox Marxists' search for a more genuine bourgeois class, distinct from the state, continues, with occasional sightings reported, but the evidence is patchy and limited, interestingly enough, to those countries where the excesses of patrimonialism have been somewhat curbed (Leys, 1978; Swainson, 1980: Beckman, 1982; Fauré & Médard, 1982; Crook, 1983; Tangri, 1985).

Bates' scepticism about the prospects for change in the policies of African states is based on his analysis of why it is in the interest of particular groups and in accordance with political imperatives to perpetuate certain economic inefficiencies. The logic of the patrimonial model is even more unpromising: the sheer survival of the political elite and the extraction of the means to fuel its ethno-clientelist networks are the dominant principles, so much so that all other interests are sacrificed in a downward — and highly irrational — spiral, or 'negative entropy' as Price terms it (Price, 1984). The experiences of Ghana in 1972–83 and Uganda in 1971–86 provide strong evidence for acceptance of such a proposition (see Chazan, 1983). If it is accepted, then the focus of the argument shifts to the question of what capacity might be realistically expected in an African state to administer any kind of reform programme, whether capitalist, socialist or peasant-based. The commonest feature of the current literature, whether it concerns the socialist or non-socialist countries, is, indeed, the renewed concern for order, and the damaging effects of a lack of it even in mundane areas such as basic public services, infrastructure or provision of statistics. As Mars points out, this 'corrosive doubt' about state capacity derives from a model of the state which virtually 'excludes regeneration in the forseeable future' (Mars, 1986, p. 16; cf. Sandbrook, 1985, p. 127; Young *et al.*, 1981, p. 159; Young, 1982, p. 321 and 1984, p. 80; Hart, 1982, p. 104; Hyden, 1983 and 1985; Hodder-Williams, 1984, p. 233; Tordoff, 1984, p. 150; Price, 1984; Luke, 1986; Jackson & Rosberg, 1985, p. 55; World Bank, 1983; Crook, 1983, p. 188; Lofchie, 1985; Lipton, 1985; Munslow, 1984, p. 220; Roesch, 1984; Cliffe & Munslow, 1985, p. 50).

The issue, then, is what can be done with the patrimonial state in its present form. Some writers argue, perhaps with historical analogies in mind, that only a full-blown capitalist transformation based on encouraging trends towards urbanization and the use of foreign capital and expertise will make any difference. What else can be expected, they ask, from a bureaucracy rooted in an agrarian pre-industrial society? Commercialization does not produce the labour discipline and rational specialization associated with the industrial revolution (Hart, 1982; Hyden, 1983 and 1985). Studies of the 'newly industrializing countries' in Asia are clearly beginning to have an impact on the consciousness of Africanists; there is speculation on the origins of Asian industrializing elites, from which are derived models of authoritarian statism (Sandbrook, 1985, p. 32; Price, 1984, p. 187; White, 1986, p.2). This problem for most analysts who advocate a capitalist path remains, however, how to get a capitalist transformation started. Some observers have become so disillusioned that they recommend in effect a recolonization of Africa. The propping-up by the international community of weak states which exist only juridically must end since they are obstacles to rational economic development. If indigenous elites are hopeless, foreign personnel or IMF leverage must be used. It is notable that the Ivory Coast's success is now openly attributed to its being run by Frenchmen (Jackson & Rosberg, 1985, p. 60; Sandbrook, 1985, p. 120). It may be suggested that in Zaire even this solution failed. How practical would it be elsewhere?

Another argument is that modest advances can be made within the patrimonial context — which, indeed, may be all that is politically feasible anyway. Some sociologists believe patrimonialism to be compatible with bureaucratic organization and able to play a positive role in state-building and integration. It is true that some of the early modern European states were built with patrimonial bureaucracies; this perception has led to an interest in the positive potential of 'personal rule' models in Africa (Roth, 1968; Rudolph, 1979; Randall & Theobald, 1985; Jackson & Rosberg, 1982). The World Bank eschews such highly speculative theory and engages with the concerns of the 'development administrationists': how to achieve practical low-level improvements in the 'capacity, responsiveness [to their subjects] and equity' of the bureaucracy (Luke, 1986). Disillusioned with remedies such as 'manpower training' or 'planning', the literature has shifted its emphasis to structural reforms such as 'decentralization' and creation of 'access' through local responsiveness and 'participation'. Brett, for instance, having asserted the irredeemable irrationality of the African state, goes on to propose that there must be 'politically controlled structures for economic intervention', which, because they will be decentralized and locally accountable, will 'meet the needs of small-scale producers'. How such structures are to emerge from the patrimonial context is of course a profoundly political (as well as puzzling) question (Brett, 1986, p. 29; Hyden, 1983; Mawhood, 1983; World Bank, 1983; Schaffer & Lamb, 1981; see also Lea & Chaudhri, 1983, p. 337).

The old issue of accountability is also raised by the World Bank — perhaps unwisely since it is here that the problems of patrimonialism are most obvious. To recommend that bureaucrats should be made more accountable to politicians (Koehn, 1983) may raise a hollow laugh in some circles, but the seriousness with which this idea is regarded by those who study socialist regimes should give pause for thought. In Mozambique, now that the government has accepted the error of its reliance on state and communal farming, the role of a party machine quite separate from the state and responsive to local opinion is regarded as crucial to the success of the new peasant-based strategy. Indeed, Cliffe sees 'local political cadres' as professionally committed to opposing bureaucratic as well as 'rich peasant' distortions of that strategy. The change in values that is necessary for administrative reform is perhaps more intimately connected to political (or religious?) action than is usually acknowledged (Cliffe & Munslow, 1985; Hanlon, 1984).

Overall, however, there is extreme caution over the prospects for getting the state to run marketing boards or input and extension services more honestly and efficiently, or to give up expensive capital-intensive agricultural projects which either fail to produce the expected results or are hijacked by patronage networks. Consequently, there is a tendency to propose solutions that minimize the role of the state; the favourite term of criticism is 'over-ambitious', the favourite recommendation for improving accountability not political cadres but market disciplines (World Bank, 1983, p. 123; De Wilde, 1984). The hostility to the state is not, however, wholly the preserve of market missionaries; it is also associated with a trend in thought which might be labelled 'peasantism'.

Rolling back the state and 'peasantism'

There is at first sight a curious similarity between the current views of the 'new right' and the radical left; both believe that peasant farmers or smallholders are the key to Africa's agricultural problems and that smallholders would do much better if the bureaucrats got off their backs. There are of course important differences in the analysis, notably in the role of the market and in the conception of who is worthy to be called a 'peasant'.

The most single-minded exponent of 'market incentives for small-holders' remains Berg, although Bates in his most recent contribution is a strong contender too (Berg, 1985; Bates, 1984). The logic of the argument is derived in essence from Bauer's original critique of the marketing boards, namely that farmers as individual entrepreneurs would invest their profits from selling crops on the world market more efficiently than government could (Bauer, 1954). It was not until the 1970s that this view became influential — first of all through the commitment of international development agencies to 'redistribution with growth' and targeting the rural poor. What this came to mean in policy terms was increasing the production or raising the productivity of small farmers (World Bank, 1975; Lea & Chaudhri, 1983; Williams, 1981). When government action (or, at least, official intentions) along these lines failed to produce results, the stage was set for the Berg Report of 1981. The justification for calling this report a revival of the Bauer hypothesis is that it views a peasant strategy as an integral part of capitalist strategy; or, as Williams puts it, 'peasants are to be understood in terms of the logic of capital ... the small farmer is seen as a capitalist farmer in miniature' (Williams, 1981, pp. 30–1). It is this clear-eyed view of the peasant as a petty commodity producer with the interests of an owner of the means of production — however meagre — that distinguishes the Berg position from that of the radical peasant populists. Anyone familiar with the history of cocoa growing in Ghana and the Ivory Coast or of coffee and commercial food-farming in Kenya knows that the logic of the market is to start a chain of accumulation and differentiation. Bauer, Swynnerton and others hoped that an indigenous bourgeoisie would thus emerge. What remains unproven is whether it has in fact led to an increase in the productivity of agriculture (Munro, 1984, p. 49; Hart, 1982, p. 153; Gbetibouo & Delgado, 1984, p. 125). Also unproven, of course, is the counter-factual proposition that export-crop farmers, left to themselves, could have furthered a process of economic development more effectively than the governments which have appropriated their surpluses (see below).

Another unresolved ambiguity in the neo-Bauerist approach is the relationship between the policy of encouraging rural petty capitalism and that of encouraging large agri-business projects — as in Nigeria, the Ivory Coast, Malawi and Kenya — many of which depend for their success on the state patronage networks so abhorred by the free marketeers (Watts & Shenton, 1984; Forrest, 1981; Lee, 1983; Livingstone, 1985; see also Shepherd, 1981, and Beckman, 1981, for similar developments in Ghana). Arguments about the relative economic efficiency of smallholder versus large-scale production are unresolved because of the more urgent concern to find policies that both bypass the state and yet at the same time encourage private enterprise.

Concern over the implications of a market strategy and with conflicts of interest between different strata of the peasantry, the state and large capitalists is by contrast the hallmark of those who have been dubbed 'ethno-populists' (Robertson, 1984, p. 296; see also Kitching, 1982, Chap. 4, on 'neo-populism'). For them, a peasant policy means a concentration on helping poor peasants, who are likely to be those who cultivate marginal land, do not grow export crops or migrate to employment. There is a deep suspicion of any policy that seeks to encourage production for the market or export (as opposed to food) crops or that enables some farmers to become richer than others. Peasant farming is seen as in conflict with 'capitalist' farming, and the suggestion that increasing production to supply urban or international markets is a way forward is attacked as 'not necessarily compatible with the interests of rural producers' (Heyer, Roberts & Williams, 1981, pp. 2 and 5). Virtually all state schemes of rural development are also attacked as either misguided or positively harmful. Coulson's account of the record of the Tanzanian government as consistently wrong in every respect over the past thirty years is typical of the work of many scholars concerned with that country; the blame for the betrayal and failure of 'peasant socialism' is placed squarely on the bureaucracy. The right policy is said to be one of trusting the peasants because they know best how to develop agriculture in a way that serves their needs (Coulson, 1981).

As Robertson notes, the belief that ordinary folk know best 'inspires an outright rejection of national development planning' (Robertson, 1984, p. 296). For some writers the belief is a guide to action and research. Chambers urges that development experts should spend their time learning from the peasants about local ecology and farming systems. But for Chambers this eminently sensible suggestion is more than a methodology; it is a crusade to assert the worth of indigenous knowledge as against that of expariate experts (although he does not fall into the trap of asserting that European science has *nothing* to contribute) (Chambers, 1983, pp. iii, 86, 201; cf. Adams, 1981). Although Chambers does not ignore the problem of political feasibility, his scepticism about the record of development planning to date is tempered by a continuing faith in the ability of the state to implement rational reforms and hence in its amenability to the power of patient persuasion that things could be done better. Practical help for the poor, he argues, is largely a matter of working with the imperfect agencies that exist, and circumventing, persuading or if need be challenging the power of local or national elites. Chambers' commitment to peasant spontaneity is, certainly, more general and therefore more consistent than the position of those who purport to espouse a 'socialist' defence of the peasantry. They are forced to discriminate between the kinds of states and the kinds of peasants they are prepared to support.

Some of the socialist writers committed to a defence of the peasantry are prepared to accept many of the implications of the Bauer/Berg line. Williams concludes a study of the marketing boards in Nigeria with the assertion that, on this issue, 'socialists should support free trade' (Williams, 1985,p. 13). And Beckman's masterly studies of the conflict between the state and cocoa farmers in Ghana (Beckman, 1976 and 1981) could as easily support the policy conclusions of Bauer and Berg as the assertion that African states are supporting 'rich' farmers and capitalists against the poor. In Kenya the real achievements of smallholder farming in the 1970s have been acknowledged by both Heyer and Swainson (Heyer, 1981; Swainson, 1986). The problem for the socialist who accepts the Bauerist argument is, however, that it is difficult to escape the capitalist logic of a policy that favours leaving cash-crop farmers to invest and/or consume their own surpluses, and is hostile to 'bureaucratic' planning and 'monopolistic' state intervention.

For others, the obsession with suppressing a *kulak* class enables them to evade the problems (for a socialist) of neo-Bauerism (Raikes, 1975; von Freyhold, 1979). The virtue of peasant spontaneity is denied to cash-crop farmers, who are stigmatized as 'capitalist' farmers (i.e. not peasants) because, it is asserted, they may, in contrast to food-farmers, employ labour or have larger cash incomes. Both assertions would seem to be inaccurate in so far as they ignore the considerable differentiation that exists among cash-crop farmers — many are 'poor smallholders', just like food farmers (Killick & House, 1983; Gbetibouo & Delgado, 1984) — and also ignore the petty capitalist characteristics of all smallholder production. Why confine the label 'peasant' to the poorest of farmers, and within that category to food growers, when the dividing line between peasant and capitalist is more properly to do with scale, the division of labour and the form of capital invested? (cf. Hart, 1982, pp. 13 and 156–8).

For those who study the socialist states, a commitment to peasant virtue is specifically tempered by the hope that 'the party' will both prevent a peasant-based strategy from developing spontaneously into rural capitalism and slay the bureaucratic dragon (Cliffe & Munslow, 1985). Cliffe is careful not to 'blame' the peasants for the failures of the socialist regimes' attempts to transform agriculture; but it would be unfair, in the light of his continuing commitment to agrarian transformation, to label him a 'peasantist'. The state, he concludes, must approach the peasants in a more tactful manner, using dedicated cadres to ensure that development projects reach the poor for whom they were intended, and to listen to peasant views and interests. He even recognizes that there may be structural reasons for the friction between state and peasantry; but he does not draw from this recognition as do others, the conclusion that the 'socialist project' may itself be incompatible with a peasant-based policy, and lead inevitably to 'bureaucratic collectivism' (Sandbrook, 1981, p. 206). He converts the difficulties into practical questions of how to prevent bureaucratic distortions of the intended transformation (Cliffe & Munslow, 1985, pp. 47 and 51). But the 'peasantist' or populist approach is also flawed if it refuses to accept the results of peasants' spontaneous responses to market opportunities and, whilst being anti-state, condemns the state for not intervening to curb the outcomes of differentiation (Heyer, Roberts & Williams, 1981, p. 10; cf. Kitching's critique of the populist attitude to economic development in general: Kitching, 1982, p. 180).

State capacity and the 'non-price' factor

The Bates model, as outlined earlier, describes the impact of the state in three markets crucial to agricultural producers in Africa. In two of these — producer prices and producer inputs — the state's intervention is, in most countries, effected through institutions such as marketing boards and development corporations which are amenable to political and administrative analysis. (In some cases even the third market for consumer goods has been subject to state-controlled importing or retailing operations.) The common judgement of these institutions is that they are inherently and systematically harmful because they are subject to certain political imperatives: the state's need for revenue, which must be drawn from the agrarian sector but is used to favour urban and bureaucratic interests, and its need to maintain political control. Alternatively, the patrimonial model shows such institutions to be not only systematically corrupt and inefficient but also not amenable to rational reform. The implications of both models are that producer incomes could be much higher and therefore agricultural development stimulated if excessive marketing costs and taxation were reduced. And, as Bauer originally argued, this would be best achieved by reducing state involvement and allowing private traders to do the buying and marketing. But this change is difficult if not impossible to accomplish for the systemic reasons already given.

Both the rational state and the patrimonial state models therefore invite solutions to the problem of agricultural development which attempt to side-step the issue of state capacity by advocating either market or bypassing strategies. It may be argued, however, that neither model offers sufficient justification for these strategies, first because of inherent flaws in their comparative logic and second because they fail to address the real issue of institutional capacity in African economic development.

The neatness of the 'rational coalition of interests' model is disturbed by the variety of actual outcomes in different countries. It is not always true, for instance, that the state systematically transfers resources from farmers to the urban sector. In Senegal, the groundnut marketing and agricultural development institution ONCAD became a 'Frankenstein's monster'; a patronage machine that got out of control and transferred resources to the groundnut sector, principally to the big patron farmers, the Mourides, but also to the peasants, through higher prices. And, in spite of the higher prices, the peasants (and their local collaborators) continued to benefit from a parallel market that deprived the state of a majority of the harvest. ONCAD had to be closed down as the state sought other means both to revive and re-establish control over the industry (Caswell, 1985). In Malawi, the marketing board used its surpluses from peasant production of export crops — tobacco and tea — to encourage a massive expansion in plantation production of the same crops and to subsidize maize and rice farmers (Livingstone, 1985).

Neither is it always the case that the state keeps food prices low in countries where there is a 'food crisis'; and, in any case, economists are by no means agreed that prices are the main determinant of African food production. According to Bequele, the stagnation in Ghanaian food production during the 1970s was accompanied by a rise greater in producer prices than in retail prices, whilst cocoa production for export continued to slump as a result (?) of massive drops in the real producer price. The Ghanaian case is especially debatable — and especially important in so far as Ghana is often cited as the leading example of what went wrong with African agriculture in the 1970s. Beckman argues that the retail price rises were absorbed by traders benefiting from overall shortages caused by the black market, whereas Bequele finds in rural labour shortages a 'supply side' explanation of the high prices. Moreover, as Ghai & Smith comment, the food price inflation was not, as is commonly asserted, dampened by overvaluation but rather exacerbated 'as the foreign exchange shortages intensified'. Ghana experienced the most rapid increase in consumer food prices of all the seventeen countries for which information was available in the period 1968–80 (Ghai & Smith, 1987, pp. 80 and 125). Interestingly enough, the shortages coincided with a massive expansion in large-scale rice production in the north, financed by state patronage and mostly sold in the black market. Shepherd argues that the rice boom both caused a shortage of labour and an intensification of peasant agriculture — which nevertheless 'impoverished' the northern peasantry! The expansion of rice production failed, apparently, to ease the 'shortage' of food and the retail price inflation (Bequele, 1983; Beckman, 1981; Shepherd, 1981).

In Nigeria too (which, in contrast to Ghana, was enjoying an oil boom in the 1970s) the prices of domestic food crops rose relative to export crops as urban demand soared; yet it is alleged that food production stagnated to a far greater extent than can be explained by competition from imported food. And this in a country where the state, because of oil revenues, did not need to raise a surplus from peasant production at all! (Collier, 1983).

Even the assumption that marketing boards and state intervention in agricultural markets are necessarily harmful to agriculture turns out on closer inspection to be contested. Kenya has been cited as an example of a country that has maintained high producer prices — above export parity levels — for staple food crops and that has successfully developed smallholder farming in both the food and export crop sectors (Heyer, 1981). Bates would argue that this is because Kenya is one of the few countries where agrarian interests have been able to influence the ruling elite; yet they have not abolished the marketing boards, and Bates' model in any case assumes that the ruling elite has used state patronage to benefit privileged large farmers (whites and their successors) rather than smallholders. But, as Swinson has argued, Kenya's most notable recent success has been smallholder tea-growing, a success linked to the efforts of an efficient and successful state agency, the KTDA (Swainson, 1986). It is also clear that one must distinguish the impact of a marketing board on the success or failure of an agricultural sector from the social changes taking place within that sector. This at least is the implication of the work of other economists who have argued that the success of a prosperous section of the middle and large farmers in Kenya has been achieved against the background of constantly worsening domestic (rural–urban) terms of trade which leave the majority of smallholders poorer (Killick & House, 1983, p. 58).

Even more startling is the case of the Ivory Coast, which in all comparisons of African agricultural performance leads in output, incomes, food production per capita, exports and the success of its export-based smallholder strategy (Ghai & Smith, 1987). Again, for Bates, this outcome follows from the primacy of agricultural interests in the Ivorian political structure, a view of Ivorian politics increasingly challenged by political analysts (Fauré & Medard, 1982; Hecht, 1983; Bakary, 1984; Sandbrook, 1985; Watts & Bassett, 1986). It might be thought that such a country would have escaped the evils of marketing boards, and in a sense this is true; the major export crops — coffee and cocoa — are still bought and may still be exported by private traders. But there is nevertheless a state price-setting agency, the Caisse de Stabilisation, which accumulates surpluses through the familiar mechanism of taking the difference between the world price and a local price which it has determined. And the characteristics of this system have been very little different from other African export economies. No less than nineteen parastatal corporations are involved in the agricultural sector; huge surpluses have been transferred to the urban and industrial sectors; the exchange rate has been over-valued (although not as drastically as Ghanaian or Tanzanian currencies) (Gbetibouo & Delgado, 1984; Hecht, 1983; Michel & Noel, 1984, p.93).

According to Gbetibouo, Ivorian cocoa farmers received on average about 50 per cent of the Abidjan FOB price between 1960 and 1975, dropping to one-third during the cocoa boom of 1976–80 — very similar to other African producers (Rimmer, 1984, p. 170; Bates, 1981, Appendix B). Moreover, the 'nominal protection coefficient' for 1976–80 — i.e. the ratio of the domestic producer price to the net world price converted as a 'real' exchange rate — was 0.38, compared to Ghana's 0.40 and Nigeria's 0.50 (Gbetibouo & Delgado, 1984, pp. 125–8). Obviously some account must be taken of the extreme unreality of Ghana's exchange rate during this period — a point admitted by Gbetibouo, who notes that the protection coefficient he gives for Ghana cocoa is 'unadjusted'. Teal argues that Ghana's domestic inflation caused 'real' producer prices to drop more than threefold between 1960/64 and 1975/79, while in the Ivory Coast real prices remained almost constant (Teal, 1986, p. 275). But Teal's figures have been updated by Gbetibouo, who estimates that by 1983 the real producer price of cocoa in the Ivory Coast was only 60 per cent of its 1975 value (using the Abidjan African CPI), whilst Lee calculates that the 'real gross revenue per hectare' for cocoa and coffee between 1960 and 1976/7 did not keep pace with the rise in GDP and claims that farmers' gains were insignificant (Lee, 1983, p. 110; Gbetibouo & Delgado, 1984, p. 131). Whatever the truth of the figures, it is known that considerable smuggling of cocoa from Ghana to the Ivory Coast has occurred and it is clear that the main motivation of Ghanaian traders was to get paid in CFA francs (or their black-market cedi equivalent); but since it was the official under-valuation of foreign exchange in Ghana that made smuggling so attractive, we cannot make any deductions from this evidence about the real value of Ivorian prices to Ivorian producers.

Attempts to explain why Ivorian farmers continued to expand production, while apparently being subject to the same kind of 'taxation' and transfer of surpluses to bureaucratic and urban interests as other African producers, are few and tend to emphasize the total package of incentives offered to Ivorian producers. Gbetibouo assesses the 'non-price' factors— an efficient buying system, good roads, good extension services, plentiful labour supply — as being the key determinants. Rimmer too emphasizes these factors, interpreted as reduction in producers' costs, and also argues that, taking account of the wide availability of imported goods, the real domestic producer price for export crops must have retained comparative advantage (relative to other crops) (Gbetibouo & Delgado, 1984, p. 129; Rimmer, 1984, p.245). It is the political question, however, that remains most intractable, in so far as Bates' model fails to account for a state which transfers large surpluses from peasant farmers to the bureaucratic elite, whilst simultaneously encouraging peasant farming.

Overall, it is clear that the presence or absence of marketing boards that extract a surplus and the dominance of urban interests are not necessarily associated with either low producer prices or transfers to non-agricultural groups; and that, even when they are, they do not necessarily explain the success or failure of agricultural development — even that based on commercial smallholders. This has been recognized by some writers: Hesp, for instance, argues that Bates' model does not apply very easily to food marketing and that for governments to set prices is more complex than it appears once the problem of relativities between various crops is faced (Hesp & van der Laan, 1985, pp. 19 and 24). Lofchie points out that price increases 'may have no effect whatsoever unless accompanied by a number of other improvements in the economic environment in the countryside', and pleads for an end to the debate between 'interventionist versus noninterventionist strategies' (Lofchie, 1985, p. 183). Similar points are made by Faber & Green (1985) and by Colclough — the latter arguing strongly that price mechanisms simply cannot work in the conventionally predicted ways in such imperfect markets as those of Tropical Africa (Colclough, 1985, p. 27). The latest systematic comparative survey by the economists Ghai & Smith concludes that the data 'do not show any correlation between producer prices and overall agricultural performance' in the majority of Tropical African countries, and that non-price factors 'have probably had a stronger negative effect on agricultural performance that price levels' (Ghai & Smith, 1987, p. 52). These conclusions differ significantly in their emphasis from an earlier economic study by Bond, who had argued that supply responses to price changes were positive for both individual crops and aggregate agricultural production, although only the long-term elasticities for individual crops were of 'fairly sizeable magnitudes' (Bond, 1983, pp. 710, 716 and 723). Ghai & Smith use more recent data than Bond, and the latest United Nations International Comparison Project techniques for calculating 'real purchasing power prices'. Nevertheless, they are rightly more cautious about the validity of much of the data, and, whilst not disagreeing with the proposition that individual crops may be price-responsive, come to a correspondingly different conclusion on the aggregate significance of prices. The great variety of price trends for food and export crops in different countries cannot be correlated with either good or bad performance and certainly contradicts the 'stereotype' that all African governments have followed policies that depress real agricultural prices (Ghai & Smith, 1987, pp. 162–3).

Even the assumption that agricultural policies systematically favour urban interests can be challenged by those familiar with recent conditions in Ghana, Uganda and Zaire. As Price points out, the *kalabule* economy benefits only a restricted circle of official insiders and their trading accomplices; most urban consumers in fact suffer high food prices and daily extortions, along with the breakdown of the urban economy generally (a factor that also looms large in the gloom of expatriate development experts!). It would also seem implausible to suggest that African governments have been slow to repress urban workers' protests (Price, 1984; Sandbrook, 1985, pp. 74 and 144).

Clearly the rational interest model of the African state does not produce a clear or consistent picture of which interests are being served by agricultural policies or institutions. Is it the case then that 'policies' are simply the irrational by-product of whatever methods a rapacious

patrimonial elite uses to appropriate state resources, and that this elite
is therefore incapable of implementing 'rational' policies through more
effective institutions? On the issue of inherent capacity there are
empirical lessons that may serve at first sight to question the pessimism
induced by the patrimonial model.

The success of Ivory Coast agriculture shows that the marketing board
issue is to some extent a red herring. It is not a question of whether there
is a state monopsony; it is whether the functionally necessary marketing
system can be run efficiently and benignly. (This is not to imply that the
effect of the system on the various interest groups could or should be
neutral. Benign in this context means serving the interests of farmers.)
The Ivory Coast and other examples — Zimbabwe and Kenya — show
that it is not impossible for the state to do it. From the point of view of
the individual cocoa farmer, for instance, what is required is a marketing
system that ensures prompt payment of the best proportion of the world
market price over the season, preferably with advances given by honest
buyers, together with a good road system and research and input
services such as SATMACI provides in the Ivory Coast (cf. Young,
Sherman & Rose, 1981, p. 118; Gbetibouo & Delgado, 1984, p. 128). In
the past, Ghanaian producers, particularly large farmers who indulged
in cocoa-broking themselves, demanded competition among buyers as
the best way to ensure fair prices and honest treatment. But the history
of cocoa in Ghana shows that the physical and economic conditions of
cocoa exporting lead inevitably to combination amongst buyers. The
reasons are very simple and compelling: the need to cope with the risks
of a futures market set in London or New York. It is as well to remember
that it was this logic that lay behind the behaviour of private traders in the
1930s and 40s — behaviour that led to the most widespread rural revolts
that West Africa has ever seen. Nor did the reintroduction of private
local buyers into the Ghanaian industry between 1969 and 1972 show
any better results. No doubt the abandonment of statutory price fixing
could benefit farmers in the short term, but, as the Ivory Coast shows,
it is not necessary for agricultural growth. Experience does not sustain
the assertion that only private traders can cope with the needs of the
export crop industries (Jones, 1982). The difficulties of the free market
position are perfectly exemplified in De Wilde's argument that, having
abolished its harmful monopolistic marketing boards, the state must
ensure that competition, accountability and an appropriate price system
are maintained (De Wilde, 1984). In the context of export crops sold on
the world market, this is the logic of Canute.

Can we agree then with those who see the patrimonial state as
capable of effectiveness and amenable to reform, in spite of the
deep pessimism inspired by the assertions of structural irrationality?
Sandbrook tentatively suggests that the 'benevolent neo-patrimonialism'
of the Ivory Coast is as good a model as we are likely to get. Others focus

on the 'personal rulership' aspect (Jackson & Rosberg, 1982), although, as Kenya after Kenyatta showed, a functioning bureaucracy is probably a more powerful explanation of regime survival than the influence of one individual. Nevertheless, it would seem to be deeply unsatisfactory to leave the argument there. The question of what distinguishes a 'good' from a 'bad' patrimonial state remains unanswered. Those who assume that the pathologies of current patrimonial states in Africa can be ignored or bypassed, letting 'capitalism' or other world historical forces do their work, would do well to consider the following picture:

each Minister recruits his own department; there are no standard conditions of service, and 75% of all appointments are patronage based. Parallel with this service, which performs all the recurrent functions of government, are civil servants funded by the 'development' budget, which comes mainly from overseas aid and represents the bulk of total resources. Donors insisted on the creation of a planning agency, recruited separately, to which the most skilled personnel are assigned and paid at the same rate as foreign experts. A study of the Health Ministry discovered that 31 steps were necessary to disburse money, both inside and outside the Ministry; initial determination of the availability of money is clouded and it appears that the Chief of Accounting makes such a determination according to criteria that are largely undocumented and unknown to others. There is excessive dominance by the executive branch of government and most honest or competent [nationals] leave the country; skilled people have to work in a milieu of low morale, extremely poor administrative communications, excessively centralized structures, lack of essential working materials and low salaries. Public employment has doubled in the decade 1970–80.

Of course this description is not of Africa but of Haiti in a recent report on administrative reform (Garcia-Zamor & Mayo-Smith, 1983). Nearly two hundred years after independence, neither capitalism nor overseas aid experts bypassing the patrimonial state have had much effect. Even the most cautious optimism would seem misplaced in the absence of a deeper analysis of the nature of patrimonialism and its different forms.

We return then to the crucial question: how can the relative effectiveness of systems such as that of the Ivory Coast be understood and replicated within states possessing predominantly patrimonial bureaucracies?. Since both successful and unsuccessful cases share this characteristic, a strong case can be made for the centrality of the organizational factor in explaining the ability of certain states to create institutions capable of sustaining both markets and public policies. In this respect it might be helpful to distinguish between patrimonialism and the politics of patronage. As apologists for British Colonial Office once argued, patronage is not necessarily incompatible with efficiency! (Furse, 1962). Clearly some states have been able to develop positive or institution-building forms of patronage, and in this sense relative efficiency is the end result of a deeper process.

'Efficiency' is, of course, a concept that begs many questions, but the sense in which it is used here derives from the current administrative literature on 'compliance' and 'bureaucratic politics' (Dunsire, 1978; Guy-Peters, 1978). In African states, the issue of compliance — getting people in organizations to do their jobs or to carry out instructions within the parameters of the discretion allowed to them — is still a live one (Crook, 1983). In this environment Goodsell's defence of the fundamental values of bureaucracy is wholly relevant: 'a system for applying laws uniformly and precisely and for delivering standardized services to all eligible individuals. It also incorporates the goal of official detachment from personal interest or favouritism' (Self, 1985, p. 154). Efficiency is simply an old-fashioned word that may still be used — in spite of Murray's objections (Murray, 1983) — to describe what happens when an institution has become sufficiently institutionalized for impersonal compliance procedures to work routinely, and with minimum disruption, whilst permitting bureaucratic politics. When an institution is established as a going concern, individuals or groups may compete informally to maximize discretion or win influence in a way that nevertheless accepts the formal roles imposed by the hierarchy and the overriding interests of the organization itself. Indeed, one of the characteristics of bureaucratic politics is said to be their concern with the goal of organizational survival or advantage. This may be contrasted with the politicization of bureaucracies which renders them impotent through destruction or subversion of formal roles and their replacement by personal ties. Compliance ceases to be routine, and the organization becomes literally incompetent, i.e. inefficient.

In arguing for the centrality of organizational development, then, it is suggested that the escape from destructive patrimonialism into more benign forms of patronage is a product of the emergence of a public realm initially within particular institutions rather than the state as a whole. The first positive sign is the creation of an 'agency ideology' or organizational ethos. It is no good whistling hopefully for the Weberian legal or technical rationalities, since virtually all attempts to introduce such rationalities from the outside have so far failed (as development administrationists freely admit). Compliance is associated with a logic of collective action which could emerge from a well-founded political movement (Brett's 'politically controlled structures'), but again need not be predicated on such a rare phenomenon in contemporary African reality. Such organizational strength existed in Ghana in the late 1950s and early 1960s (Crook, 1983) and perhaps exists in contemporary Mozambique or Tanzania (how else can one explain the survival of such regimes through unparalleled economic failure?) In the Ivory Coast less heroic factors may be at work, but what is similar is that institutions operate as 'going concerns' within which there is organizational commitment, and compliance mechanisms that work. Hence, the water supplies get delivered and the electricity bills get collected! The commitment may come from politics, religion — or simply expatriate administrators.

The conclusion of this discussion is that the patrimonial characteristics of African states are destructive unless something is done to convert them into more benevolent forms. They cannot just be left in the hope that persuasion or the rational pursuit of interests will eventually make things better.

Many of the authors surveyed above agree that a more rationally bureaucratic, efficient state is an absolute essential if there is to be any improvement in agricultural policies and their implementation in Africa (Sandbrook, 1985; Hart, 1982; Lofchie, 1985; Hyden, 1983; Young, Sherman and Rose, 1981; Tordoff, 1984; Bryceson, 1985;). An efficient (rational, honest) state is a necessity in Africa because without it the conditions that farmers need cannot be created and even market-based price strategies will be subverted. But we know little enough about how to achieve such as result, which is why it is suggested that we try to learn from the experience of successful cases.

References

Adams, A. (1981), 'The Senegal River Valley — what kind of change?' in Heyer, Roberts & Williams (1981).

Arhin, K., Hesp, P. & van der Laan, L. (1985), *Marketing Boards in Tropical Africa*, London, Routledge & Kegan Paul.

Bakary, T. (1984), 'Elite transformation and political succession' in Zartman & Delgado (1984).

Barker, J. (ed.) (1984), *The Politics of Agriculture in Tropical Africa*, Beverly Hills, Sage.

Bates, R.H. (1981), *Markets and States in Africa*, Berkeley, University of California Press.

— (1983), *Essays on the Political Economy of Rural Africa*, Cambridge, Cambridge University Press.

— (1984), 'Some conventional orthodoxies in the study of agrarian change', *World Politics*, **36**.

Bauer, P.T. (1954), *West African Trade*, Cambridge, Cambridge University Press.

Bauer, P.T. (1984), *Reality and Rhetoric*, London, Weidenfeld & Nicolson.

Beckman, B. (1976), *Organising the Farmers: Cocoa Politics and National Development in Ghana*, Uppsala, Scandinavian Institute of African Studies.

— (1981), 'Ghana 1951–78: the agrarian basis of the post-colonial state' in Heyer, Roberts & Williams (1981).

— (1982), 'Whose state? State and capitalist development in Nigeria', *Review of African Political Economy* **23**.

Bequele, A. (1983), 'Stagnation and inequality in Ghana' in Ghai & Radwan (1983).

Berg, E. (1985), 'The potentials of the private sector in Sub-Saharan Africa' in Rose (1985).

Bond, M.E. (1983), 'Agricultural responses to prices in Sub-Saharan African countries', *IMF Staff Papers* **30**.

Brett, E.A. (1986), 'State power and economic inefficiency: explaining political failure in Africa', *IDS Bulletin*, **17**.

Bryant, C. & White, L. (1984), *Managing Rural Development: Peasant Participation in Rural Development*, W. Hartford, CT, Kumarian Press.

Bryceson, D. (1985), 'The organization of Tanzanian Grain Marketing' in Arhin, Hesp & van der Laan (1985).

Callaghy, T.M. (1979), 'The difficulties of implementing socialist strategies of development in Africa: the first wave' in C.G. Rosberg & T.M. Callaghy (eds), *Socialism in Sub-Saharan Africa*, Berkeley, University of California Press.

— (1984a), *The State-Society Struggle: Zaire in Comparative Perspective*, New York, Columbia University Press.

(1984b), 'External actors and the relative autonomy of the political aristocracy in Zaire' in Kasfir (1984).

Carter, G.M. & O'Meara, P. (eds) (1985), *African Independence: The First Twenty-Five Years*, London, Hutchinson.

Caswell, N. (1985), 'Peasants, peanuts and politics; state marketing in Senegal, 1966–80' in Arhin *et al.* (1985).

Chambers, R. (1983), *Rural Development: Putting the Last First*, London, Longman.

Chazan, N. (1983), *An Anatomy of Ghanaian Politics: Managing Political Recession*, Boulder, Colorado, Westview Press.

Clapham, C. (ed.) (1982), *Private Patronage and Public Power*, London, Frances Pinter.

Cheema, G.S. & Rondinelli, D. (eds) (1983), *Decentralization and Development: Policy Implementation in Developing Countries*, Beverly Hills, Sage.

Cliffe, l. & Munslow, B. (1985), 'The politics of agrarian transformation in Africa', paper presented to the Conference of the Political Studies Association, Manchester.

Colclough, C. (1985), 'Competing paradigms — and lack of evidence — in the analysis of African development' in Rose (1985).

Collier, P. (1983), 'Oil and inequality in rural Nigeria' in Ghai & Radwan (1983).

Conyers, D. (1984), 'Decentralisation and development: a review of the literature', *Public Administration and Development*, **4**.

Coulson, A. (1981), 'Agricultural policies in mainland Tanzania' in Heyer, Roberts & Williams (1981).

Crook, R. (1983), 'Bureaucracy and politics in Ghana: a comparative perspective' in P. Lyon & J. Manor (eds). *Transfer and Transformation: Political Institutions in the New Commonwealth*, Leicester University Press.

De Wilde, J.C. (1984), *Agriculture, Marketing and Pricing in Sub-Saharan Africa*, Los Angeles, University of California African Studies Center.

Dunsire, A. (1978), *The Execution Process, Vol. 2: Control in a Bureaucracy*. Oxford, Martin Robertson.

Faber, M. & Green, R.H. (1985), 'Sub-Saharan Africa's economic malaise' in Rose (1985).

Fauré, Y-A. & Médard, J-F. (1982), *Etat et Bourgeoisie en Côte d'Ivoire*, Paris, Editions Karthala.

Filippi–Wilhelm, L. (1985), 'Traders and marketing boards in Upper Volta' in Arhin *et al.* (1985).

Forrest, T. (1981), 'Agricultural policies in Nigeria, 1900–78' in Heyer, Roberts & Williams, (1981).

Francis, P. (1984), 'Consequences of the 1978 land nationalization in Nigeria', *Africa* **54**.

Furse, Sir R. (1962), *Aucuparius*, London, Oxford University Press.

Garcia-Zamor, J.C. & Mayo-Smith, I. (1983), 'Administrative reform in Haiti: problems, progress and prospects', *Public Admin. and Development*, **3**.

Gbetibouo, M & Delgado, C.L. (1984), 'Lessons and constraints of export crop led growth: cocoa in Ivory Coast' in Zartman & Delgado (1984).

Ghai, D. & Radwan, S. (1983), *Agrarian Policies and Rural Poverty in Africa*, Geneva, ILO.

Ghai, D. & Smith, L. (1987), *Agricultural Prices Policy and Equity in Sub-Saharan Africa*, Boulder, Colorado, Lynne Rienner Inc.

Good, K. (1986), 'The reproduction of weakness in the state and agriculture: the Zambian experience', *African Affairs*, **85**.

Guy-Peters, B. (1978), *The Politics of Bureaucracy*, New York, Longman.

Hanlon, J. (1984), *Mozambique: the Revolution Under Fire*, London, Zed Books.

Hart, K. (1982), *The Political Economy of West African Agriculture*, Cambridge, Cambridge University Press.

Hecht, R.M. (1983), 'The Ivory Coast economic "miracle": what benefits for peasant farmers?', *Journal of Modern African Studies*, **21**.

Hesp, P. & van der Laan, L. (1985), 'Marketing Boards in Tropical Africa: a survey' in Arhin *et al.* (1985).

Heyer, J. (1981), 'Agricultural development policy in Kenya from the colonial period to 1975' in Heyer, Roberts & Williams.

Heyer, J., Roberts, P. & Williams, G. (1981), *Rural Development in Tropical Africa*, London, Macmillan.

Hodder-Williams, R. (1984), *An Introduction to the Politics of Tropical Africa*, London, G. Allen & Unwin.

Hopkins, A.G. (1973), *An Economic History of West Africa*, London, Longman.

Hyden, G. (1980), *Beyond Ujamaa in Tanzania: Underdevelopment and an Uncaptured Peasantry*, London, Heinemann.

— (1983), *No Shortcuts to Progress: African Development Management in Perspective*. London, Heinemann.

— (1985), 'Urban Growth and Rural Development' in Carter & O'Meara (1985).

Jackson, R.H. & Rosberg, C.G. (1982), *Personal Rule in Black Africa: Prince Autocrat, Prophet Tyrant*, Berkeley, Univesity of California Press.

— (1984), 'Popular legitimacy in African multi-ethnic states', *Journal of Modern African Studies*, **22**.

— (1985), 'The marginality of African states' in Carter & O'Meara (1985).

Jones, D.B. (1982), 'State structures in new nations: the case of primary agricultural marketing in Africa', *Journal of Modern African Studies*, **20**.

Jones, W.O. (1960), 'Economic man in Africa', *Food Research Institute Studies* **1**.

Joseph, R. (1984), 'Class state and prebendal politics in Nigeria' in Kasfir (1984).

Kasfir, N. (1984), *Class and State in Africa*, London, Frank Cass.

Killick, T. & House, W.T. (1983), 'Social justice and development policy in Kenya's rural economy' in Ghai & Radwan (1983).

Kitching, G. (1982), *Development and Underdevelopment in Historical Perspective*, London, Methuen.

Kochanek, S.A. (1985), 'The politics of regulation; Rajiv's new mantras', *Journal of Commonwealth and Comparative Politics*, **23**.

Koehn, P. (1983), 'The role of public administrators in public policy making: practice and prospects in Nigeria', *Public Admin. and Development*, **3**.

Lea, D. & Chaudhri, D. (eds) (1983), *Rural Development and the State*, London, Methuen.

Lee, E. (1983), 'Export-led rural development: the Ivory Coast' in Ghai & Radwan (1983).

Leys, C. (1971), 'Political perspectives' in D. Seers & L. Joy (eds), *Development in a Divided World*, Harmondsworth, Penguin.

— (1978), 'Capital accumulation class and dependency; the significance of the Kenyan case', *The Socialist Register 1978*.

Lipton, M. (1977), *Why Poor People Stay Poor: Urban Bias in World Development*, London, Temple Smith.

— (1985), 'Research and the design of a policy frame for agriculture' in Rose (1985).

Livingstone, I. (1985), 'Agricultural development strategy and agricultural pricing policy in Malawi' in Arhin *et al.* (1985).

Lofchie, M. (1985), 'Africa's agrarian malaise' in Carter & O'Meara (1985).

Luke, D.F. (1986), 'Trends in development administration: the continuing challenge to the efficacy of the post colonial state in the Third World', *Public Admin. and Development*, **6**.

Mars, T. (1986), 'State and agriculture in Africa: a case of means and ends', *IDS Bulletin*, **17**.

Mawhood, P. (1983), *Local Government in the Third World: the Experience of Tropical Africa*, Chichester, J. Wiley.

Michel, G. & Noel, M. (1984), 'The Ivorian Economy and alternative trade regimes' in Zartman & Delgado (1984).

Munro, J. Forbes (1984), *Britain in Tropical Africa 1880–1960*, London, Macmillan, for Economic History Society.

Munslow, B. (1984), 'State intervention in agriculture; the Mozambican experience', *Journal of Modern African Studies*, **22**.

Murray, D.J. (1983), 'The World Bank's perspective on how to improve administration', *Public Admin. and Development*, **3**.

Newbury, M.C. (1984), 'Dead, buried or just underground? The privatization of the state in Zaire', *Canadian Journal of African Studies* **18**.

Price, R. (1984), 'Neo-colonialism and Ghana's economic decline; a critical assessment', *Canadian Journal of African Studies*, **18**.

Raikes, P. 91975), 'Ujamaa and rural socialism', *Review of African Political Economy*, **3**.

Randall, V. & Theobald, R. (1985), *Political Change and Underdevelopment*, Basingstoke, Macmillan.

Rimmer, D. (1984), *The Economies of West Africa*, London, Weidenfeld & Nicolson.

Robertson, A.F. (1984), *People and the State: an Anthropology of Planned Development*, Cambridge, Cambridge University Press.

Roesch, O. (1984), 'Peasants and collective agriculture in Mozambique' in Barker (1984).

Rose, T. (ed.) (1985), *Crisis and Recovery in Sub-Saharan Africa*, Paris, OECD.

Roth, G. (1968), 'Personal rulership, patrimonialism and empire building in the new states', *World Politics*, **20**.

Rudolph, L.I. & Rudolph, S.H. (1979), 'Authority and power in bureaucratic and patrimonial administration; a revisionist interpretation of Weber', *World Politics*, **31**.

Sandbrook, R. (1981), 'Is socialism possible in Africa?', *Journal of Commonwealth and Comparative Politics*, **19**.

— (1985), *The Politics of Africa's Economic Stagnation*, Cambridge, Cambridge University Press.

Saul, J. (1979), *The State and Revolution in East Africa*, London, Heinemann.

Schaffer, B. (1969), 'The deadlock in development administration' in C. Leys (ed.) *Politics and Change in Developing Countries*, Cambridge, Cambridge University Press.

— (1978), 'Administrative legacies and links in the post colonial state; preparation, training and administrative reform', *Development and Change*, **9**.

& Lamb, G. (1981), *Can Equity Be Organised?* Farnborough, UNESCO, Gower.

Schoepf, B.G. & C. (1984), 'State, bureaucracy and peasants in the Lufira Valley', *Canadian Journal of African Studies*, **18**.

Self, P. (1985), *Political Theories of Modern Government*, London, G. Allen & Unwin.

Shepherd, A. (1981), 'Agrarian change in Northern Ghana' in Heyer, Roberts & Williams (1981).

Swainson, N. (1980), *The Development of Corporate Capitalism in Kenya*, London, Heinemann.

— (1986), 'Public policy in the development of export crops: pineapples and tea in Kenya', *IDS Bulletin*, **17**.

Tangri, R. (1985), *Politics in Sub-Saharan Africa*, London, James Currey.

Teal, F. (1986), 'The foreign exchange regime and growth; a comparison of Ghana and the Ivory Coast', *African Affairs*, **85**.

Tordoff, W. (1984), *Government and Politics in Sub-Saharan Africa*, London, Macmillan.

Von Freyhold, M. (1979), *Ujamaa Villages in Tanzania: analysis of a Social Experiment*, London, Heinemann.

Watts, M. & Shenton, R. (1984), 'State and agrarian transformation in Nigeria' in Barker (1984).

Watts, M.J. & Bassett, T.J. (1986), 'Politics, the state and agrarian development: a comparative study of Nigeria and the Ivory Coast', *Political Geography Quarterly*, **2**.

White, G. (1986), 'Developmental states and African agriculture: an editorial preface', *IDS Bulletin*, **17**.

Williams, G. (1976), 'Taking the part of the peasants' in P.C.W. Gutkind & I. Wallerstein (eds), *The Political Economy of Contemporary Africa*, Beverly Hills, Sage.

— (1981), 'The World Bank and the peasant problem' in Heyer, Roberts & Williams (1981).

— (1985), 'Marketing with and without marketing boards: the origins of state Marketing Boards in Nigeria', *Review of African Political Economy*, **34**.

World Bank (1975), *The Assault on World Poverty*, Baltimore.

— (1981), *Accelerated Development in Sub-Saharan Africa: an Agenda for Action*, Washington DC.

— (1983), *World Development Report*, Washington DC.

Young, C., Sherman, N. & Rose, T. (1981), *Co-operatives and Development; Agricultural Politics in Ghana and Uganda*, Madison, University of Wisconsin Press.

Young, C. (1982), *Ideology and Development in Africa*, New Haven and London, Yale University Press.

— (1984), 'Zaire: is there a state?' *Canadian Journal of African Studies*, **18**.

Zartman, I.W. & Delgado, C. (eds) (1984), *The Political Economy of Ivory Coast*, New York, Praeger.

9 The African Food Crisis of 1982–1986: A Provisional Review

John Borton and Edward Clay

Acknowledgements

The authors would like to thank Douglas Rimmer of the Centre of West African Studies at Birmingham University, Professor M.B. Gleave of the Department of Geography, Salford University, and the other participants at the ESRC Conference on Rural Transformation in Tropical Africa, as well as Ray Bush of the Department of Politics at Leeds University and Tony Jackson of OXFAM who have commented on earlier drafts of this paper.

Introduction

It is perhaps still too soon to provide a 'balanced' review of the recent 'African food crisis'. Until much more research has been done, such complex happenings are the subject of conflicting interpretations of issues, such as the relative importance of the causal factors and the effectiveness of the international early warning systems that had been put in place after the food crisis of the early 1970s.

We have attempted to survey those academic contributions that are available, together with some of the extensive, but generally unavailable, material produced by the various institutions involved in the response to the crisis; these include the governments of the affected countries, the various multilateral and bilateral donor agencies and the non-governmental organizations (NGOs). Our intention is to clarify the scope of the debate on the nature or the crisis, its causes and the issues raised by the response to it. We also highlight areas that are considered to be in particular need of further research.

A problem of the published literature commented upon by several authors (e.g. Allison & Green, 1985) is the extent to which the diversity of economic, political and environmental conditions in Sub-Saharan Africa is obscured by the attempt at generalizations for the whole region. Even a cursory review of the documentation reveals that the recent food crisis and the responses to it have involved widely differing experiences within, as well as between, countries. Our approach, which allows us to show the problem raised by generalizations about 'the African food crisis' is to consider selected cases. We have focused in the second half of the paper on the specific experiences in Ethiopia, Kenya and Botswana. The concentration on three cases better documented in the English language literature has made our task of review more manageable. This case approach we hope will identify 'issues' for further research and subsequent attempts to synthesize recent experiences.

Statistics and definitions

Food production

A production index which has been widely reproduced is that based on United States Department of Agriculture data of per capita food production for the period 1961–65 to 1983, comparing trends in Sub-Saharan Africa, Latin America and Asia (World Bank, 1984). The decline in Sub-Saharan Africa's per capita food production appears in stark contrast to the increases in the other two regions. The index shows a variable rate of decline, with the most severe falls occurring during 1969–73 and 1981–83. The fall between 1982–83 appears to have been the most dramatic for two decades. The updating of the index indicates a levelling-off in 1984 and a significant recovery in 1985 (USDA, 1985; Lofchie, 1986). In some countries, such as the CILSS group, Ghana, Zimbabwe and Kenya, the recovery appears to be dramatic, with record production levels being recorded in 1985 and 1986 (Club du Sahel, 1985). Consequently, international food policy discussions are currently as much dominated by problems of short-term surpluses as they are by considerations of scarcity.

Food imports

Food imports to Africa, both commercial and food aid, have increased significantly since the 1960s. Annual average cereals imports, which were 1.18 million tonnes during 1961–63 and 2.35 million tonnes during 1969–71, increased dramatically to 8.7 million tonnes during 1980–82 and peaked at 12.7 million tonnes in 1984/5 (World Bank, 1984; Benson & Clay,1986).

Food availability

An important question is whether food imports managed, in aggregate terms, to offset the decline in domestic food production. Treating cereals separately, recent data prepared by the World Food Programme (using a slightly different definition of Sub-Saharan Africa than that used by the World Bank) show that per capita availability during the period 1979/80 to 1984/5 peaked at 147.9 kg. in 1981/2. Thereafter, the figures show a significant fall to 136.8 kg. in 1982/3 and 123.4 kg. in 1983/4 (Benson & Clay, 1986).

Of course, cereals contribute only part of the total food supply in Africa. In an attempt to see what the trends in total food availability were in the twenty worst-affected countries (as defined by the FAO/WFP Task Force), WFP have compiled indices for 'apparent total caloric food consumption' (Benson & Clay, 1986). Care does need to be taken in drawing any significant conclusions from such data as they are bound to obscure considerable variations between and within countries. Nevertheless, per capita calorie consumption in the twenty countries appears to have been below 1970 levels up to 1976 and above 1970 levels between 1978 and 1982. Thereafter, the per capita index fell steeply. In view of the recovery in production in many countries noted earlier, it is realistic to expect that when the index is updated it will show a fairly steep increase during 1985 and 1986.

The definition of a food crisis

As the statistics above show, Sub-Saharan Africa was considered to be experiencing a problem of stagnant or declining food production long before the dramatic declines between 1982 and 1985 which many understand to be the 'food crisis' proper (FAO, 1983). The literature on the chronic food problem was extensive before the food crisis began in earnest.

Though some referred to this as the Agrarian Crisis (Berry, 1983), others discussed it as an Economic Crisis because of the two-way relationship between the state of the agriculture sectors and the national economies (World Bank, 1981). Occasionally all the crises were lumped together under the term 'The African Crisis'.

So what is meant by the 'African food crisis'? Are we to use it to describe the chronic problem, or the acute problem that appears to have occurred between 1982 and 1985? Curiously, we have not come across satisfactory definitions of the specific term 'food crisis' in the literature. Definitions are available for 'famine' (Cutler, 1985 and Sen, 1981) and for 'food security' (FAO, 1984a; Lipton & Heald, 1984; World Bank, 1986a). Those for food security emphasize access to sufficient food. Thus, a recent Policy Study by the World Bank defines food security as 'access by all people at all times to enough food for an active and healthy life' (World Bank, 1986a). The same study distinguishes between 'chronic' and 'transitory' food insecurity and sees famine as 'the worst form of transitory food security'. In view of the over-use of the word 'crisis' in relation to Africa, transitory food insecurity is probably a more useful, though less handy, term to describe the phenomenon referred to as the 'African Food Crisis'. For the purpose of this paper we take the period covered by the food crisis to be from 1982 to 1986. The implicit definition of this crisis in most writing is of a process in which governments and ultimately the international donor community became involved in extraordinary actions or responses to what was perceived to be famine and the risk of famine in many parts of Africa.

Whilst on the subject of definitions, it is worth noting the working definition of emergencies used by a major institutional actor in the response system, the World Food Programme. Emergencies are defined as: 'urgent situations, in which suffering or loss of livestock [has occurred] and which the Government concerned has not the means to remedy; and it is a demonstrably abnormal event which produces dislocation in the life of a community on an exceptional scale' (WFP, 1970).

The emphasis on a government's ability to cope with a situation is to be expected of an agency of the United Nations, a family of institutions that regards all governments with deference. Nevertheless, there is considerable amibiguity over whether or not a government requires external assistance in order to cope. For instance, during the present drought Botswana has received substantial tonnages of food aid, even though it maintains its international financial reserves at a very high level. Thus, in 1984, Botswana's gross international reserves were equivalent to 6.3 months of import coverage, whilst the average for Sub-Saharan Africa was 1.6 months (World Bank, 1986c). When such ambiguity is combined with the severe economic difficulties experienced by most countries (see below) and the increasing tendency of governments and donors to view food aid as a significant economic resource (Stevens, 1986), it does raise the possibility that some governments might have exaggerated the extent of an emergency to gain access to the resources of the International Emergency Food Reserve (IEFR) and bilateral emergency assistance. The lack of alternative sources of finance to cope with the short-term balance of payments and economic adjustment problems makes emergency food aid an attractive resource.

The validity of the statistics

The two main sources of Africa-wide production data are the Food and Agriculture Organisation (FAO) and the United States Department of Agriculture (USDA). Both rely heavily on data provided by African governments. The FAO publishes data supplied by the governments with little modification, as is the practice of United Nations specialized agencies. The USDA makes some adjustments on the basis of its assessment of the reliability of the data and their historical consistency (Paulino & Tseng, 1980). However, with regard to the data used in Global Information and Early Warning System, it should be noted that the FAO draws on information from a variety of government and non-government sources when making its estimate of expected production. Such estimates are revised throughout the crop cycle as more information becomes available (FAO, 1987). Several writers note that the accuracy of African food production statistics is seriously open to question (Berry, 1984; ODI, 1985). In many countries, the overwhelming proportion of food produced is for own consumption by farming households. Agricultural census and sample surveys are subject to many sources of error. Increased government regulation of agricultural marketing during the 1970s provoked widespread resistance and evasion by producers and traders. The result appears to have been varying combinations of: the development of illegal or 'parallel' markets; higher consumption levels by subsistence households' and some decline in output (Harriss, 1979; Hyden, 1983). These factors lead Berry (1984) to suggest that:

It is likely that official statistics have diverged further and further from actual output in recent years, but we do not know the magnitude or, in many cases, even the direction of the divergence.

The temptation for a government to manipulate production data to increase the size of its food deficit for aid negotiation purposes has already been noted.[1] Equally, some governments appear to have accepted initially excessive estimates of production shortfalls and, acting in good faith, overcommitted their own scarce financial resources. Africa did experience a food crisis. The incidence of famine is proof of the most awful kind that there was a severe food crisis in several countries. But the unreliability of the data implies that researchers should re-examine with care prevailing notions of the extent and sources of the crisis at a country and regional level.

The extent and severity of the crisis

The drought-induced, or drought-intensified, food crisis appears to have been the worst for several decades. Whereas the severe drought of the early 1970s affected countries in the Sahel and the Horn, the recent crisis affected not only these, but also countries in Southern and Eastern Africa (Christensen & Witucki, 1986). Indeed, only those countries in the central western part of the region appear to have been unaffected.

According to the FAO, twenty-two African countries were facing serious food shortages by May 1983 when the Director-General launched a special appeal for increased aid to the affected counties. By the end of 1983 this list had increased to twenty-four countries. It increased to twenty-seven by September 1984 and fell to twenty-one in December 1984. [2] By late 1986 the list had been reduced to Cape Verde, Ethiopia, Sudan, Angola, Mozambique, Botswana and Lesotho (FAO, 1986b).

According to Gill (1986), the lists were 'almost certainly too long', and they were publicly criticized by British-based NGOs (Foreign Affairs Committee, 1985). It was not until early 1985 that the FAO highlighted the worst-affected countries (FAO, 1985a). Sudan was left off the list until late-1984, even though it was clearly experiencing severe food deficiency before then, apparently because the government was reluctant to acknowledge that it had a problem (Gill, 1986).

The problematic nature of such lists is further illustrated by the case of Cape Verde. This small state has experienced continuous drought since the late 1960s and is dependent on imports for over 90 per cent of its food grain consumption. Most of these imports are satisfied by programme food aid. Intensification of drought in 1985 made only a minor difference to the overall food balance (Binsbergen, 1986).

The severity of the crisis is virtually impossible to assess objectively. No reliable estimates are available of the numbers who died as a direct result of the food crisis. Journalists occasionally talk of 'up to three million' (eg. ITN News, 5 September 1986). Some 250,000 are estimated to have died in the Sahel Drought and Ethiopian famine of the early 1970s (Wijkman & Timberlake, 1984; Rivers *et al.*, 1976). In February 1985 the UN Office for Emergency Operations in Africa estimated that 150 million people living in twenty critical countries were affected, of whom 30 million were seriously affected and 10 million had abandoned their homes in search of food and water (cited in UNOEOA, 1986). There is general agreement that the worst-hit countries were Ethiopia, Sudan, Mozambique, Chad and Mali where famine or widespread starvation occurred (FAO, 1985a; ODI, 1985; USAID, 1986).

Sources of crisis

A range of overlapping and interacting factors have been cited as contributing to the food crisis (Berry, 1984). Some factors such as abnormal rainfall patterns clearly have a direct causal link, whilst other factors, such as the erosion of traditional coping mechanisms or the international debt crisis, have a less direct link but have undoubtedly contributed to an increased level of vulnerability of many countries or of groups within these countries.

At the outset it is worth pointing out that four out of the five worst-affected countries were beset by civil war or externally financed insurgency. In looking for the sources of the crisis we need to look not only at these five, but also at the reasons why so many areas were affected and what it was that made rural populations more vulnerable.

Within the literature there is a tendency to give particular attention to facets of the crisis and its underlying causation that reflect the background discipline of those making the contributions. Thus, environmental scientists are more likely to explore and lay greater stress on matters such as climatic change and land degradation (e.g. Timberlake, 1985). In contrast, economists attach greater importance to the impact of a sharply deteriorating external environment since 1979. For our part, we do not claim to be objective, but, recognizing contributions by researchers writing within different discourses, we offer a 'map' of the debate on the crisis. We feel it helpful to say in advance that we do not see any one cause of the crisis, preferring instead to view it as a 'concatenation process' whereby a complex mix of events and processes variously interact in time and space (Currey, 1984).

Rainfall and climatic trends

All writers agree that poor rains and drought were a significant factor in contributing to the food crisis. Most accounts describe a common pattern. For example:

Poor rains in 1982, 1983 and 1984, in the southern African countries, led to the worst food crisis of the century. The Sahel countries ... and the countries in the horn of Africa ... had more localised droughts in 1983 followed by widespread drought and famine in 1984, especially in Chad, Mali, Sudan and Ethiopia. [Overseas Development Institute, 1985.]

However, there is a disagreement over the relative importance of the poor rains and inconsistency between accounts of the chronology of the poor rains.[3]

There are several reasons why such differences can occur. Firstly, few countries in Africa are well covered by rainfall recording stations. In some cases the coverage has worsened as a result of the economic crisis. Thus the Meteorological Services Department in Ghana was only able to pay its staff intermittently and recording equipment was not maintained. During 1983 only four of the twenty-two synoptic stations were reporting and the Department had only one functioning vehicle (Ussher, Acting Deputy Director, Meteorological Services Department: personal communication, 1985).

Secondly, rainfall in arid and semi-arid areas of Africa is highly variable both spatially and temporally (Jones, 1986). Localized droughts can occur in areas not covered by the rainfall recording network. A few high-intensity storms can precipitate an entire season's rainfall, making the aggregate total appear 'normal', yet crops may fail owing to the long dry periods between such events. Taken together, such factors make it difficult to use such terms as 'good', 'bad' and 'normal' with any real objectivity.

Agro-meteorological models offer a more accurate method of measuring the effect of highly variable rainfall on cereal crops than simple recordings of rainfall. An example of such a model is that developed by Frere and Popov which measures the moisture satisfaction indices for the main crops throughout the growing season (FAO, 1979). The FAO is presently assisting several African governments to set up such monitoring capacities as part of national and regional early warning systems (e.g. FAO, 1983). But it remains to be seen whether such systems will be maintained once external funding is phased out.

In a recent review of climatic trends, Wigley & Farmer (1986) show convincingly that for Sahelian Africa there has been a general decline in rainfall beginning in the mid-1950s and note the 'unprecedented length and severity of the [recent Sahel] drought compared with other droughts of the instrumental period'. For eastern Africa, trends in average rainfall are less clear (Ogallo, 1984). Recent work in central and eastern Kenya failed to discern any strong trends or cycles within the instrumental period, though it was acknowledged that 'dramatic changes [had occurred] on the time scale of a century or more' (Downing, Mungai & Muturi, 1985). In southern Africa, Tyson has asserted the existence of a quasi-twenty year oscillation of ten predominantly wet years followed by ten predominantly dry years and, in 1979, on the basis of this model, predicted with unerring accuracy that southern Africa would experience: 'a series of below normal rainfall years in the eighties and that extended droughts of the kind experienced in the sixties will again be experienced in the eighties' (Tyson, 1979).

Several hypotheses have been put forward to explain those trends that have been identified on the continent, such as increasing levels of carbon dioxide, sea surface temperatures and atmospheric dust. None have been conclusively proven (Wigley & Farmer, 1986). The possibility of human activities accentuating existing climatic trends, through what are refered to as bio-geophysical feedbacks, has attracted considerable interest. Thus, Charney (1975) has suggested that vegetation changes caused by overgrazing or deforestation would cause albedo (surface reflectivity) changes which could act to amplify or prolong an existing drought.

The economic crisis

All agree that the severe economic problems experienced by Sub-Saharan Africa contributed significantly to the food crisis (e.g. Timberlake, 1985; World Bank, 1986c; Lofchie, 1986; Office of Technology Assessment, 1984). Low-income Africa is poorer in 1986 than it was a generation ago in 1960 (World Bank, 1986c). Because of the extent of poverty in the region, it is considered to be more vulnerable to disasters than richer areas of the world, less able to cope without external assistance and more likely to experience a higher death toll as a result of disasters (Wijkman & Timberlake, 1984; Cuny, 1983).

Per capita annual GDP, which had been growing by an average of 2.75 per cent in the first half of the 1970s, slowed down to 0.2 per cent during the second half of the decade. Thereafter, per capital GDP consistently declined, the average for 1980–84 being minus 4.4 per cent (World Bank, 1986c).[4] The declines experienced by most countries resulted in severe cuts in government expenditure and shortages of foreign exchange. The level of public service provision was reduced and shortages of even the most basic goods became a way of life in many countries. The effects of the economic problems on the levels of support to African farmers, health care and poverty have been well documented (UNICEF, 1984; Chambers, 1985; Howell, 1985).

There is now a substantial body of literature on the economic crisis in the region. Much of it has been in the form of contributions to the debate stimulated by the publication by the World Bank in late 1981 of the report 'Accelerated Development in Sub-Saharan Africa: An Agenda for Action', (World Bank, 1981). Although not a totally new analysis of Sub-Saharan Africa's economic problems (Allison & Green, 1985), the report's emphasis on 'domestic policy inadequacies' and implicit preference for an enhance role for markets and consequent reduction in the role of the state were controversial.

The subsequent debate has been between those who see the economic crisis as primarily a product of external shocks (e.g. G.K. Helleiner cited in Green, 1986) and those who see the problem largely in terms of the failures of domestic policy (e.g. Sender & Smith, 1984). Gradually the two camps have moved from their original positions and there is now a large measure of common understanding (Allison & Green, 1985; Sender & Smith, 1984). In reflecting on the debate, Colclough (1985) notes that, 'protagonists on all sides have been particularly prone to erect "straw men" in their contributions' and blames this partly on the poor data available and the high degree of generalization employed. Though some have deplored the fact that 'as the flow of words has increased the crisis in Africa has deepened' (Please & Amoako, 1984), many would probably agree that 'the dialogue ... has clearly been necessary and in many respects positive' (Allison & Green, 1985).

Recognizing the risk of considerable over-simplification, it is useful to set the context in terms of a brief account of the background to the economic crisis, beginning with the external environment. In the mid-1970s many of the non-oil exporting countries experienced a boom and bust cycle in the prices of their main export earners — coffee, cocoa, groundnuts, beef, sugar, sisal and phosphate (World Bank, 1984). Public revenues increased dramatically in many countries and governments sharply increased their spending. Some borrowed heavily from abroad on the strength of their creditworthiness and in the expectation of continuing high export earnings. Much of the additional revenue and credit went into large public investments, many of which contributed little to economic growth or to generating foreign exchange (World Bank, 1984).

When the collapse in prices came, it was exacerbated for the oil-importing countries by the oil price shock of 1979–80 which resulted in dramatically increased fuel import bills and substantial falls in the level of foreign exchange reserves. Governments were reluctant to reduce their spending and some, tempted by interest rates that then appeared attractive, continued to borrow, thereby storing up debt-servicing problems for the future. Estimates of the total external debt in 1984 are as high as $130–135 billion, giving an average debt service ratio in the region of 35 per cent (Green & Griffith-Jones, 1985). With the deep recession in the Western industrial economies, the terms of trade for non-oil primary commodities continued to fall, declining by 27 per cent in current dollar terms between 1980 and 1982. This was equivalent to a 2.4 per cent decline in GDP for the low-income group of countries in the region (World Bank, 1984).

During the 1970s many governments pursued policies and managed their economies in ways that were distinctly biased against agriculture (Bates, 1981). Thus, at the beginning of the downturn in commodity prices, many governments delayed in reducing the high export taxes imposed during the boom period (Roberts, 1986). They were also slow to adjust their official exchange rates as a result of their desire to keep imports (primarily for consumption in the urban areas) cheap. Exchange rate over-valuation was particularly severe in, for example, Ghana, Tanzania and Nigeria (World Bank, 1986b). The result was the uncompetitiveness of many African exports and lack of incentive to producers of export crops to maintain their production. This led to reduced output, smuggling into neighbouring countries offering higher real producer prices and declines in the shares of the markets held by several African countries. This exacerbated the balance of payments and foreign exchange problems.

Many governments had become heavily involved in agricultural marketing, ostensibly as a way of preventing exploitation of producers and consumers by private traders. In many countries 'de jure' public monopolies sell agricultural inputs, market outputs and in some cases distribute consumer goods (Bates, 1981). The performance of many of these parastatals has been poor and in some cases they have accounted for a significant proportion of government spending (e.g. Ellis, 1982). Prices to urban consumers have often been held down, effectively taxing rural producers. As noted earlier, the result has been to reduce the amount sold through official channels. With the reductions in government revenues and intensified foreign exchange difficulties from the late 1970s, the performance of parastatals worsened, farmers were poorly supplied with inputs and shortages of even basic consumer goods became common — probably leading to an even greater withdrawal of producers from the money economy. In consequence many countries and their rural populations were by 1981/2 highly vulnerable to further shocks.

Demographic pressure

The population of Sub-Saharan Africa is growing at 3.1 per cent per annum, faster than that of any other continent, and its 1980 population of 359 million will probably double by the turn of the century and significantly more than triple by the year 2020 (World Bank, 1984). This is unprecedented in human history and exerts considerable pressure on the region's natural resources and social systems.

Environmental degradation

Opinion is divided on the overall quality of the region's soils. The long-held view has been that they are of inherently poorer quality and more fragile than in more temperate areas (e.g. Gourou, 1953; Kamarck, 1976; Lofchie & Commins, 1984). Some soils, such as the volcanic soils of the Kenyan Highlands, are recognized to be rich in nutrients, but they are seen as exceptions to the rule (Office of Technology Assessment, 1984). The long-held view has been questioned by Moss (1981), who has pointed to numerous instances from more temperate areas where deforestation, over-grazing and over-cultivation have resulted in 'ecological disasters'.

Most agricultural systems in Africa are rainfed and are considered to make extensive use of land (i.e. to be 'land intensive') as a result of the widespread practices of shifting cultivation and employing long fallow periods (Levi & Havinden, 1982). Only limited use is made of manure and off-farm inputs (Ruthenberg, 1980). Irrigation plays an insignificant role in arable production in the region. In most countries, less than 5 per cent of the cultivated area is under irrigation, compared to around 30 per cent in India. In only two countries (Madagascar and the Sudan) does irrigated land account for more than 10 per cent of the cultivated area (World Bank, 1981; Eicher, 1985). Thus, most agricultural production in Sub-Saharan Africa is considered to be of the 'low input–low output' type and yields per hectare of staple crops are lower in Africa than in Asia or Latin America (Office of Technology Assessment, 1984).

The danger that rapidly increasing human and animal populations may lead to reduced crop or grazing yields, physical degradation and ultimately the loss of topsoil through erosion or desertification is widely recognized (Boserup, 1965; UN Conference on Desertification, 1977; Lagemann, 1977; Blaikie, 1985). Some writers have placed considerable emphasis on the contribution of environmental mismanagement to the food crisis. Both Timberlake (1985) and Tinker (1985) use the phrase 'environmental bankruptcy' to describe the situation. Tinker comes dangerously close to stating that human disasters are caused primarily by environmental mismanagement. Despite the extraordinary difficulties of quantifying the extent of the problem, McPherson (1984) has estimated that, with the current rate of soil loss, Africa could experience a decline in its potential rainfed crop production of about 15 per cent during the next two decades.

The relationship between population growth and environmental degradation is, however, extremely complex and, to make matters more difficult, several authors have noted the lack of comprehensive and quantified studies of the subject (Sandford, 1983; Eicher, 1985). Agricultural systems in the region are by no means static, there being numerous examples of innovation and adaptation in response to increasing population densities (Gleave & White, 1969; Gleave, 1980; Ruthenberg, 1980). Despite such adaptations, it is nevertheless quite possible that, in many instances, they are simply unable to keep pace with the additional demands being exerted by the unprecedented rates of population growth being experienced. It is probably reasonable then to agree with the World Bank (1984), 'that part of the decrease in agricultural output per capita in the 1970s can be explained by population pressure on arable land'.

The failure of agricultural research

The inability of domestic food production to keep pace with the rate of population growth and the successes of the 'Green Revolution' in Asia have led to a questioning of why agricultural research in Africa has not emulated the Asian experience. Spending on agricultural research and extension in Sub-Saharan Africa appears high in comparison with South Asian countries. Other factors are therefore identified to explain the poor performance of agricultural research in the region: a low output of research in relation to the high cost of the scientists (many are donor-funded expatriates); the spread of scientists among a large number of small research stations (reflecting the number of countries with comparatively small populations and a lack of regional co-operation); and the high turnover of both local and expatriate staff (Lipton, 1985). Even more significant in terms of food production in the region is the bias towards export crops and rich people's productd (Pinstrup-Anderson, 1982).

Social transformation

A prominent theme in radical writing is the effects of capitalist penetration on African agriculture (Berry, 1984; Palmer & Parsons,

1977; Hart, 1982). Evidence suggests that the process often results in the breakdown of indigenous social structures and practices that afforded a significant measure of food security (Cliffe & Moorsom, 1979). In many cases, modern structures have shown themselves unable to replace the levels of food security formerly enjoyed (Appeldoorn, 1981). A problem of such analyses is that data on the degree of security afforded by the original structures is hard to come by. We do know, however, that Ethiopia, for example, has been famine-prone for several centuries (Pankhurst, 1986; Aseffa, 1986). Even if it can be proved for other countries that the pre-capitalist structures did cope, it is questionable whether they could have coped with the much larger populations now living in the more arid areas. And not everywhere has the process of capitalist penetration led to a reduced level of food security. For example, the people of rural Botswana have probably fared considerably better during the present drought than during drought of equal severity during the pre-colonial era.

Wars, refugees and superpower rivalry

Sub-Saharan Africa is generally considered to suffer from considerable political instability (World Bank, 1984; Office of Technology Assessment, 1984). According to Tinker (1985), the past twenty-five years have seen over seventy coups and the assassination of thirteen heads of state. Another expression of the degree of instability is the high proportion of refugees in Africa. With only one-tenth of the world's population, Africa contains at least one-quarter of the world's refugees (World Bank, 1984); in 1982 there were just under 2.7 million in Africa (UNHCR cited in ODI, 1983) and the number has almost definitely increased since. According to the Overseas Development Institute (1983), the numbers have grown rapidly over the last ten years, as the result of increased armed conflict and civil strife coupled with natural disaster and economic instability.

As well as being a product of the region's instability, Africa's refugees must also count among one of its contributory causes since, despite the assistance provided to them by the UNHCR and WFP, a large refugee population can place an 'enormous strain on already fragile economic and social systems and limited natural resources' (ODI, 1983). The aggregate statistics show 1 in 200 Africans to be a refugee (World Bank, 1984), but this hides the very high concentrations in a few countries. Thus, in 1982, the figures were 1 in 7 in Somalia, 1 in 21 in Burundi and 1 in 32 in Sudan (UNHCR cited in ODI, 1983). The environmental impact of Somalia's large refugee population has been described by Young (1985).

Students of African politics and international relations tend to see the root causes of such instability in terms of the problems of post-colonial African states (e.g. tribalism, nonsensical borders) and the exploitation of these problems by foreign powers (Hyden, 1983).

The two superpowers are identified as the major exploiters of such problems and it is seen as no accident that the strategically important Horn of Africa should account for well over half of Africa's refugee population (Halliday & Molyneux, 1986; King, 1986). Some states within the region, notably Libya and South Africa, are also seen as causing instability, apparently without any direct support from either of the superpowers.

Instability is considered to have contributed to the food crisis in a variety of ways. For example, in Ghana political instability contributed to the decline in food availability, partly by making it more difficult for farmers to market their produce. However, it was often difficult to separate the role of political instability from that of economic factors (Borton & Shoham, 1986).

In countries experiencing civil war, far more than the farm-to-market trade suffers. Crops can be destroyed by opposing forces or go untended through fear of attack or the farmers' absence. Critical as such events may be, the crucial factor is the disruption caused to the transport system and efforts to bring food into the area from outside. Within the literature, there is almost unanimous recognition of the role of the civil wars in Ethiopia, Chad, Mozambique and Sudan in propelling what were food crises resulting from drought, environmental and economic problems into full-blown famines (ODI, 1985; Office of Technology Assessment, 1984; USAID,1986; WFP, 1986a; Tickner, 1985).

Response to the crisis

The literature that is presently available on the response to the crisis can be broadly divided into two categories. The output by journalists working in the affected areas has been prolific, but it often depicts the response in terms of theatre and protagonists. A formal literature of agency performance in certain countries is now available, written either by the agencies' own staff or by independent researchers working on commissioned studies (e.g. WFP, 1986a; USAID, 1986; Pearson, 1986; Borton *et al.*, 1986). We can only review what happened using these sources of information.

Much of the journalistic literature describes the response purely in terms of the unprecedented levels of external assistance provided by donor agencies, NGOs and the general public in the wealthier countries. The internal response by governments, indigenous NGOs and the general public (both those directly affected and those less affected) is often overlooked. Many governments used foreign exchange reserves to import food on a commercial basis. Thus Kenya purchased some 378,000 tonnes of maize in 1984/5 at a cost of US$ 60 million

(World Bank, 1986d). Tanzania purchased some 84,000 tonnes of maize from Thailand in 1984 (Borton & Holt, 1986), at a time when its foreign exchange reserves were reduced to only nine days' import coverage (World Bank, 1986). In Kenya a National Relief Fund was launched by the President and has been well supported by citizens. In Sudan's severely affected Darfur Province, York (1985) has noted how branches of the Red Crescent Societies spread rapidly across the Province as local community leaders, teachers, health workers and merchants formed relief committees and later chose to turn them into Red Crescent branches.

Nevertheless, the international response was undoubtedly massive (World Bank, 1986c; Foreign Affairs Committee, 1985). Information is more readily available on the amount of food provided for relief than on financial assistance, which can be difficult to separate from normal flows. Total cereals food aid to Sub-Saharan Africa averaged 1.13 million tonnes over the five years from 1975/6 to 1979/80, and from 1980/81 to 1983/4 it averaged 2.58 million tonnes. In 1984/ 5 it increased to 4.95 million tonnes (Benson & Clay, 1986). The proportion of food aid approved for emergency relief also increased sharply, from only 14 per cent of receipts in 1979/80 to 51 per cent in 1984/5 (Benson & Clay, 1986).

Financial donations by the Western public were unprecedented — totalling several hundred million pounds (Twose, 1985). The level of the response is thought to have been increased above that to previous famines by the involvement of Western pop musicians in fund-raising and by public shock at the contrast between famine in Africa and the growing 'grain mountains' in the EEC. Pressure by the public is thought to have been a significant factor in increasing the level of response by Western governments (Gill, 1986).

Among the points raised by the evaluative literature is that the timing of the response by donors was often poor, particularly in Ethiopia (WFP, 1986a). There was more information-sharing among donors than during previous emergencies. The creation of the Africa Task Force Secretariat within WFP in early 1985 enabled donors to see when and where gaps in the requirements would occur (WFP, 1986a). At the country level, agency coordination varied considerably, being thought excellent in Ethiopia but poor in the early stages in the Sudan (WFP, 1986; Gill, 1986). The success of NGO fund-raising, combined with a preference by donors to rely on NGOs rather than untrusted or incapable agencies of host governments, resulted in unprecedented demands being made on the capacity of certain NGOs (Finucane in Clay & Everitt, 1985). Too great a reliance on resources provided by one donor can jeopardize the effectiveness of an NGO's response (Borton *et al.*, 1986). More resources should be put into ensuring a higher level of preparedness in the future (WFP, 1986a; USAID, 1986; Borton *et al.*, 1986).

The crisis in the case study countries*

Kenya

Kenya experienced its worst drought for several decades during 1984 (FAO, 1984b; World Bank, 1986d; Borton, 1987). The feature that made the drought so unusual was the failure of the 1984 'long rains' in Central and Rift Valley Provinces — the country's arable heartland.

Initial estimates by the Government of the severity of the situation were overly pessimistic and as additional information became available so the estimates of the cereal import requirement were gradually revised down throughout 1984. Thus, in its initial appeal to donors in June 1984, the Government estimated the total cereals import requirement to be between 1.3 and 1.5 million tonnes (FAO, 1984b). Eventually the donors, following FAO recommendations, supplied some 285,000 tonnes and the Government purchased a total of 572,000 tonnes.

As a result of some of the imports arriving late and the bumper harvest in 1985, maize stocks rose to the unprecedented level of 800,000 tonnes in February and Kenya was forced to re-export 126,000 tonnes of the less popular imported yellow maize at a considerable financial loss (World Bank, 1986d). This problem of lagged response and excess stocks after good rains is now widespread in the region.

The response strategy adopted by the Government was to give priority to 'market relief', i.e. to maintaining supplies of the staple cereals through the existing marketing channels, and it was to this end that the Government undertook such a substantial programme of commercial imports. It was intended that relief to those badly affected would be through the creation of temporary labour-intensive public works schemes and, in areas not covered by such schemes, by way of free-food distributions (Ray, 1984; Borton & Stephenson, 1984). In the event, the public works schemes were scaled down considerably, owing to limited implementation capacity, and the free-food distributions expanded to reach up to 1.5 million recipients.

Although the Government apparently failed to respond to the regional drought that affected northern and eastern areas of the country during 1983, it is generally considered that the Government dealt promptly and decisively with the much more serious situation in 1984 (World Bank, 1986d; Cohen & Lewis, 1987). The early decision to embark on a substantial commercial import programme has been identified as being crucial to the comparative success of the relief programme, since the commercial imports tided the country over until donated supplies began arriving in significant quantities in 1985. Kenya's ability to purchase contrasts with many other countries in the region. It can be largely

* This section is heavily based on Borton, 1987.

attributed to the maintenance of tea and coffee exports during 1984 at levels comparable with previous years and to the substantial increase in world tea prices during 1984.

In stressing the positive role of the Government, there is the possibility that the level and promptness of support by the donor community may be underestimated. The readiness of Western donors to support the Government's relief programme in the months immediately following its appeal in June 1984 has been contrasted by journalist to the support offered to Ethiopia during the same period. No less than 90 per cent of the food distributed through the governments free food distribution system was provided by the United States Government. Another problem with the above assessments is that they take a macro-perspective. The effectiveness of the relief programme at the district and village levels remains to be conclusively established. Significant increases in malnutrition were detected during the second half of 1984 by a nutrition research project operating in Embu District (Neumann et al., forthcoming).

Cohen & Lewis (1987) have contrasted Kenya's success in averting a famine with the absence of the kind of permanent institutional structures designed specifically to cope with national crises. They argue that Kenya's experience demands that international agencies should rethink their advocacy of and support for the creation of such structures in drought-prone countries. Care needs to be taken in drawing such conclusions from Kenya's comparative success. The poorly developed early warning system cannot be said to have been tested by the failure of the long rains in 1984, which was clearly apparent to officials in Nairobi well before the first crop surveys were carried out. Though severe, the drought was not prolonged in the main arable areas, and it is not clear how the system would have held up had it been placed under greater pressure.

Botswana

Botswana has been experiencing a severe and prolonged drought since the failure of the 1981/2 rains. The drought has caused significant increases in livestock mortality rates and dramatic reductions in domestic crop production and the income of rural households. Although the drought broke in many of the neighbouring countries in 1985, the 1984/5 rains in Botswana were well below the long-term average and the country remains on the FAO's list of 'Affected Countries'. It is nevertheless questionable whether the country has been experiencing a food crisis in the sense that the term has been applied elsewhere, for starvation has been averted and increases in malnutrition have been limited (Morgan, 1985; Hay, Burke & Dako, 1985). Botswana's experience is therefore in contrast to that of many other countries and is worth examining to see why this should be the case.

The primary reason for Botswana's success in mitigating the effects of the drought has been the unusually comprehensive and effective relief programme mounted by the Government, which has attracted praise from a variety of sources (Borton, 1984; Holm & Morgan, 1985; Bush, 1985; Hay *et al.*, 1985; World Bank, 1985a). The Relief Programme has four main components, namely food relief, cash for work projects, water relief, and agriculture/recovery projects.

The food relief component involves the distribution of approximately 40,000 tonnes each year to some 600,000 beneficiaries, equivalent to 60 per cent of the total population. Approximately 90 per cent of the food is donated, with the remainder being supplied by the Government to fill any gaps occurring in the arrival of donated shipments (Borton, 1986). The effectiveness and wide coverage of the distribution system has been shown by a recent survey of six rural villages in several parts of the country (Hay *et al.*, 1985). The exceptional outreach of the feeding programmes is largely attributable to the heavy investment in rural infrastructure (schools, health facilities and water supplies) by the government during the 1970s and early 1980s (Borton, 1984; Hay *et al.*, 1985).

The second component of the Relief Programme, the cash for work (referred to locally as labour-based relief) projects, involve the creation of temporary public works projects in most villages in the country. Some 50-70,000 participants are provided with temporary work each year, and it has been calculated that the wages paid during 1984 and 1985 replaced an estimated 35 per cent of the value of the crops lost owing to the drought (Morgan, 1985).

The water relief component of the Programme involves the acceleration of the Central Government's borehole drilling and equipment programme and the allocation of funds to district councils to provide water to villages whose normal sources have dried up. The agriculture/recovery projects involve a package of measures designed to help reduce stock losses and to assist arable farmers to take full advantage of the rains when they arrive. Obviously the Relief Programme is not without its problems (Borton, 1984). The World Food Programme intends to reduce its level of assistance to the Programme as a way of encouraging the Government to introduce targeting to those within the Vulnerable Group category who are more seriously affected (WFP, 1986b).

Nevertheless, the achievements of the Relief Programme are many. The literature identifies the following as its strengths (Borton, 1984; Morgan, 1985).

1. The effective national Early Warning System enables the prediction of the likely harvests as early as the February of each year and this gives almost four months' notice before the start of each year's Programme. Such time is crucial in initiating the 'gearing-up' process

and in enabling an early request to donors for assistance.

2. The early commencement of the Programme (in the June of 1982 at the time when the first failed harvest was being gathered) 'bought time' for the system to gain momentum and for early problems to be resolved before the performance of the Programme became critical. Similarly, it enabled relief to be provided in the villages at a stage well before people were forced to leave their homes in search of food and before participants in the labour-based relief projects became too weak to work.

3. A non-drought supplementary feeding programme had been operating in the country since the 1960s and this meant that the food distribution component of the Relief Programme built on systems already in place.

4. The prior agreement within the government on the beneficiary groups avoided the need for a time-consuming clarification and assessment process by donors.

5. There was a sound committee structure at both central and local government level.

In looking for the underlying factors accounting for the Programme's success, the following points have been emphasized:

1. Internal stability (Colclough & McCarthy, 1980).

2. The comparatively wealthy and well-managed economy (per capita GDP is US$ 960 — World Bank, 1986b) has given the Government considerable flexibility in the design and implementation of the Relief Programme (Borton, 1984; Harvey, 1985).

3. There is a strong commitment by the Government to the Programme (Cutler, 1986; Holm & Morgan, 1985).

4. Despite its relative wealth, Botswana continues to enjoy popularity with the Western donor community. In 1984 per capita net receipts of Official Development Assistance were US$ 102, whereas the average for Sub-Saharan Africa was only US$ 18 (World Bank, 1986b).

5. The comparatively small size of the population (940,000 at the time of the 1981 Census), whilst presenting some logistical problems, makes it easier for the Government to mount an effective Programme and for donors to make donations which, measured in their own terms, are small, but which to Botswana are highly significant (Borton, 1984).

6. The excellent regional transport infrastructure (Borton, 1984).

7. Because the country experiences drought so frequently, the Government has had considerable incentive to develop an effective Relief Programme. The Government has been prepared to accept criticism of its efforts and to integrate the lessons from each Programme into the design of the next (Holm & Morgan, 1985; Borton,

1984). Taken together, these factors have enabled a gradual fine-tuning of the system.

In conclusion, the Programme involves a comprehensive set of measures with good coverage of the country, which can be expanded as required. The key elements of a successful response system, outreach and flexibility, are therefore present.

Ethiopia

Following the 1972–74 Ethiopian famine and the almost simultaneous famine in the Sahel, there were calls in international forums, such as the 1974 World Food Conference, for the creation of structures to predict and prevent famine. It was felt that, if such structures existed, national and international resources could be mobilized earlier to prevent a recurrence of the situation. In Ethiopia, a result of this was the creation of the Relief and Rehabilitation Commission (RRC), which, even before 1984, was a large and powerful government agency (Cutler & Stephenson, 1984). Given the resources put into the RRC and similar, though smaller and less ambitious, agencies in other countries in Africa, a crucial question is why the system failed. Several reasons have been given in the literature.

Part of the answer must lie in the atrocious statistical base for judging food production and availability in Ethiopia. For instance, according to both FAO and USDA, indices of per capita food production stood at levels above those of their base-year periods (1974–76 in the case of FAO and 1976–78 in the case of USDA) until 1984, when they both fell substantially — the FAO index to 90 and the USDA index to 98 (FAO, 1984a; 1985a; USDA, 1985). Such 'food balance' indices need to be treated with considerable caution, since they obscure regional differences, include areas outside government control and rely on out-of-date population estimates. First reports of starvation in Wollo came in 1983, just one year after a bumper harvest that had supposedly produced the highest index for a decade (Baulch, 1985). The FAO Production Yearbook of 1983 took the total population to be 33.7 million, whilst the country's first-ever national census carried out between March and September 1984 produced a figure of 42 million (World Bank, 1985b).

A widely-held view in the literature is that the RRC was guilty of exaggerating its food aid requirements in the years up to 1984 and that this resulted in a growing scepticism amongst donors, possibly fuelled by the unpopularity of the Mengistu regime, towards the RRC's appeals during 1983 and 1984 (Cutler, 1985; Gill, 1986). There were certainly strong incentives for the RRC to do so. Although Ethiopia is the poorest country in Sub-Saharan Africa (World Bank, 1986b), in 1983 it received the lowest levels of development assistance (World Bank, 1984). In addition, the Government in Addis Ababa was devoting considerable resources to waging wars against secessionist movements in Eritrea and Tigray. No less than 40–45 per cent of the GNP is estimated to be expended on the wars (Cutler, 1985; Baulch, 1985). In these circumstances, emergency assistance was the only channel of bilateral aid not severely constrained by the lack of an agreed framework between the Government and donor agencies.

Controversy continues on the precise chronology of action in 1984 and, by implication, on the balance of responsibility for the tragedy. The relative importance of the Government's revolutionary celebrations in diverting national efforts and imposing travel restrictions on foreigners, and the failure of external assessments (most notably that by the FAO/WFP in May 1984) to highlight Ethiopia's more serious plight during a continent-wide crisis are examples of issues in the debate (Gill, 1986; Aseffa, forthcoming; Lemma, 1985). This is a subject for further study by contemporary historians of Ethiopia and international affairs.

Some issues concern social science analysis more directly. For example, Cutler & Stephenson (1984) focus on response to and uses of information by government and agency officials in Ethiopia. Within bureaucratic donor institutions, individuals were preoccupied with palliative responses to a progressively deteriorating situation. Only media intervention precipitated a global awareness and triggered a massive response commensurate with the gravity of the situation. Social science research on famine warning systems has been primarily concerned with technical problems of identifying and calibrating improved indicators (see, for example, Cutler, 1985). In contrast, little attention is accorded to how information is processed and filtered within bureaucratic institutions.

The role of the media in the international emergency response process had already been raised by Shawcross (1984) in a study of the Kampuchean emergency. The Ethiopian famine has once again shown this to be a rich and important subject for research.

Political factors appear to have played a significant role in the failure to respond to the numerous early warning signals. That this should be the case in the most extreme food crisis for a decade should not lead to a perception of early warning systems as attempting technical fixes to political problems. The cases of Kenya and Botswana show that early and decisive action is important in determining the effectiveness of response. Early warning is clearly a necessary but not a sufficient condition for effective response.

Perhaps the understandable interest in the Ethiopian famine will pose a wider problem for research. A pathology of extreme cases is a potentially dubious basis for generalizing on important issues of public policy. One could therefore question the usefulness of a concept such as 'famine studies' as distinct from social science analysis of food security problems and policy practice. Our other examples show the need for a more systematic review of drought preparedness strategies, from household to national levels, covering a wider range of country experiences.

Conclusions and implications for future research

The food crisis was the product of a number of interacting factors. The permutations of these factors varied significantly between countries. Drought, internal political and economic factors and the unfavourable external economic environment were significant contributory factors in most countries. However, the external environment was not entirely unfavourable, for the world cereal markets were overhung with surpluses and it was possible for some countries, such as Kenya, to buy their way out of serious problems. This had not been an option during the 'World Food Crisis' of the early 1970s.

Retrospective evaluations do suggest that food aid mitigated the situation. The early warning systems put in place since the early 1970s were helpful where the internal political context and relationships with the international donor community were favourable.

In this review we have deliberately given attention to two of the 'success stories'. We would ask whether it would be more useful, where we are examining highly complex systems, to give more attention to those that in some sense are functioning, rather than to become preoccupied with the extreme cases. The process of understanding the causation of complex systems is difficult and the debate may remain inconclusive. Witness for instance the continuing acrimonious debate on the Bengal Famine of 1943.

We therefore suggest for discussion that priority areas for research should include countries such as Botswana, Kenya, Zimbabwe and Cape Verde, as well as Ethiopia and Sudan. Again, in the Sahel, the experiences of Niger and Burkina Faso are just as significant as those of Mali and Chad.

We have drawn attention to the incomplete nature of evidence in the environmental debate. Here is an area that requires systematic and multi-disciplinary research. Agricultural systems are comparatively well researched, whereas the food system viewed as an integrated production and consumption system is less well understood. We will never know with any degree of accuracy how many people were affected and how severely. We believe that the study of how food systems respond to stress and interventions to provide food security and post-disaster relief should be a high priority for research.

One lesson of the recent crisis is that rural development cannot be sustained without putting in place a robust system of food security. A lesson of the previous food crisis is that agencies very quickly take a view on what institutional changes are required to improve response but that their interest soon lapses. Research is needed to keep the issues alive.

Notes

1   These problems are not unique to Africa. Both deliberate manipulation and unintended biases resulting from 'rule of thumb' procedures have been documented elsewhere, for example in Bangladesh (Boyce, 1985).

2   The countries on the FAO list at the end of 1983 were: Cape Verde, Mauritania, Mali, Burkina Faso, Senegal, Gambia, Guinea-Bissau, Guinea, Ghana, Togo, Benin, São Tomé and Principe, Chad, Central African Republic, Ethiopia, Somalia, Tanzania, Mozambique, Zambia, Zimbabwe, Botswana, Swaziland and Lesotho. By September 1984 Morocco, Kenya and Rwanda were added to the list, whilst Swaziland was dropped. By December 1984 Gambia, Guinea–Bissau, Guinea, Ghana, Togo, Benin, Central African Republic, São Tomé and Principe had been dropped, whilst Niger, Sudan, Burundi and Angola had been added (FAO, 1985b).

3   For instance, in mid-1983 the US Department of Agriculture reported that: 'Favourable weather across coastal West African countries led to slight increases in cereal production in 1982/3 for most of the region, excluding Gambia and Ghana (USDA, 1983).' Christensen and Witucki, writing over two years later, describe the situation in the same period and region in rather different terms: 'Abnormal weather patterns disrupted crop production in many countries throughout 1983. Coastal regions from the Ivory Coast to Nigeria suffered from an unusually severe dry season during late 1982 and early 1983.' (Christensen & Witucki, 1986).

4   The countries showing the greatest declines between 1970 and 1981 were Ghana, Chad, Zaire, Zambia and Liberia. Not all countries had low or negative per capita GDP growth rates: Botswana, Sudan Lesotho and Cameroon enjoyed average annual increases above 3 per cent over this period (World Bank, 1984).

References

Allison, C. & Green, R. (1985), 'Towards getting some facts less snarled?' *IDS Bulletin*, **16** (3): 1–18.

Appeldoorn, G. Van, (1981), *Perspectives on Drought and Famine in Nigeria*, London, Allen & Unwin.

Aseffa, A. (forthcoming), 'Ethiopian famine' in Curtis, D., Hubbard, M. & Shepherd, A., *Preventing Famine*', London, Methuen.

Bates, R. (1981), 'Markets and States in Tropical Africa: The Political Basis of Agricultural Policies', Berkeley, University of California Press.

Baulch, R. (1985), 'Entitlements and the Ethiopian famine', unpublished dissertation, University of Sussex.

Benson, C. & Clay, E. (1986), 'Food aid and food crisis in Sub-Saharan Africa: statistical trends and implications', *Disasters*, **10** (4): 303–16.

Berry, S. (1983), 'Agrarian crisis in Africa? A review and an interpretation', paper prepared for the Joint Studies Committee of the Social Science Research Council and the American Council of Learned Societies.

Berry, S. (1984), 'The food crisis and agrarian change in Africa: A review essay', *African Studies Review*, **27** (2): 59-112, June: Los Angeles.

Binsbergen, A. Van, (1986), 'Cape Verde: food aid resource planning in support of a national food strategy', paper for WFP/ADB Seminar 'Food Aid for Development in Sub-Saharan Africa', Abidjan, 8–11 September, Rome, World Food Council.

Blaikie, P. (1985), *The Political Economy of Soil Erosion in Developing Countries*, Harlow, Longmans Development Studies.

Borton, J. (1984), *Disaster Preparedness and Response in Botswana*, London, Relief and Development Institute.

Borton, J. & Stephenson, R. (1984), *Disaster Preparedness In Kenya*, London, Relief and Development Institute.

Borton, J. (1986), 'Food aid management in Botswana', background paper for the WFP/ADB Seminar 'Food Aid for Development in Sub-Saharan Africa', Abidjan, 8–11 September.

Borton, J., with Holt, J. (1986), *A review of the 1984/5 CRS Emergency Programme in Tanzania*, London, Relief and Development Institute.

Borton, J, & Shoham, J. (1986), *A Review of the 1983/4 CRS Emergency Programme in Ghana*, London, Relief and Development Institute.

Borton, J., Shoham, J., D'Souza, F. & Holt, J. (1986) *A Review of CRS Emergency Programmes in Three African Countries: Executive Summary and Recommendations*, London, Relief and Development Institute.

Borton, J. (1987), 'The 1984/5 Drought Relief Programme in Kenya: A provisional review', a report prepared for the Overseas Development Administration, London.

Boserup, E. (1965), *The Conditions of Agricultural Growth*, London, Aldine.

Boyce, J. (1985), 'Agricultural growth in Bangladesh 1949/50–1980/81: a review of the evidence', *Economic and Political Weekly*, 27th March.

Bush, R. (1985), 'Drought and famines', *Review of African Political Economy*, No. 33.

Chambers, R. (1985), 'The crisis of Africa's rural poor: perceptions and priorities', Institute of Development Studies, Discussion Paper 201.

Charney, J. (1975), 'Dynamics of deserts and droughts in the Sahel', *Quarterly Journal of the Royal Meteorology Society*, **101**: 193–202.

Christensen, C. & Witucki, L. (1986), 'Food policies in Sub-Saharan Africa' in S. Commins, M. Lofchie & R. Payne, *Africa's Agrarian Crisis*, Boulder, Lynne Rienner.

Clay, E. & Everitt, E. (eds) (1985), 'Food aid and emergencies: a report on the third IDS Food Aid Seminar', Institute of Development Studies, Discussion Paper 206.

Cliffe, L. & Moorsom, R. (1979), 'Rural class formation and ecological collapse in Botswana', *Review of African Political Economy*, No. 15/16.

Club du Sahel, (1985), 'Report on Meeting of Network on Strategies for Promoting Food Self-Reliance in Sahelian Countries'.

Cohen, J. & Lewis, D. (1987), 'Role of government in combatting food shortages: lessons from Kenya 1984–85', in M. Glantz (ed.), *Drought and Hunger in Africa: Denying Famine a Future*, Cambridge, Cambridge University Press.

Colclough, C. (1985), 'Competing pardigms — and lack of evidence — in the analysis of African development' in T. Rose (ed.) *Crisis and Recovery in Sub-Saharan Africa*, Paris, OECD.

Colclough, C. & McCarthy, S. (1980), *The Political Economy of Botswana*, Oxford, Oxford University Press.

Commins, S., Lofchie, M. & Payne, R. (eds) 1986, *African's Agrarian Crisis*, Boulder, Lynne Rienner.

Cuny, F.C. (1983), *Disasters and Development*, Oxford, Oxford University Press.

Currey B. (1984), 'Coping with complexity in food crisis management' in B. Currey & G. Hugo (eds), *Famine as a Geographical Phenomenon*, Dordrecht, Reidel.

Cutler, P. (1985), 'The use of economic and social information in famine prediction and response', a report prepared for the Overseas Development Administration, London.

Cutler, P. (1986), 'Food security in nine African countries: Botswana, Ethiopia, Ghana, Kenya, Mali, Sudan, Tanzania, Zambia and Zimbabwe', London, Overseas Development Administration

Cutler, P. & Stephenson, S. (1984), *The State of Food Emergency Preparedness in Ethiopia*, London, Relief and Development Institute.

Downing, T., Mungai, D. & Muturi, H. (1985), 'Drought climatology in central and eastern Kenya' in *Climatic Variability and Agricultural Production in Central and Eastern Kenya*, Nairobi, National Enviornment Secretariat.

Eicher, C. (1985), 'Agricultural research for African development: problems and priorities for 1985–2000', paper prepared for a World Bank Conference on Research Priorities for Sub-Saharan Africa, Bellagio, 25 February – 1 March.

Ellis, F. (1982), 'Agricultural pricing policy in Tanzania', *World Development*, **10** (4): 263–83.

FAO, Food and Agriculture Organization (1979), 'Agrometeorological crop monitoring and forecasting', Plant Production and Protection Paper No. 17, Rome.

FAO, Food and Agriculture Organization (1983), 'An early warning system for regional food security', report prepared for SADCC Countries, Rome.

FAO, Food and Agriculture Organization (1984a), 'World food security: selected issues and approaches', Committee on World Food Security, Rome.

FAO, Food and Agriculture Organization (1984b), 'Assessment of the agriculture, food supply and livestock situation: Kenya', Rome, Office For Special Relief Operations.

FAO, Food and Agriculture Organization (1985a), 'Food and agriculture situation in African countries affected by calamities in 1983–85', Report No. 7. FAO/WFP Task Force, Rome.

FAO, Food and Agriculture Organization (1985b), 'World food report', Rome.

FAO, Food and Agriculture Organization (1986a), 'Food outlook', Rome.

FAO, Food and Agriculture Organization (1986b), 'Food supply situation and crop prospects in Sub-Saharan Africa: special report', September 1986. GIEWS, Rome.

FAO, Food and Agriculture Organization (1987), 'Review of improvements in the global information and early warning system in the current biennium and measures taken to strengthen national early warning systems', 12th Session of Committee on Food Security (CFS 87/7), Rome.

Foreign Affairs Committee, (1985), 'Famine in Africa', Second Report Session 1984–85, London, House of Commons.

Gill, P. (1986), *A Year in the Death of Africa: Politics, Bureaucracy and the Famine*, London, Paladin.

Glantz, M. (ed.) (1987), *Drought and Hunger in Africa: Denying Famine a Future*, Cambridge, Cambridge University Press.

Gleave, M. (1980), 'Some further thoughts on population density and agricultural systems in West Africa', in E. Simpson (ed.), 'The rural agricultural sector', papers presented at a meeting of the Developing Areas Study Group of the Institute of British Geographers, University of Newcastle upon Tyne.

Gleave, M. & White, H. (1969), 'Population density and agricultural systems in West Africa' in M. Thomas & G. Whittington (eds), *Environment and Land Use in Africa*, London, Methuen.

Gourou, P. (1953), *The Tropical World* (1st ed.), London, Longman.

Green, R. (1986), 'The IMF and stabilisation in Sub-Saharan Africa: a critical review', Institute of Development Studies, Discussion Paper 216.

Green, R. & Griffith–Jones, S. (1985) 'External debt: Sub-Saharan Africa's emerging iceberg' in T. Rose (ed.) (1985), *Crisis and recovery in Sub-Saharan Africa*, Paris, OECD.

Halliday, F. & Molyneux, M. (1986), 'The Soviet Union and the Ethiopian revolution', *Third World Affairs*.

Harriss, B. (1979), 'There is method in my madness — or is it vice versa? Measuring agricultural market performance', *Food Research Institute Studies*, **17**.

Hart, K. (1982), *The Political Economy of West African Agriculture*, Cambridge, Cambridge University Press.

Harvey, C. (1985), 'Successful adjustment in Botswana' *IDS Bulletin*, **16** (3): 47–51.

Hay, R., Burke, S. & Dako, D. (1985), 'A socio-economic assessment of drought relief in Botswana', draft report to the Inter-Ministerial Drought Committee, Gaborone, Ministry of Finance and Development Planning.

Holm, J. & Morgan, R. (1985), 'Coping with drought in Botswana: an African success, *Journal of Modern African Studies*, **23** (3): 463–82.

Howell, J. (ed.) (1985), *Recurrent Costs and Agricultural Development*, London, Overseas Development Institute.

Hyden, G. (1983), *No Shortcuts to Progress*, London, Heinemann.

Jones, M. (1986), 'Conservation systems and crop production' in L. Foster (ed.), *Agricultural Development in Drought-Prone Africa*, London, Overseas Development Institute and the Tropical Agriculture Association.

Kamarck, A. (1976), *The Tropics and Economic Development*, Baltimore, Johns Hopkins Press.

King, P. (1986), *An African Winter*, Harmondsworth, Penguin.

Lagemann, J. (1977), *Traditional African Farming Systems in Eastern Nigeria*, Munich, IFPO-Institut Weltforum Verlag.

Lemma, H. (1985), 'The politics of famine in Ethopia', *Review of African Political Economy* No. 33.

Levi, J. & Havinden, M. (1982), *Economics of African Agriculture*, Harlow, Longman.

Lipton, M. & Heald, C. (1984), 'African food strategies and the EEC's role: an interim review', Institute of Development Studies, Sussex.

Lipton, M. (1985), 'The place of agricultural research in the development of Sub-Saharan Afric' in *IDS Bulletin*, **16** (3): 14–23.

Lofchie, M. (1986), 'Africa's agricultural crisis: an overview' in S. Commins, M. Lofchie & R. Payne (eds) (1986), *Africa's Agrarian Crisis*, Boulder, Lynne Rienner.

Lofchie, M. & Commins, S. (1984), 'Food deficits and agricultural policies in Sub-Saharan Africa', *The Hunger Project Papers No. 2*, San Francisco.

McPherson, M. (1984), 'Checking land destruction: immediate gains and future benefits', *Journal*, World Resources Institute, Washington.

Morgan, R. (1985), 'The development and application of a drought early warning system in Botswana, *Disasters*, **9** (1): 44-50.

Morgan, R. (1986), 'From drought relief to post-disaster recovery: the case of Botswana', *Disasters*, **10** (1): 30–4.

Moss, R. (1981), 'Ecological constraints on agricultural development in Africa', *African Research and Documentation* **25**: 1–12.

Neumann, C. et al. (forthcoming), 'Impact of the 1984 famine on food intake and nutritional status in Embu District, Kenya', in T. Dowing et al., *Drought in Kenya: Lessons from 1984/5*, Boulder, Lynne Rienner.

Ogallo, L, (1984), 'Temporal fluctuations of seasonal rainfall patterns in East Africa', *Mausam* **35**, Meteorological Department, India.

ODI, Overseas Development Institute (1983), 'Refugees and the Third World', Briefing Paper, London.

ODI, Overseas Development Institute (1985), 'Africa's food crisis', Briefing Paper, London.

Office of Technology Assessment, (1984), 'Africa tomorrow: issues in technology, agriculture and US foreign aid', Washington, OTA.

Palmer, R & Parsons, N. (eds) (1977), *The Roots of Rural Poverty in Central and Southern Africa*, London, Heinemann.

Pankhurst, R. (1986), 'The history of famine and epidemics in Ethiopia prior to the twentieth century', Relief and Rehabilitation Commission, Addis Ababa.

Paulino, L. & Tseng, S. (1980), 'A comparative study of FAO and USDA data on production, area and trade of major food staples', IFPRI Research Report 19.

Pearson, R. (1986), 'Lessons from famine in Sudan 1984–86', Report to UNICEF, Khartoum.

Pinstrup-Anderson, P. (1982), *Agricultural Research and Technology in Economic Development*, Harlow, Longman.

Please, S. & Amoako, K. (1984), 'The World Bank's report on accelerated development in Sub-Saharan Africa: a critique of some of the criticism', *African Studies Review*, **27** (4): 47–58.

Ray, T. (1984), 'Drought assessment: Kenya', Nairobi, USAID.
Roberts, J. (1986), 'Economic, social and institutional constraints', in *The Agricultural Dilemma in Africa*, London, ODA.
Rose, T. (ed.) (1985), *Crisis and Recovery in Sub-Saharan Africa*, Paris, OECD.
Rivers, J., Holt, J., Seaman, J & Bowden, M. (1976), 'Lessons for epidemiology from the Ethiopian famine', *Annales Société Belge de Médecine Tropicale*, **56**, 4/5: 345–57.
Ruthenberg, H. (1980), *Farming Systems in the Tropics*, Oxford University Press.
Sandford, S. (1979), 'Towards a definition of drought' in *Symposium on drought in Botswana*, Gaborone, Botswana Society.
Sandford, S. (1983), *Management of Pastoral Developments in The Third World*, London, Overseas Development Institute.
Sen, A. (1981), *Poverty and Famines: an Essay on Entitlement and Deprivation*, Oxford, Clarendon Press.
Sender, J. & Smith, S. (1984), 'What's right with the Berg Report and what's left of its critics?', Institute of Development Studies, Discussion Paper 192.
Shawcross, W. (1984), *The Quality of Mercy: Cambodia, Holocaust and Modern Conscience*, London, Andre Deutsch.
Stevens, T. (1986), 'After the famine: food aid policy and management issues in Sub-Saharan Africa', *Food Policy*, August.
Tickner, V. (1985), 'Military attacks, drought and hunger in Mozambique', *Review of African Political Economy*, No. 33.
Timberlake, J. (1985), *Africa in Crisis: The Causes, The Cures of Environmental Bankruptcy*, London, Earthscan.
Tinker, J. (1985), 'Environmental bankruptcy in Sub-Saharan Africa', paper presented to CIDA/North–South Institute/InterPares symposium, Ottawa, January.
Twose, N. (1985), *Fighting The Famine*, London, Pluto Press.
Tyson, P. (1979), 'Southern African rainfall: past, present and future' in T. Hinchey (ed.), *Symposium on Drought in Botswana*, Gaborne, Botswana Society.
UN Conference on Desertification (1977), *Desertification: An Overview*, Conference Document A/Conf. 74/3.
UNICEF (1984), 'State of the world's children', New York.
UNOEOA, UN Office for Emergency Operations in Africa, (1986), 'Special Report on the emergency situation in Africa: review of 1985 and 1986 emergency needs', New York.
USAID, US Agency for International Development(1986), 'The US response to the African Famine, 1984–86', Washington, DC.
USDA, US Department of Agriculture (1983) 'World food aid needs and availabilities, 1983', Economic Research Service, Washington.
USDA, US Department of Agriculture (1985), 'World indicies of Agriculture and food production 1975–84', Statistical Bulletin No. 730.
Wigley, T. & Farmer, G. (1986), 'Rainfall' in *The agricultural dilemma in Africa*, papers of the 1985 ODA Natural Resources Advisers Conference, the Overseas Development Administration, London.
Wijkman, A., Timberlake, L. (1984), *Natural Disasters: Acts of God or Acts of Man?*, London, Earthscan.
World Bank (1981), 'Accelerated development in Sub-Saharan Africa: an agenda for action', Washington.
World Bank (1984), 'Towards sustained development in Sub-Saharan Africa: a joint programme of action', Washington DC.
World Bank (1985a), 'Economic memorandum on Botswana', Washington.
World Bank (1985b), 'Sector review: Ethiopia population, health and nutrition', Washington DC.
World Bank (1986a), 'Poverty and hunger: issues and options for food security in developing countries', Washington.
World Bank (1986b), *World Development Report 1986*, Oxford University Press.

World Bank (1986c), 'Financing adjustment with growth in Sub-Saharan Africa, 1986–90', Washington DC.

World Bank (1986d), 'Kenya: policies and prospects for restoring sustained growth of per capita income', Washington DC.

WFP, World Food Programme (1970), 'Food aid and related issues during the second development decade', Report of the Intergovernmental Committee, Seventeenth Session, Rome.

WFP, World Food Programme (1986a), 'Executive Directions' report on evaluation of WFP emergency response to the Africa food crisis', Rome.

WFP, World Food Programme (1986b), 'Budget increases for CFA approval: Botswana project 324 Exp. 1', Rome, WPME.

York, S. (1985), 'Report on a pilot project to set up a drought information network in conjunction with the Red Crescent Society in Darfur', *Disasters*, **9** (3): 173–8.

Young, L (1985), 'A general assessment of the environmental impact of refugees in Somalia with attention to the Refugee Agricultural Programme', *Disasters*, **9** (2): 122–33.

Index